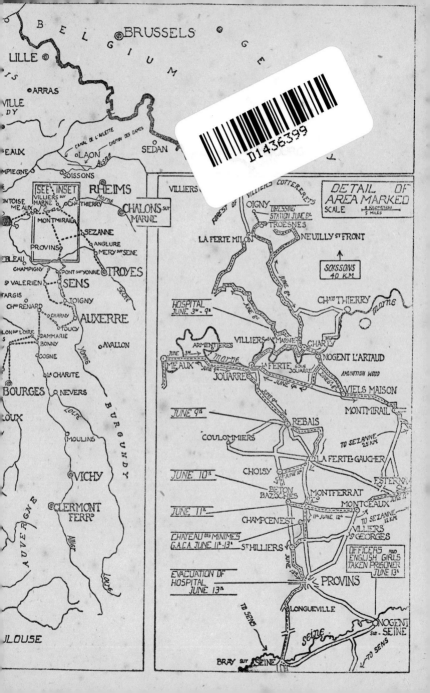

The Road To
BORDEAUX

THE ROAD TO
BORDEAUX

C. DENIS FREEMAN
AND DOUGLAS COOPER

ILLUSTRATED BY EDWARD ARDIZZONE

London 1942
READERS UNION LTD. and THE CRESSET PRESS

Made 1942 in Great Britain

PRINTED BY THE GARDEN CITY PRESS LTD. LETCHWORTH AND PUB-
LISHED BY READERS UNION LTD., DUNHAMS LANE, LETCHWORTH

TO THOSE WHOM WE LEFT BEHIND

You must forgive
this personal record written without your consent or know-
ledge. To apologise for writing a book about you is absurd,
but to have written it without apologising would also be
absurd. We did not enlist in the French Army for the sake
of writing our memoirs. It was never our intention to use
you, or the events of the tragic month of June, 1940, which we
endured together, for our own gain. But we have been impelled
by circumstances to tell our story. It was in Plymouth that the
thought first came to us, when we realised that grave injustice
was being done to the French people and to the French Army.
So many were being made to pay for the faults of so few.
Nobody more than our small Section had experience of the
fortitude of the French soldier and of the tragic bewilderment
of the French people. We, two Englishmen in that awful rout,
felt that it was our duty to recount what we had seen and heard.
Many of the incidents we have recorded will seem petty, but it
was only with them that a complete picture could be built. What
is important is not the detail of our daily existence but the
sequence of greater events into which it fits. Some of your names
have been changed : you will understand the reasons. We have
had no news of you since we left : some of you are prisoners,
some are lost, all of you are certainly less fortunate than our-
selves. But wherever you are, we know that each one of you will
not give up the fight until France is again free. Perhaps, then,
after the victory, we may meet again in the same beautiful
Paris where we first met.

CONTENTS

There is a Time, when Toil must be preferr'd
Or Joy, by mistim'd Fondness, is undone.
A Man of Pleasure is a Man of Pains.

EDWARD YOUNG, Night Thoughts, Night VIII.

*Will not let war obtrude on my work, yet obsessive return to it
in thought. War is now the reality, civilian life unreality,
luxury ; it is essential to make contact with it and see one's
standards (the artistic creations which one believes in and
defends, one's æsthetic) in this new light. One cannot ignore
a war which one wishes to see successfully concluded, on which
the continued creative activities of one's artist friends and con-
temporaries will depend. Freedom and security of artists
threatened. Man of average sensibility will settle down and be
happy under any system—Germany is full of them, Russia too.
Fascism has no room for the artist—nor Communism : both
should inspire, but both anti-artistic. French soldiers, my
friends, fighting and dying for what I believe in. Can one
ignore them while they die ? Can I wait (in retreat) till it is all
over ? Picasso showed the way in " Guernica ". Soldier is
called on to defend values he cannot understand. Can I possibly
accept his sacrifice while acknowledging no responsibility?
France, a last corner of culture and civilisation, threatened
with extinction. Even if in the end I can still only reject and
condemn the war, I will at least have seen and shared.*
From COOPER'S DIARY, *May 25th, 1940.*

We wish to express our gratitude in particular to Professor Denis Saurat, of the Institut Français, for his valuable encouragement ; to the Baroness Budberg for numerous suggestions and continual help; to Iris Palmer and to Dr. Basil Mackenzie for ceaseless labours on the script and proofs, also to Commander V. H. Goldsmith.

C. D. F.
D. C.

London, October, 1940.

PARIS

WE MET AGAIN in Paris at the end of March. As I
got out of the train, I said to myself : " This is my
third and final attempt to get involved." I was sunburnt
and well after an enforced ski-ing holiday among the de
luxe refugees in St. Moritz. When I had left six weeks
earlier, having been officially told that no use could be
found for my services, Freeman had said : " They will
need you one day when everyone is an octogenarian."
So I returned to Zürich with its Furtwängler concerts,
first nights with Emil Jannings, Gieseking recitals,
German guest singers at the Opera, Paul Valéry talking
to a sold-out hall on " *La Guerre et l'Amour*," and as the
counter-attraction (England's unique attempt at publi-
city) a concert by the English Singers. In this atmosphere it was scarcely surprising that one should fall a
victim to claustrophobia. I tried to listen to Jung's
weekly lecture, the best intellectual stimulant and the
subtlest anti-Nazi thought, but was driven away by the
pencils of the snobbish American women, scratching
with ignorant adulation, in long- and short-hand, his
verbatim text. So it was Paris for the third time.

* * *

I found Cooper sitting at a writing-table on the sixth
floor, behind the largest and most vulnerable area of
plate glass in Paris, looking with hope and childish
delight on his favourite view across the Seine at the
façade of the Louvre.

" This time I've come to do something. Things must
be different with Reynaud."

I answered truthfully that it had made a difference.
There was more confidence, determination and
activity ; the charity ladies and their good works, who
earlier on had sprung up overnight like mushrooms,

9

had almost disappeared, and those who worked *worked*. I was not too discouraging, but I knew in fact that things had not yet changed, and there was still no demand for volunteers.

I had returned to Paris on October 13th, having left it on the day war was declared. When the relief work on which I had been engaged had come to an end I had re-offered my services in any capacity in which they would prove useful. I had been rejected by the medical authorities a year before, so now voluntary work alone was open to me, but apart from working on a propaganda play for the B.B.C., *The Siege of Warsaw*, I was still inactive. Unfortunately I had found that men who genuinely wanted work were greeted in many official quarters with apathy.

Although Cooper's talents might have been usefully employed in many directions, everywhere I watched him meet with polite refusal, until one day, a few weeks later, he told me that he had been asked by a department of the French Red Cross to help in the organisation of circulating lending libraries to the front line troops.

It was a war of inactivity, and it was still possible, even after the shock of hostilities in Norway, to think of helping the soldiers in France to employ their leisure hours profitably.

*   *   *

Spring came to Paris with a rush after one of the coldest and most paralysing winters imaginable. Thousands of people not actively concerned in the conduct of the war threw off their feeling of impotence and numbness, and came back to life and the capital. For the first time since October, children were playing in the Tuileries and the Luxembourg Gardens. The café terraces were full again, and on Sundays as large a crowd as usual was taking its promenade in the sun on the Champs Elysées, in the Bois or at Versailles.

First the magnolias in the gardens of the Avenue Gabriel came into bloom. Next came the chestnut trees, greener and whiter and fresher than ever. Less overcrowded than usual, emptier of motor traffic, Paris had a peculiar air of nostalgic beauty, and as the women, gaining courage, once more wore coloured dresses and gay hats, so the town decked itself as though defying destruction. At the corner of the new Pont des Beaux Arts, four seated Republican ladies in flowing robes were built on to their plinths, while on the embankment below, two small gardens were planted beside the river. Behind the cathedral of Notre-Dame and in the courtyard of the Louvre, gardeners were at work, filling the beds with flowers. After five months, Léger completed his largest canvas, "*Les Saltimbanques,*" the war's first masterpiece. The heroic note of patriotism was sounded by a new production of *Cyrano de Bergerac* at the Comédie Française, with *décor* by Bérard : even the young Rostand found time to write and produce a play : a new and trivial comedy by Cocteau made its appearance at the Bouffes : *Médée*, a new work by Milhaud, with *décor* by André Masson, was produced at the Opéra on the stage which a few days earlier had been filled by Maurice Chevalier and Gracie Fields. People still went to the theatres and music-halls, the Parisians dined out as usual—the Germans, we were constantly told, would sooner or later starve—at least three-quarters of the *boîtes* had closed, but the few remaining open were full. The *guignol* in the Luxembourg, with Hitler and Goering, was a big draw ; the mid-day celebration at the Madeleine was still the fashionable one. There were even races at Longchamps, and the Entente was weekly cemented by some form of inter-allied sporting event. Many walls were covered with the double poster, " *Chantons quand-même !*—Let's sing all the same ! " Friends came from London on week-end visits, and most English women in the freshly decorated Ritz bar wore uniform. There was still " Paris by Night " for them, they were blinded by finding a Paris less dark than London.

But life was not really so normal. The French were adapting themselves to circumstances. There were three days a week without meat, except for *agneau de lait*, which was classed as fish : three days without alcohol and three other days without pastry or confectionery, so that the devotees of *baba au rhum* were only able to enjoy it on Sundays. In the restaurants hors d'œuvres were limited, only one meat dish of 100 grs. was allowed, and butter was served only with cheese or sardines. Coffee and sugar were difficult to find, and prices had risen considerably. Coal and wood were almost unobtainable, and next winter's minute ration cards had just been issued (as well as a decree governing the period allowed for central heating) when the cold spell came to a sudden and fortunate end. All but the Government Monopoly cigarettes disappeared. A considerable proportion of shops in the main thoroughfares had shut down. Very many tube stations were closed, only a reduced service of buses was running, taxis were scarce and at night practically non-existent. All cafés and places of entertainment had to close at a stated hour, which for a long time was 10 p.m., though ultimately this was prolonged until midnight. Several times a week, by night and by day, one heard the anti-aircraft guns in action.

Paris was defying destruction, *les gens de l'arrière* were fighting to keep the flame of culture and civilisation burning, to preserve an atmosphere, a calm to steady the nerves of the men on leave.

So it seemed to us then. Perhaps to-day one should look afresh and ask if we were not deceived. Naturally it was a pleasure to live in Paris ; the town itself made life pleasant. It was a pleasure, too, to be among

French people, for they had not changed either. This was possibly their undoing. What seemed to us then an heroic attempt to preserve to the utmost something which everyone knew and loved, to preserve a spontaneity, a wit, a superiority over events, may in fact have been a mere refusal to face facts. Did the French people, one must ask oneself, deliberately turn their back on the war? Was it too remote? Too distasteful?

Certainly the French over-saturation with politics had reached its highest pitch. *Plus ça change, plus c'est la même chose.* This had produced among the people a disinterested attitude to the outcome of the *political* struggle. Their great desire was to win the war, but they wanted someone to inspire them to victory. They were far from indifferent to the outcome of the *military* struggle. Unfortunately the one attitude was to prove fatal to the other.

There were, of course, still a few million left-wing voters, both inside and outside the army; in a rational community used to thinking for itself, and almost unique in that respect, it was only natural that there should be. One cannot make people abandon their political convictions simply by imprisoning a handful of their elected representatives. There were also vested interests, those who were not prepared to abandon rights and privileges, those to whom business, not *patrie*, came first.

The French are a paradoxical nation. They appear mean, selfish, tight-fisted; possession means a great deal to them. On the other hand, they are the most generous givers of ideas, and England has profited by them often enough in the last century and a half. Let us not forget that the French knew, more profoundly than the English, the meaning of modern warfare. They had been invaded in 1870, and bled white by the Prussians. They had been invaded again in 1914, a large part of their country destroyed and the flower of their manhood wiped out by these same Germans. Had it not been the Allied politicians who, at Versailles, had frustrated the natural guarantees of security demanded by Clemenceau ? The Tiger had been gelded ; the next generation of Frenchmen went into the present war after twenty years of impotence.

It is no use recriminating now over the causes of France's downfall, over who betrayed whom, if treachery there was. For one thing the facts are not available, for another the Third Republic was always a bastard and an unlucky child from birth. Frenchmen of every party recognised that its days were numbered, but they were all determined to fight in its defence until the invader had been destroyed. When their country was threatened all factions united, thinking it better to preserve a form of society inside which they could agree to differ, than to have one faction supreme at the price of surrender. The idea of France transcends the present tragedy ; recrimination is superfluous.

The general feeling was really one of suspense, a feeling that some terrific eruption was inevitable, because, as in the old problem of the immovable meeting the irresistible, here were two gigantic forces patiently facing each other behind their impenetrable lines of defence, and each speculating on the internal collapse of the other. This continued state of passivity was really foreign to the logical French mind. The French had no intention of taking the offensive, they could not afford the waste of human life ; as Daladier said, " *le français se fait rare.*" But in their hearts they knew that the enemy must and would find a battle ground. " Which way will Hitler come ? " was the inevitable trend of conversation.

Meanwhile the soldiers begged for books and newspapers to occupy their minds during the long weeks of enforced idleness. It was indeed a " war of nerves," and the most difficult one for the French temperament to

deal with. In the middle of this came the trial of the
Communist deputies, which aroused no great opposition
even among the Communists themselves, whose sym-
pathies were divided. The B.E.F. were in the north,
guarding the Belgian frontier ; a strong force was waiting behind the Alps ; a vast and magnificently trained
and equipped army under Weygand was in Syria. The
Maginot Line was undoubtedly impregnable, though
ironically enough, just because of its very existence, it
would probably never be called on to justify itself. A
few shells were exchanged over the Rhine, rival loud-
speakers blared across No Man's Land, patrols brought
in occasional prisoners, but the major activity seemed to
be with the R.A.F. and the British Navy, whose exploits
became a legend.

No one expected the solution to be simple, but no
one expected anything as sudden as the attack on
Denmark and Norway.

The surprise was colossal. But surprise soon gave
way to satisfaction at the fantastic successes of the
British fleet, and gradually the feeling of security
returned. Norway was, after all, a long way away,
and, as Reynaud pointed out in a speech, though
Germany might have started with " a tactical success "
it had undoubtedly made " an enormous strategic
error." It is true that all leave was stopped and everyone recalled immediately to their units. Uniforms disappeared from the streets, and for several days families
were without news of husbands and sons. The fight
went on, and each edition of the newspapers had reports
of successful operations ; but when *The Times* started
preparing the British public for the sad, if inevitable,
withdrawal from Trondheim, it disappeared silently
from the Parisian bookstalls. The illusion that all was
going well was officially upheld until finally publication
of the facts could be put off no longer. The public was
aghast. Hitler's sudden action in Norway had saved

the life of the Reynaud Cabinet, and looking back now one cannot help wondering whether there was not already a spirit of defeatism in certain Ministries.

After a fortnight leave was reinstated, and with an effort Paris started to return to a semblance of normality, though everyone really knew that the war had now started in earnest. It was realised that our first effort had ended in a setback. An explanation, and prompt correction, was essential in both Allied countries. Reynaud with difficulty survived debates in the Senate and Chamber of Deputies. France looked to England and followed hotly the debate in the House of Commons which led to the resignation of Chamberlain. The combination of Reynaud and Churchill, the man who, more than anyone else, inspired the French with confidence, was felt to be businesslike and invincible. From now on, the mistakes of Norway could not be repeated.

" With our national character so impressionable, so ardent in exploiting a first success, so easily discouraged at the first defeat, we ought to devote ourselves to winning the first success." The words of General Charreton, proved false in 1914, came into their own again in 1940.

Looking back, less than two months later, those first ten days of May seem even more unreal than at the time. One tried to take advantage of familiar pleasures while they still lasted, but there was an atmosphere of nervousness and strain as the pace quickened. Again one ate with friends on leave, but their state of mind had changed ; they could no longer accept the unreality. They no longer tried to crowd every pleasure Paris could offer, every diversion they could find, into each hour of their short leave. They railed against the apparent apathy of the civilians to the war, to the indifference shown when air-raid warnings sounded. They wanted life at home to be strict, rigid, spartan as was their life at the front. Their whispered criticisms of Gamelin were almost open statements and what seemed less important was their negative attitude to the Government. There was no apathy in the attitude of the soldiers to the war, their main pre-occupation was the apathy of the civilian. What they wanted was, in fact, a form of martial law.

*   *   *

On the night of May 9th, we were all together in Cooper's apartment. After dinner I had gone round there with two English friends of mine who were returning from a ski-ing holiday in the Italian Alps. We found the painter André Masson and his wife, as well as some French soldiers who had been dining there. Conversation was animated. The soldiers were criticising the careless attitude of the civilians to Alerts. One told how he had insisted upon his mother dressing and going downstairs to the *abri*, much to the old lady's horror. We all secretly sympathised with the old lady ; so many months of ineffectual air raids had made one indifferent—and in any case one did not seem to be more secure in musty wine-cellars than in one's own bed. We must have seemed uninterested, because a young aviation officer, with the face of a Renaissance angel and one of the highest flying decorations with *palmes*, suddenly remarked, with great charm but con-siderable conviction, that he was often tempted to drop one of his bombs on Paris " just to wake people up." With tact Cooper moved the conversation on to my friend's broken leg, for, like all good skiers, she had not escaped uninjured. This had delayed her in Italy, and she encouraged us with her impressions of the anti-German feelings among the people of that country.

Masson took the conversation off the war, and told of his latest experience at the Opéra. The night before had been the *première* of a new production designed by him and it had been ruined, he said, by a combination of

trade unions and lavatories. The *mise-en-scène* had
followed the lines of *Coq d'Or* : the singers were
grouped at the sides, while the action was mimed by
dancers in the centre of the stage. For the singers he
had designed rigid costumes to create the effect of a
frieze. At the dress rehearsal, a fussy and pompous
little man appeared, explaining that he represented the
trade union of chorus singers, and that he must protest at costumes which made it impossible for the
singers to obey the call of nature during the acts.
Masson's suggestion that they might visit the lavatory
either before or after the acts met with a look of
astonishment. The chorus had always obeyed the call
of nature during an act, if necessary, and would
continue to do so. The result was something of a dead-
lock, but the chorus won by non-co-operation : they
kept their voices in on the first night.

Masson's story was a relief and for a short time we
talked of literature, art, our friends, just as one has
always done in Paris. We forgot the war, we forgot the
time, too.

At 4 a.m. the sirens shrieked, and the war came to
Paris. A few minutes later the sky was full of aeroplanes.
The anti-aircraft guns banged with more insistence than
ever before, and the early dawn was bright with tracer
bullets. The raid over, we all went home.

We awoke to find that Germany had violated Dutch
and Belgian neutrality.

*   *   *

The next few days were days of intense activity and
excitement. Hitler had made the obvious move, and
still everyone was surprised. Here was the great test.
Churchill was busy forming his Cabinet in England :
all soldiers in France were immediately recalled :
decree followed decree curtailing civil liberties : air-
raid followed air-raid, and the guns were scarcely ever
silent : the Whitsun holidays were cancelled : every

enemy alien rounded up—and still the German advance went on.

Almost immediately the streets of Paris filled with
refugees arriving in heavily loaded cars, and after a few
days they appeared in their thousands by car, train and
boat, bringing with them an amazing collection of tales
of fantasy and horror. Their plight was terrible and a
great many were in tears ; some had spent as much as
seven days driving from Brussels to Paris. Many of the
cars had the roof covered with a mattress as additional
protection, while plenty bore the marks of bullets. As
the German advance continued through the Ardennes
and then across the French frontier, the problem
reached enormous dimensions. Refugees streamed into
Paris, and no praise can be too high for the magnificent
way in which the authorities dealt with them.
Thousands were fed, clothed and housed each night,
and moved on southwards in the morning to make
room for more. Canteens and reception centres sprang
up everywhere to deal with the chaos in the stations.
The bus services were cancelled altogether to help in
the evacuation, and as much as possible of the refugee
motor traffic was diverted through the suburbs.

All places of entertainment were closed, newspapers
reduced to a single sheet, and all music forbidden in
radio programmes, so that one was left with nothing
but unconvincing news bulletins repeated once an hour.
" On les aura " was the general catch-phrase—but no
one seemed to know where or when. Something
seemed to have broken down, but no one despaired ;
there was talk of a second Battle of Waterloo, a reverse
of Sedan, a new Battle of the Somme.

The atmosphere was perfect for false news, especially
as official sources were so resolutely reticent. One
realises now how the Press and the Radio were muzzled,
gagged and buried alive, by caution and fright, in a
winding-sheet of red tape. They poured out from their

mausoleum a flood of lies and inaccuracies. It was not so much deliberate prevarication that caused the trouble, as omission and suppression of vital news, which produced a result worse than deliberate false-hoods. A half-truth is a dangerous thing ; it has the semblance of reality. The statements read in the press and heard over the air were repeated and added to, embroidered and decorated, and repeated again until they became travesties of the travesty that begat them, more dangerous than any high explosive shell. A vast part of the public believed what it was told. What reasons had they for doubting it ? " I read it in the papers "—" I heard it on the wireless," was the usual answer to a doubt expressed after too tall a story.

Rumours grew to absurd proportions : parachutists were reported everywhere, and one had even landed on the Place de la Madeleine, but he turned out to be a deflated observation balloon. The peak was reached on May 16th, when the Germans were reported to have taken Laon and Reims, and the Government said to have left Paris. At this moment, the Parisians them-selves added to the congestion by starting to leave hurriedly. There was an afternoon of panic, greatly encouraged by a heavily reduced train service which had come into effect only that morning. We were even confronted with the not unfunny spectacle of a lady of our acquaintance setting out for the station with five trunks, two fur coats, a canary in a cage and, for some inexplicable reason, a bright blue feather boa wrapped round her neck. But, like thousands of others, she was unable to get away, and was obliged to return home in time to hear Reynaud's vigorous speech denying the truth of all these stories.

The next day Churchill came to Paris for a consulta-tion. The situation was critical. On the 18th came the news that the Allies had withdrawn west of Brussels, followed in the evening by a so-called fighting speech from Reynaud, referring to traitors and measures to deal with them, and announcing the dismissal of Gamelin and Daladier and the appointment of Pétain and Weygand. Weygand, it was felt, could only bring victory " *quand la patrie est en danger* "—and the French remembered the words of Foch. But there were plenty of people who questioned whether the appointment had been made soon enough to avert catastrophe, and who were seriously alarmed that, at such a moment, a War Minister dismissed for incompetence should be rewarded with the Ministry of Foreign Affairs—even if only until the public had recovered from the shock. Pétain was certainly very old, but he was known to be very active during the few hours he could work daily. It was like running up the Tricolour, but little did they know then that it was the beginning of the end of the Third Republic. His recent diplomatic successes in the new Spain of his former and devoted pupil, General Franco, had temporarily obscured his lack of anglophil sentiments, and his record in the last war. It was a pity that no one remembered his epitaph at the Ecole de Guerre : " If this man ever rises above the rank of major, it will be the end of France." Reynaud had made his first miscalculation : he now had to fight, in addition, the defeatists he himself had brought into his Cabinet.

*   *   *

With so much happening so quickly, Freeman and I were rapidly coming to the conclusion that our rather sedentary occupations should be exchanged for more active ones. My work of organising lending libraries now seemed absurd. At my headquarters, things began to change rapidly : books were forgotten as hourly the demand grew for ambulances, X-ray lorries, and other medical equipment. So it was a great relief when a contingent of these arrived safely in Paris after a three-day dash from the bombardment of Liège. They were to have been a gift from Belgian ex-servicemen, and were still not fully equipped, but it was a small matter to finish them and send them on to where they were urgently needed. We were faced with the problem of getting drivers, as previously only military drivers had been allowed and now no soldiers could be spared. St. Quentin and several other towns had fallen ; the German attack, diverted from Paris, was pushing towards the coast ; in the east, too, the situation was critical. At this point, the Ministère de la Guerre passed a new order militarising our organisation as the Section Sanitaire Automobile du Front, and leaving us to organise a corps of volunteer drivers. I found myself faced with the alternatives of doing nothing or signing an engagement with the French Army. I had two days to think it over, though my mind was made up.

Freeman, with whom at dinner next evening I discussed my decision and the reasons for it, was delighted, and said at once that he completely shared my point of view. When he left me that night I had recruited another volunteer.

I had given him detailed instructions on how to proceed because I had to attend the first meeting of the volunteers in the morning. Freeman found it was quick work to enlist, as we were due to leave in under a week. There was a lot to be done and very little time in which to do it. It was the morning of King Leopold's betrayal, and crowds were outside the Belgian Embassy, screaming " *Mort au Roi !* " as Freeman walked down the street to the British Embassy. It was an extraordinary scene. The Garde Républicaine from the Elysée Palace were even called out to quell the infuriated Belgians, who only twenty-four hours earlier would have died for the man they were now cursing.

Armed with the necessary authorisation from the British Military Attaché, which was quickly given, it was only a question of hours before Freeman had signed his papers, and when we met for lunch he had already been accepted. Even I was a little surprised at the speed with which it had all been arranged, and I was delighted because it made certain that we would both be included in the same Section.

I had been able to prepare him a little for our curiously assorted international brigade of fellow-drivers, with whom I had been working in the morning, and whom he first saw in the afternoon. We had all been summoned to headquarters to have our credentials examined by a representative from the Ministère de la Guerre, and to receive instructions about uniform and the equipment which was needed.

The headquarters were at an apartment in the Avenue Hoche. We were received in a large half-bare room to which the air of luxury still clung. The walls were covered by a series of those spurious modern paintings which are calculated to perplex the innocent visitor in advance and dispose him to believe in his host's superior intelligence. Ranged round the room on chairs, piles of blankets and a variety of packing cases, sat the thirty odd volunteers, watching each other curiously. By the end of the day we each had papers authorising us to buy and wear the regulation uniform, for after the alarming experiences in Holland it had been made impossible to purchase any item of French military kit without producing a host of documents.

Next morning began the scramble to have everything ready in time. We paraded in the morning and again in the afternoon on the third floor of a garage behind the Ecole Militaire, where the ambulances were kept. Our *Chef de Section*, Henri Caillemer, was a pleasant and conscientious young man, nervous and willing, with a bent to literature and a few " *Notes et Critiques* " in the Nouvelle Revue Française to his credit. The relationship established itself as between master and

unruly pupils. There were invariably a certain
number of absentees, engaged on visits to the tailor and
similar shopping excursions. We were encouraged to
examine the ambulances and acquaint ourselves with
their mechanism, to read and digest the book of instructions. Enough petrol and oil were provided to
allow the engine to run, but there was no question of
going for a test drive. The cars were mostly Citroëns
of a straightforward type, and had been presented to
the organisation by such widely different donors as
Persil Ltd., the State of Tonkin, and the French colony
of Rio de Janeiro. The interior was fitted to take three
stretchers, or alternatively four people seated, (*trois
couchés ou quatre assis*, in the words of the official description), so it was quite roomy ; the chassis was solid, the
bodywork largely three-ply wood with a strengthening
of metal, the outside was painted olive green, and on
the roof was a large red cross on a white ground.

The next event was the arrival of the military *cadre*,
the representatives of the Army, who were to take
charge of us. There were six of them, a lieutenant, a
maréchal des logis (the equivalent of a sergeant), a
mechanic, a cook, an accountant and a general assistant. The lieutenant, M. Bouveret, was small and dark,
a *soldat de carrière*, ambitious, going to the front for the
first time and not quite happy about the chances of
being able to cover himself with glory at the head of
such a unit. He would have liked to enforce discipline,
but lacked confidence in himself, and decided from the
first day that it was simpler to appeal to us as a *corps
d'élite* to set an example with our behaviour.

On the second day we were led to barracks, where, as
a first reminder of the seriousness of the work we were
about to undertake, we were each asked to provide
the name of a relative or friend in France with whom
the authorities should communicate *en cas d'accident*. As
we waited about in a dark and narrow passage, it was

depressing to hear our Belgian and Dutch companions
desperately trying to think of someone they knew.

After this began the distribution of the equipment
provided by the French Army. First, gas masks. They
were thrust on one's head, and with a mechanical
repetition of only one phrase : " Can you breathe
now ? " " Yes "—then, after manipulation : " Can
you breathe *now* ? " " No." " *Bien* "—one went away
slinging over one's shoulder the sack containing a
masque à gaz, type l'éléphant. There followed a scramble
for a tin hat of the right size, a solid, dark green object
shaped like a coal-scuttle bearing on its front a grenade
stamped with R.F. After the preliminary shock of its
terrific weight, one realised that it was well-balanced
and not too uncomfortable. We then formed a circle
in front of a shed, and rotated round and round like
ponies in a circus ring, being given another piece of
accoutrement each time we passed the door. *Musette*
(the French haversack), tent-pegs, props, cord, a
quarter of a canvas tent (we were to sleep in parties of
four)—we soon had a formidable pile. Then came the
collection of aluminium ware—water bottle, *gamelle* (a
double-decker combination of soup-bowl and plate,
equally intended as frying-pan or kettle, called in
English " dixie "), a cup, spoon and fork, and a bread-
tin. Lastly, a small grey package labelled *pansement individuel*, a bandage for one's personal use in case of
necessity. Then we were complete.

There was an enormous rush to get us ready and off.
We only had three more days. The time was easily
filled with questions and answers, the final equipping
of the cars with buckets, brushes, thermos flasks for the
wounded, picks, spades, tools, cans for extra petrol and
oil, and competitive speeches from our two lieutenants
who were already disputing the right to the final word.

Nor was our practical training in First Aid neglected.
We spent one whole afternoon in the carbon monoxide

fumes of our third floor garage, watching an elaborate
professional display by military stretcher-bearers of the
correct way to open and shut, mount and dismount,
carry and set down a stretcher. Another part of the
course dealt with handling the wounded. One man was
sent to lie in a far corner, and in parties of four we
scurried over to pick him up, bearing well in mind
whether he could use both arms or only one, both legs
or neither, had a bullet in the head or an internal
haemorrhage. As with all text-book cases, it worked
like clockwork under the eyes of a commanding officer,
but within a few days we were to find that things worked
really quite differently.

By the end of the week everyone was in uniform,
petrol tanks full, tyres inflated, and we were ready to
leave. But in true French style we had to go through a
ceremony first. Wearing our steel helmets, we drove in
solemn convoy through the streets of Paris to the inner
courtyard of the Invalides, where we drew up in two
lines. Here we were received by a group of high French
officers and the *Présidente* of our organisation, in
uniform. She was the Corsican-born wife of the owner
of the right-wing paper " *Gringoire*," and beside her
stood the *Vice-Présidente*, her friend, the active Jewish
wife of a famous left-wing Jewish lawyer. A third figure,
in a uniform of his own design, a male Vice-President,
was Bernard Faÿ, a famous French literary figure and
professeur at the Collège de France. M. Faÿ looked
slightly uncomfortable as he stood there holding the
bénitier during the short service which followed, when
we were addressed in stirring terms and blessed by a
dignified old Cardinal in scarlet and lace. We did not
learn till afterwards that, during a hectic drive down
from Montmartre, the holy water had been spilled over
M. Faÿ's trousers, and that instead of being sprinkled
over us it was slowly forming a pool at his feet. However, what the blessing lacked in liquid it made up for

in fervour. The Cardinal was then hustled away before a pastor (the head of the Protestant Church of France) could be introduced. He was tall, sad and puritan, dressed in a black lounge suit, and spoke in a voice of thunder which contrasted sharply with the beautiful tones of the Cardinal. He guaranteed on behalf of God to take personal responsibility for the conscience of any of us who were not quite reconciled to the morality of the war. Having delivered his homily, he insisted on being personally introduced to those of his faith, after which our spiritual armament was complete. But this was not the end of our ceremonies. Again we formed a convoy and drove this time by way of the Place de la Concorde and the Champs Elysées to the Arc de Triomphe, where we had to lay a wreath. That marked the end of our preparations, and when we went home that night it was to pack and get ready for our departure on the following morning.

VILLIERS-SUR-MARNE

Monday, 3rd June.

THE *rassemblement* was at 6.30 a.m. at the Ecole Militaire, where the ambulances had been parked and under guard since the previous evening. We arrived about half an hour before with our luggage, which, in common with the others, we proceeded to stow away. We had also had the foresight, and it caused a great deal of amusement, to bring with us a very large sack of tinned food. We had taken the advice of our soldier friends who had seen active service.

Punctually at 6.30 there was a series of piercing blasts on a whistle, the accepted sign in the French army that something is about to happen. It was for the roll-call, and strangely enough everyone was present. There we all were, twenty ambulances and thirty drivers, some of us going in pairs. We were the only two Englishmen among a group consisting of eleven Frenchmen, five Dutch, five Belgian, a Cuban and a Guatemalan.

We were joined by a compact, humourless little group of six Norwegians. They looked aloof, dumb and faintly superior, and we did not really take to them. Their lack of physical charm, like their ambulances, was covered by a splendid display of flags, badges and silver stars glittering everywhere. Their chief, a burly figure of a troll, in its old Norwegian sense, had got himself appointed an assistant *Chef de Section*. He introduced himself in unintelligible French with a name which we only heard as ' Jack-and-Jim,' and as this he became known. They were cold Nordic people, and mostly unable to speak or understand French.

After the roll-call we were given a series of final instructions, especially concerning the procedure for

B 29

moving off and the significance of various signs blown on the whistle. Thus, one blast meant get into the car, two blasts start the engine and put out the left hand when it is running, three blasts move off in line. There was also a little dissertation on how to behave in case of an air-raid or machine-gunning while on the road. Here it was pointed out that if the ambulance was empty it should be hidden under the nearest tree while the driver took shelter, whereas if it was full of wounded it should still be hidden as effectively as possible, but the driver must naturally remain at the wheel.

Then, too, the elaborate procedure of driving in convoy was explained at length, for we were accompanied by a kitchen lorry as well as a breakdown van, whose duty it was to come last of all. The route, and the name of the place which was to be our destination, was only given to the first car, in which sat the two lieutenants, and to the breakdown van, so that if anyone was in distress he had to wait for this lorry. As all the cars were new, we were prepared for the usual crop of running-in mishaps.

Finally came the order from Caillemer to hoist our flags, for we had a Red Cross and a Tricolour, one to put on each side of the ambulance. We were to leave Paris *en tenue de gala*. However, this was suppressed almost immediately by Bouveret, and so we had our first practical experience of the *ordre* and *contre-ordre* technique which is so essential a part of the French military machine.

By this time the personalities who had come to give us a formal send-off had all assembled in the courtyard, as well as a good number of devoted friends and relations who, because of war-time regulations, were only allowed to look on from behind the *grille*. We drew up in formation in numerical order : our car was No. 12. The car in front of us was driven by the charming and distinguished Belgian actor, Raymond, who led

the second half of the convoy. We were told he was our *brigadier* : this was good news. Behind us, No. 13, was a Dutchman, Erwtemans, who was amusing and gay. When we were all in line, the whistle blew and, saluting our chiefs, the convoy moved off.

It had been whispered that we were going to Epernay or Verdun, at any rate there was no doubt that we were going east, where the heaviest fighting was then taking place. In any case, we knew our duties were in the front line. We threaded our way through the main streets of Paris, though not without some difficulty. A military convoy among the normal traffic of a busy city is a cumbersome affair.

The crowds looked at us in silence as we passed, the women did not wave and smile as usual, but it was more from apprehension than from lack of sympathy. They thought of their own men, for they knew what the Red Cross meant. Again we passed through the Place de la Concorde, down the Quai du Louvre and on along the river past the Gare de Lyon to the Porte de Vincennes. Shepherding us through streams of cross-traffic meant a great deal of work for the commanders, especially as obstinate lorry-drivers would insist on breaking up the convoy. We stopped and started with monotonous regularity, until at last we were on an open road. We were running our cars in, so that we never touched more than 30 km. an hour. We envied the generals, liaison officers and despatch riders who flashed past us in both directions.

For those who have never experienced driving in convoy, we can only say that it is not only a bore but a nightmare. By some inexplicable law, the further one is away from the leader the faster one has to travel, no matter how slowly he may be moving. The general rule is to leave a gap of 25 yards between the cars as a precaution against bombing and machine-gun attacks. By the time one has avoided the private cars which come between, and the pedestrians who play a perpetual game of hide-and-seek, one usually finds that the rest of the convoy has taken quite another turning at the cross-roads. A regular trick of the leader seems to be an inveterate habit of calling a halt at the moment when he has reached the top of some long hill, leaving his followers, whose brakes are not always what they should be, to slide gracefully downwards into each other. When two convoys meet at a cross-road, precedence depends not on the size or speed, but on the strength of voice of the officers in charge. If their vocabularies and vocal chords are evenly matched, it works like the weft and warp.

After we had passed Vincennes, we quickly realised what it meant to be in the military zone. There were barricades at intervals along the roads, sometimes formidable, with concrete and barbed wire, sometimes formed by turned-up carts and the remains of lorries. They were mostly guarded. We passed woods where anti-aircraft batteries were concealed and every crossroad was policed by the military. Forests were being cleared for action, trenches dug, and gun emplacements prepared: we left Paris with the feeling that its defences were well under way. Once we took cover as unidentified aeroplanes passed overhead.

About midday, by which time we had covered scarcely 40 km., we were driven off the road into two lines on the grass verge, under a double avenue of trees. A despatch rider had warned us of approaching aircraft, and as far as we could see down the long stretch in front of us, ammunition lorries, cars, everything was stationary. We all seized the opportunity to eat. It was a princely display. Adoring families seemed to have pressed into each hand a parcel of " dainties " for the journey : there were finely-cut chicken sandwiches, *pâtés*, smoked salmon, and the best bottles of burgundy and claret. We had a *rôti de veau*. In ten

minutes the alarm was over and the traffic started to
move on.   Our appetites were just beginning to be
satisfied—we had not eaten since 6 a.m.—when the
lieutenant decided that we might as well prolong this
timely stop and ordered lunch to be cooked. Most of us
hung around the kitchen lorry, helping to chop wood
and distribute the ration of wine. For an hour or so the
little cook, Lenoir, cursed and grumbled at his brand
new installation : he assured us that the food would be
uneatable because he had to prepare it in such a
hurry. At last it was ready ; we sat down in the blazing
sun and were amazed to find that he had produced,
over a wood fire, one of the most delicious pieces
of beef we had ever eaten. We ate on the grass, feeding
out of our bright new *gamelles*. We felt rather like
children with a new toy. The lieutenants, asserting their
superiority, ate in considerable discomfort at a small
card table. It was suspiciously like a school treat.

Suddenly our meal was disturbed by a terrific din.
Guns blared out from all the woods around us, and
above the noise of shell-fire we could hear the drone of
a vast number of aeroplanes. There was an immediate
cry of " *Casques et Masques !* " and we rushed back to the
trees. Across the field we could see an enormously long
goods train puffing by. It was the main line, and an
important objective. The Germans were evidently flying
very high, and the most we could see, as we looked up
into the clear blue sky, was an occasional flash of sunlight on the wings. We heard the rattle of machine-
guns as the French fighter 'planes engaged them, and
the zoom of their engines as they climbed and dived.
Radio cars and mobile anti-aircraft batteries tore
past us down the road. There was no doubt the Boche
were going towards Paris, and judging by the time they
took to pass over our heads, we knew that there must
have been hundreds. The sound receded slowly, and
rather thoughtfully we went back to our beef.

Soon after this we moved on. We passed through Meaux, crossed the Marne, and then on to La Ferté-sous-Jouarre, where we took the road to Charly. Here we turned left, and we realised that we were not going to Epernay after all.

A few kilometres on, we came to Villiers-sur-Marne, and just beyond the village stopped outside a large *château*, in front of which was a sign-post " *Hôpital Complémentaire*." So this was our destination.

We turned in through the imposing entrance gates, passing on our right the old gatekeeper's tower, which was now marked "Control Office" ! We drove on round the lawn past the two-storied eighteenth century *château*, and followed a road which led up the steep hill behind. On the top, we saw at once several large concrete buildings, while dotted about on the hillside were two or three smaller ones. We drove up the narrow, winding road, and stopped in front of the largest one.

It was an enormous edifice of modern design, with five storeys and a frontage of at least three hundred feet, with balconies running the whole length. All the window-panes had been painted blue, but the paint was starting to fall off, and a great many of them were broken. No great effort of the imagination was needed to realise at once that it could only have been meant for a sanatorium. It appeared desolate. The only signs of life were a few disinterested wounded soldiers, watching our arrival from a second-floor balcony in the right wing. It stood stark, blank and white, in an open space, surrounded by the melancholy remnants of a former park. There were trees here and there below it, while just above, on the ridge of the hill, a few sad pines had been left standing, presumably only to screen the water tower.

The environment was perfect for stimulating the disappointment of those whose only thought was to find themselves immediately in the middle of the

battle. As we got out of our cars, the grumbling started.
Soon everyone had a complaint; even Caillemer
seemed discontented. Needless to say, the Norwegians
had no reactions, while we, with typical English
dumbness, expressed no amazement either, realising
that one might normally expect to operate from a base,
and believing the army incapable, at such a critical
moment, of sending us to a place where our services
would be wasted.

Our first move was to unload the ambulances completely. Then, carrying our personal luggage, we were
led endlessly up the stone staircase to the fifth floor,
which was to be our quarters. The lift, of course, did
not work. We found a long straight passage, off one
side of which opened a series of rooms. The other side
consisted almost entirely of windows, from which we
looked out over a large strength of countryside, into
which the eye was led along a road starting right below
the hospital. The country was wooded and undulating
and the road ran back between two lines of hills. The
scene was fresh, green and peaceful, and looking its
most beautiful in the evening sunlight. There was no
suggestion of a war in progress; it was the perfect
atmosphere for a rest cure in the country.

The rooms were small and completely bare, except
for a certain amount of filth and broken glass lying
about on the red tiled floor. There were single and
double rooms, but now they had to take twice their
normal complement. We were given one of the double
rooms to share with two others, Ido M . . ., a Dutch
boy, and Pierre D . . ., who was Belgian. M . . . was
twenty-two, and had lived most of his life in France;
he was more than half-way to becoming an *avocat*, but
since the war had been working in the Ministry of
Information. He was a little mystified by our perpetual
need to laugh, but he did try his best, and after all he
was a solid Hollander. We judged him to be the spoilt

child of rich parents, but he was a pleasant, sociable
young man. D . . . was remarkable. He was tall and
handsome, and at first sight looked not a day over
thirty. In fact he was forty-five, and the father of a boy
already mobilised in the Belgian Army. Our only clue to
his period was his regular habit of singing "I feel so silly
when the moon comes out." He worked hard to be the
life and soul of the party, and that was a little disturbing.
But he was very kind to us and most helpful, and we
liked him very much. He was always full of "tips and
wrinkles" learnt during military service, and as the
glamour faded, he became a sort of nice kind uncle.

Having deposited what luggage we could carry, as
a sign that the room was occupied, we went downstairs again to collect the rest. The four of us then set
about making the room habitable. On one of the lower
floors we discovered a collection of wicker *chaises-
longues*, and took one each ; in the basement were piles
of mattresses. As blankets had been supplied to us, our
beds were now complete. M . . . found a cupboard
and a table in another corner of the building, and an
old strip of carpet appeared from somewhere. Our room
almost assumed an appearance of luxury, and the others
were a little envious. But there were snags. In the first
place, it was impossible to move through the confusion
of beds and baggage except when the other three
people were already lying down. Secondly, though
there were two basins with running water, the water
did not run. Nor in fact could we, at the moment,
discover more than one tap running in the whole
building.

Having settled in and disposed of the stores belonging
to the Section, we then had to put the cars away. We
ploughed through the long grass and parked them under
the pine trees, where they were supposedly hidden from
the prying eyes of aeroplanes. But as the water tower
rose well above the trees and was a landmark for miles,

we could not help feeling that it was an excellent target.

We locked the cars, and thought we were now free to explore our new home. But Raymond appeared and detailed us off to fetch dinner at 6 p.m. Military life was beginning. We collected Lenoir and went across to Pavilion 2, the main hospital, where the central kitchen was situated. While he and the head chef poked about in the large pots on the fire, tasting and sniffing, we hung about outside feeling just like two "Bisto" children. The culinary conversation lasted awhile, and we had time to satisfy our curiosity about the whole place.

There were several *infirmiers* sitting around whom we questioned ; we learnt that it had been built by the Government as a sanatorium for civil servants. Since the war, it had been taken over by the military, and though it was almost empty at the moment, it was being re-staffed and re-equipped for immediate use. The *château* was used as offices and officers' quarters, the smaller houses for extra staff and convalescent wards, while in the three main pavilions two thousand beds were being set up. Already a large staff of doctors and surgeons had arrived, there were stacks of cotton wool, bandages and surgical equipment, and extra operating theatres were hastily being prepared.

When the meal was at last ready, we were called in to the kitchen, and our pots and pans filled. Our patience was rewarded with a few tidbits, a special mark of favour from the chef. The three of us then set off back to our own Pavilion 3, carrying a meal for forty people, a heavy load made even bulkier by the addition of several long loaves of bread. As we went through the empty corridors, we summoned everyone to table with the traditional cry "*A la soupe!*" The cry was caught up by people on the different floors, and the whole concrete shell was quickly echoing with voices and feet.

We fed in a small refectory at four long tables, at

which places had been summarily indicated by the
distribution of small bottles of wine. At the sight of
food, pandemonium broke loose. Everyone shouted at
the top of his voice, dixies and mugs clattered, and in
two seconds a group of civilised human beings were
behaving like a pack of hungry schoolboys. Soup,
roast veal and noodles was the menu, and the meal
ended when nothing more was left.

Our duties were over for the day, and with the
evening drawing on, we found ourselves exhausted and
slightly bewildered by this sudden change in our
existence. After the last conflicting weeks, during which
the responsibility for every decision, every action had
been entirely personal, one suddenly found oneself part
of a machine as remote as God himself, with decisions
and actions dictated. It was an enormous relief after
that struggle to preserve a semblance of normality.
But it was a little puzzling, for it seemed too easy a way
of escape.

As the light faded, we rolled into our flea-bags and
fell asleep.

Tuesday, 4th June
ABOUT SIX O'CLOCK next morning, everyone began
to stir. We had had no orders and heard no whistles,
but as this seemed a reasonable hour we got up. The
sun was shining brightly, and there seemed no excuse
for putting off any longer the beginning of our new
life. The first problem was water, which we needed
as much for washing as for making tea. The single tap
was in great demand, but we managed to fill a battery
of thermos-flasks, water-bottles and saucepans with
which we returned in triumph. The sight of water
being boiled and tea prepared provoked amazement
and curiosity in the others, and as they passed up and
down the passage, they peered in through our glass
windows like simple natives distrustfully watching

a missionary prepare his magic. To us it really was magic, and the familiar habit did much to lessen the shock of finding ourselves in such extraordinary circumstances.

The four of us were still washing when there was a general cry of "*Au jus!*" and we knew that it meant the coffee was ready. It was sweet, not very hot, and must have been made from acorns, or any other bean except coffee. Even if French military coffee was not up to standard, we at least had our tea, and we made a mental note to avoid the "*jus*" in future. The very word should have warned us what to expect.

At eight o'clock the whistle blew. The lieutenants, Bouveret and Caillemer, began one of their now familiar duets. Bouveret had obviously spent the night working out how to assert his control, and having no previous experience of dealing with officer cadets, for that was roughly our status, he had come to a decision with difficulty. "Discipline," he said, trying to look fierce, "is the first essential. The Section will rise at six and breakfast at seven." But as we had already done this on our own initiative, the first act of discipline fell rather flat. He went on reading a time-table and we realised that by "discipline" he meant fixed hours. "It is essential that no light be shown after dark," he continued. This again fell a bit flat, as the electric light had been cut off. Caillemer then took over and pointed out that, even when driving by night, the use of any light whatever was forbidden. A few days previously a careless driver coming up the hill had flicked on his lights for an instant, been observed by a German aeroplane overhead, and greeted with two bombs. That accounted for all our broken windows. Bouveret was not pleased, his admonition had been capped. "For some reason or other," he continued bitterly, "all of you volunteers are looked upon as *grand seigneurs* and therefore, although all the men with whom we will be working are naturally above suspicion, I suggest it would be wiser to keep all your possessions under lock and key." Then a final challenge: "In addition you will be expected to help in the kitchen and with the washing-up, also to attend to your cars yourselves and do any other odd jobs that may be necessary."

"If I see a wounded German on the road, may I run over him?" The usual series of alarmingly stupid questions had started. "When shall we go to the front?" said one. "We didn't volunteer to live a bar-racks existence," said another. In their innocence they seemed to be in an awful hurry. This appealed to Bouveret, and he softened. He confessed that he felt the same himself, but that—however tedious—we must, like him, await orders, and he was sure that within a very short time we would be in the thick of it. There were times like this, when he spoke to us as man to man, that we realised that he was fundamentally human. He wanted to be of us and with us, but suffered from an inability to make the right approach. It was a pity, because if he could only have made the contact, he would have found us solidly behind him.

The fatuous questions were brought to an abrupt end by a message from the Colonel that we were to present ourselves for inspection immediately. We marched down to the *château* and formed two very unmilitary looking lines on the lawn. The *Médecin-chef* appeared first and welcomed us, passing down the lines and noting our various nationalities. The Colonel then came out, an imposing figure with a long black beard. He addressed us at some length on the noble nature of our duties, and thanked us for the *bonne volonté* of which we had given proof by enlisting. It would not be long before he would be in need of our services. Although there might be nothing to do for a day or so, the hospital had been working full time until a week previously, and he knew it was only a question of hours before it was

again full. He advised us to take advantage of the lull
to prepare ourselves, because, when the rush came, we
would have to work day and night, and he relied on us
not to fail him. Everyone was delighted, and his parting
salute was returned in confusion by all those in the ranks
whose enthusiasm temporarily obscured their military
knowledge. Bouveret blushed with embarrassment, dismissed us and sent us off back up the hill.

Our instructions were to spend the rest of the day
cleaning our cars and putting them in order. There was
a great deal to be done, and especially inside the
ambulance itself. The stretchers and fittings had to be
greased and loosened so that even in the darkness they
would slide in and out smoothly, with the greatest
speed and precision.

At lunch time we heard the news of the aerial bombardment of Paris. It came as a great shock. Then we
remembered the hundreds of 'planes that had passed
over our heads the day before, and realised on what
a gigantic scale the attack must have been made.
The news cast a great gloom over all of us; some of our
companions were extremely worried about wives and
children whom they had left behind. There was no
means of immediate communication with Paris, but our
fears were somewhat allayed by the small casualty
figures published in the newspaper. It seemed ironical
that we should now be within a few kilometres of the
front and yet in comparative safety, whereas Paris,
which we had left only twenty-four hours earlier,
should have already been attacked.

Everything seemed to point to the fact that we had
been sent out at the moment of crisis. Now we could
understand why our Section had been so hastily
organised. We all consoled ourselves with the thought
that the next day's newspaper would at last announce
the destruction of Berlin.

In the late afternoon, the first group of five

ambulances was sent up to the front. They left quietly and
we were not told they had gone until some hours later.
In the evening, we strolled down with Ido M . . . to the
café in the village, which we found already full of
people from the hospital.   We sat at a table with
Erwtemans, who was in a gay and noisy mood, and
had with him two more of our Section, René de S . . .,
who was French, and van A . . ., another Dutchman.
   We were joined by four of the Norwegians whose
frigidity soon thawed after a few sips of Pernod, when
they realised that English, which they spoke, was the
only common language. After a little while, the oldest
and saddest Norwegian burst into " Tipperary." Everybody joined in.   Suddenly, warmed by a few more
Pernods, Erwtemans sprang to his feet and started
"God Save The King." An orgy of national anthems
followed, and all the Allied Royalty came in for a toast.
The Dutchmen solemnly thanked us for our hospitality
to their Queen (rather in the manner of one Court
Chamberlain to another), and the best joke of all was
the toast to Buckingham Palace, " the most exclusive
pension in Europe." No wonder we emptied the bottle
of Pernod.
   We hoped, when we got home, to go to bed, but the
Norwegians had a bottle of whisky and were determined to be friendly. 'Jack-and-Jim' sent a personal
message, and we felt it would be discourteous to refuse.
It was a solemn little gathering on a balcony in the
twilight, made merry with Norwegian folk-songs sung
in parts. They were still singing after we had gone to bed.

Wednesday, 5*th June*
NORWAY WAS DETERMINED to know us, and after
the morning parade they again engaged us in conversation. A sad and sheepish one, who looked particularly disillusioned, led us on to the topic of war and
politics. We knew this was a mistake, for from the

beginning it had been clear to us that, in such an international brigade, political discussion could only lead
to wounded feelings. Besides, in common with our
French friends, we had definite views on the dubious
advantages of rescuing recalcitrant neutrals. But he
was determined. He had been the Paris correspondent
of a Norwegian newspaper, then attached to the
Norwegian Chamber of Commerce; now he had come
to the war " to get copy for a book," as he put it. He
obviously had a grudge, and was burning to get it off
his chest. He worked up to it at length.

"I will never forgive the English for putting mines
along the Norwegian coast. It was a criminal thing to
do."

This was the sort of discussion which we were determined to avoid, so with an excessive display of charm,
we left him magnetised to his mines.

Food seemed to be our main preoccupation, but
perhaps this was due to the fact that for the second time
we were on kitchen duty. It was an amusing job and
we enjoyed it. During our work, we had a long conversation with little Lenoir, and when we complimented
him on his cooking he told us, to our amazement, that
he was really a Paris bus-driver. The chief cook, too,
had his secret ; he was one of the chefs at Maxim's.

The amount of washing-up which has to be done
after a meal for forty people is amazing; at least we
were given a large cauldron of boiling water from the
kitchen. After the dishes, we tackled the floor and
tables in the refectory until at last we had got them
clean. Then, as a joke, we picked a large bunch of wild
flowers in the field outside the window and arranged a
vase on each table. We thought it would appeal to the
others, and so it did, but not in the way we had expected. When they came down to the evening meal, we
were seriously complimented on the *chic* appearance
of the room. We ought to have realised that, no matter

how poor the attempt, no Frenchman would ever laugh at something that appealed to his æsthetic sense.

There had been an air of expectancy during the day. One after another, ambulances of all sizes had been driving up and unloading their wounded. Several times, aeroplanes had flown overhead ; we had heard the distant rumble of artillery and we knew from some of the *infirmiers* that the hospital was filling up. Some of our drivers had been among those returning from the front with wounded, and we heard from them that a big offensive had just been launched between Soissons and Laon. Inactivity at a moment like this seemed insupportable.

Others who had been out on different jobs had brought back some newspapers, and as we sat at table expectancy gave way to depression. The news was bad. The casualties in Paris were several times larger than the figures published the day before, and the damage more serious. Hitler, in a proclamation to the German people, had announced his war aims as " the total annihilation of Great Britain and France," and instead of the wholesale reprisals we had expected against Berlin, the Allied air fleets had bombed military objectives in Munich. Why were we still being " gentlemen " ?

We were all pretty low when Bouveret appeared, cancelled all permission to leave the grounds, and told us to prepare and hold ourselves in readiness to leave at any minute. The relief was enormous, and there was an excited rush to get ready.

We hurriedly finished our work in the kitchen and ran upstairs to wash off the day's accumulation of grease and sweat. We met Caillemer coming down. His face was covered in beads of perspiration. " It is too hot, much too hot," he complained. We remarked how glorious the weather was and how much we enjoyed the sun. " Really," he continued, " you like the sun? I only like cold countries and the winter," and puffing and sweating went on his way.

It seems odd how one reacts to little things even at moments of pressure, but Caillemer's remark seemed specially shocking at this moment, when the sun and the glorious weather were the only consolations in a world bereft of reason and sanity. We could not feel the same about Caillemer after this. Unreasonable perhaps, but such is the strength of prejudice.

We were still washing when we were called to the cars. We all drove round to Pavilion 2 and parked in formation in a sort of courtyard. In the wing on the left were the receiving ward and the main operating theatres, the central part consisted entirely of wards, while there were more operating theatres in the other wing. It was about 9 o'clock when we arrived, and still quite light. Almost immediately several of our cars were loaded with wounded and sent on the short journey to Pavilion 1, where relief surgeons were at work. All the while, innumerable large camouflaged ambulances and even commandeered charabancs were arriving with a stream of wounded. We were told that a hospital train was due at the station of Nogent-l'Artaud, some eight kilometres away, at 11 o'clock, and that our work was to fill it.

As night drew on, the scene in the courtyard appeared more and more macabre. It was almost impossible to move. Vehicles were everywhere. The drivers stood in little groups beside their cars, now quiet and subdued by their first contact with war. Elsewhere were little groups of officers, gravely discussing the turn of events and the work on hand. An occasional car would dash up with extra doctors or nurses. One in particular brought the *Pharmacien-chef* with a container of blood for transfusions, rushed from Paris by two uniformed women, one of them English. The demand for blood had been so great that the supplies of the hospital had been used up in a few hours. From time to time, a surgeon in his white cap and overalls splashed with blood would run across the courtyard.

There would be an imperative shout of "*brancardiers!*" and the stretcher-bearers would tirelessly thread their way through this confusion, loading and unloading the wounded.

Against the walls, on the ground, on steps and on the few available benches, the less seriously wounded, waiting their turn, sat huddled together in mute groups. It was hard to realise that they were human beings, they seemed shapeless and inanimate. Some were barefoot, others had lost most of their clothes, they were swathed in rough bandages, unshaven, dishevelled, their bristling faces grey with dust. They sat there clutching the few possessions they had saved from the battlefield, silent and uncomplaining, their eyes looking inwards. Where had one experienced this ghastly scene before? It all seemed strangely familiar. Then one remembered Goya, and realised that war was just as he had recorded it. He had not needed to exaggerate a single detail.

Inside the reception ward, doctors and nurses were working at terrific speed. Every available inch was covered with stretchers, there was barely space to get between them. Yet each man had to have his wounds properly cleaned and dressed and minor operations were performed on the spot. All this with very little light, for the risk of aerial attack was great. They worked in an indescribable atmosphere, hot and fœtid, a mixture of human secretions and anæsthetics. It looked like an incredible chaos, but it was handled with remarkable efficiency. The operating tables in the theatres were only free for the few moments it took to disinfect them and dispose of the used dressings.

There were continually aeroplanes overhead. We knew from the broken rhythm of their engines that

some of them were German. It was out of the question
to move before it was completely dark.

We tried to start conversations with some of the
wounded sitting outside, but, poor devils, most of
them were inarticulate and others could only speak in
disjointed sentences. We gathered that they had all
been wounded that morning or afternoon on the banks
of the Canal de l'Ailette, which the Germans were
trying to cross. The French, they said, were still
resisting magnificently, and all of them had high hopes
of victory. They spoke of the heavy German casualties
and the reckless way in which men's lives were thrown
away. They all complained that they had been un-
ceasingly machine-gunned by German 'planes without
once seeing a French fighter. "Where are the 'planes to
defend us?" was their constant cry. We were silent, but
we thought of the French airman whom we had seen
only half-an-hour before, his whole face burnt and only
a pair of yellow lips left exposed among the bandages.
These were no beaten men, but, in a spirit of quiet
determination, "just temporarily out of action," to
quote one of them.

About 11 o'clock, a window on the ground floor
in the right wing opened and stretchers were passed
out. By the light of a few shaded torches, they were
placed in the ambulances and driven off to the station.
About half the Section still remained behind and, as
the window closed, the *Médecin-chef* himself appeared
and announced that, as the railway was being bombed,
the train had been delayed for several hours. The
next lot of wounded would not be ready till 1 o'clock.

We waited in the dark, dozing in turn for a few un-
comfortable moments on the front seat of our cars.
From an ambulance that arrived, they took out a
wounded man whose monotonous half-crazed cry
"*A boire . . . A boire . . .*" tapped on our strained nerves.
But from the hardened and exhausted *infirmiers* the

only answer it drew was " Yes, yes, all in good time."
We could follow where they carried him. " *A boire . . .
A boire . . .*" echoed down the long stone corridors until
a door shut, and there was silence again.

In the doorway leading to the operating theatres, one
saw at intervals the red glow of a cigarette. It was some
surgeon who had stolen a few minutes to relax and
breathe in the fresh air. Still we waited, until at last the
window opened again.

This time the number was greater, and all our
ambulances as well as every available vehicle were
filled. Loading with such serious cases was anyhow a
complicated job by the light of only a few torches, but
when suddenly there was a cry of " Aeroplanes !
Lights ! Lights ! " and even these had to be extin-
guished, the task was formidable.

At such times the heights and depths of the human
character are laid bare, and we saw our companions
in a new light. Many of them behaved as we would
have expected, and of the rest, those with whom till
now we had made no contact, it was pretty easy in the
circumstances to form an accurate judgment. A Dutch
Catholic theological student, a turgid young man who
hitherto had only been noticeable for his overwhelming
professional friendliness and immense greed, had an
unhappy trick of peering into the faces of the wounded
and, to their intense embarrassment, muttering " *Mes
pauvres, mes pauvres.*"

Some of them were frightened of the men and
handled them gingerly as if they were freaks. Some,
through nerves, were aggressively nonchalant, while
others were dumb and useless. Still others seemed to
have an instinctive sense of how to manage them and
make them comfortable. One middle-aged man, whom
we had nicknamed " Snow-White's Grandmother,'
and who had always given the impression of enormous
efficiency, turned out to be a noisy interfering bore,

whereas Allard, a tall and distinguished-looking
Belgian, who had previously been very reserved, suddenly became the dominating character of the Section.
During that difficult and hectic half-hour, he seemed
to take control of the situation. He was calm and
gentle with the wounded and found time to help each
of us individually. He brushed aside displays of
temperament, and made order where there might have
been confusion. The fact that we were loaded with
speed and efficiency was largely due to his efforts.

The hill down to the *château*, which, in the daytime,
had seemed an easy wooded road, now seemed a nightmare. With such congestion outside Pavilion 2, and
with aeroplanes still about, it had been decided to send
us off independently as soon as we were full. The road
was narrow, and descended precipitously in a series of
short turns ; there were deep ditches on both sides, it
was pitch dark, and the overhanging trees made the
darkness literally impenetrable ; with the wounded we
could take no risks, and, having no leader to follow,
one of us had to walk in front and point the way. When
we reached the *château*, we were already shattered by
our first attempt at night-driving ; this first stage of the
journey, which by day would have been covered in
under five minutes, had now taken us thirty-five. We
reported at the Control Office and passed through the
château gates on to the main road.

The drive was straightforward though tedious, for
the surface was bad and we had to go slowly, never over
fifteen kilometres an hour. At least we were in the open
and the road was straight, with only one turning, which
was difficult to find, at Charly. Our three wounded
were very quiet, and appeared to be sleeping, so we
chatted in our own language in an undertone. It came
as a surprise to us when a voice from the back called out
plaintively in English : " How long is this bad road
going on for ? " " Not for long," we were able to reply

truthfully, for at that moment we arrived at the barricade blocking the turning to the bridge over the Marne.
The sentries stopped us with their red light and looked
at our papers. In fact, this was more or less a formality,
for they had been warned of the convoy on its way
down. We were then led through the maze of carts and
overturned lorries, drove on a few hundred yards down
the mined road, passing gun emplacements, and came
to the bridge itself, which was guarded with tanks and
blockhouses. Fifty yards further on, we turned in to
the station yard of Nogent and took our place in the
queue of cars which had already arrived.

By now it was 3 o'clock but there was still no sign
of the train. It was starting to get light. Someone commented that an aeroplane would not have much
difficulty in seeing us now ; Bouveret replied by indi-
cating a clump of trees beside the river, under which we
should hide in case of attack.

We gave our wounded a drink of water and some
cigarettes, and made them as comfortable as we
could. We felt badly that hot coffee had not been
provided for them, especially as we had thermos
flasks for that purpose. It was an omission we decided
to rectify in future, even if it meant brewing it personally. We ourselves had reached the stage of shiver-
ing, due, not to the chill morning air, but to sheer
physical fatigue. We drank a great deal of red wine,
with which we had cunningly filled one of our water-
bottles, ate some chocolate, and, curious though the
mixture may seem, we felt revived.

The waiting-room was no larger than one finds in
an English country station, yet there were well over a
hundred people inside, sitting around or on stretchers.
In a corner by themselves were two young German
airmen, badly smashed up but nevertheless able to
speak. We were curious, and talked to them in their
own language : one was from Thuringen and the other

a Sudeten. They replied evasively as though they were ashamed of having been shot down ; this was all we could extract from them.

Mixed up with all the soldiers was an old man, a civilian. He had fled from his village and was lost ; by now he was half mad, and in his madness desperately obstinate.

" I haven't eaten for two days. I won't move before I've eaten."

" You'll be fed on the train, *mon vieux*, and it won't be long now."

" I'll go all right, but I won't go till I've eaten."

They went on humouring him, but he would not believe their promises and kept up a steady flow of resistance.

Beyond the platform was a siding separated from the main line by a broad stretch of ground, where goods trains were obviously emptied and filled. This was covered with rows of stretchers which had been there several hours. The men were cold and wet from the dew ; it was a terrible sight, but it was nobody's fault. They lay there quiet and uncomplaining, with the details of their case written on an official folder tied to a button, staring upward at the morning sky, as if resigned to what the new day might bring them.

Ultimately the train backed into the siding. It was very long, and already partly filled with wounded.

We helped to carry the stretchers from the waiting-room and the yard and fix them in their place in the coaches. As we did so, we watched the men's pathetic concern for their tiny bundle of belongings now tucked into various corners of the stretcher—boots (sometimes only one), helmet, *musette*, bits of bread tied up in a handkerchief. It all seemed so useless now.

We returned to our ambulance and moved slowly with the column towards the train. Eventually we drew up beside a coach, and our three men were transferred.

As we moved them they asked where they were being sent, half doubting whether a destination had been fixed. " Troyes," we replied, " about 100 km. south of here." They seemed relieved, though they did not know where it was. Then, to our surprise, as they said good-bye, they thanked us for the care we had shown. As we drove away, we saw ragged groups of hobbling soldiers stoically supporting each other, and moving from carriage to carriage anxiously searching for a place. They were repeatedly told that there was room for all, but that they must take their turn after the stretchers. However, they were terrified of being left behind and persisted in their aimless task.

One diminutive Chasseur Alpin, who looked a mere child, said to us despondently : " They tell me I've got pleurisy, but I don't look ill, so nobody takes any notice of me." It was too much ; we stopped and handed him over to a doctor, who found him a corner. Our last sight was of the old civilian being led up the station yard, still protesting.

We drove home by daylight, and parked as usual under the trees. It was 6.30 a.m. Only the thought of bed carried us up the five flights of stairs.

Thursday, 6th June

(i)

(*The narrative is continued by Freeman*)

AS I GOT UPSTAIRS I remembered that I had forgotten to disconnect the ignition of the car ; this was a strict rule when the cars were parked. Cursing to myself, I ran downstairs and up the grass slope. When at last I had dragged myself up the five flights for a second time, by some ill-fated chance my eye was caught by the notice-board on the corner of the landing. I thought I had better see if there was anything of importance on it. I saw that Cooper and I were on guard for the day. This meant that the car had to be

at the door and one of us permanently ready to leave
for emergency calls. I went to break it to Cooper but
I found him already asleep. He was still in most of his
uniform. I tried to muster enough energy to face the
stairs again and fetch the car. I was torn between duty
and exhaustion when I heard a voice calling " Car
wanted ! " up the staircase. I had no option now, so as
briskly as I could I went outside and looked over the
banisters. It was the cook from Pavilion 2, who had
been sent by the *Médecin-chef* to fetch two cars. I told
him I would be there immediately, and went to see
who else was on guard. It was Raymond, but he had
not yet returned from the station. However, I found
Sarazinski, a podgy little Frenchman of Polish ex-
traction, who had been on guard since the previous
evening and still had another hour of duty. Although
it was not his job he was prepared to come with me,
and the two of us fetched our cars and set off together.

The hard-working staff in the reception ward had
not stopped for a moment since the previous day.
More wounded were arriving continually, and the
place was still as crowded as ever. One of the doctors'
assistants, a pretty fair-haired girl, who was resting
outside, told us that we would be wanted in a short
while to transfer some cases to Pavilion 1.

While we waited, Sarazinski and I walked up and
down in the sunshine. He was a lively, friendly fellow ;
I should say he was about thirty. He had a large
mouth and a loud voice with a curious not unpleasant
lisp. While he talked, which he did without ceasing,
everything seemed to work at once, the whole performance watered with spittle. He was slightly deaf
and that, added to the common failing of people
who spit when they talk, made him draw uncomfort-
ably near during a conversation. I used to wonder if
he would notice and think it very rude if I dodged now
and then, but I never really had the courage to try.

He told me that his family had left Poland several generations ago ; that he was Jewish and very proud of it, as indeed he was ; that he was an *avocat* and did not do too badly—for a brief moment I thought of his clients and wondered if they did any dodging. His wife and child, both of whom he adored, had left Paris to join his in-laws in the country ; he had no idea where they had gone, and was waiting for news of them.

Then he confided that he had a hobby. " You as an Englishman will understand it," he said, " I collect pipes. I have dozens—hundreds, of every shape and size. Little cheap ones bought for a few francs, and some of them excellent, up to big carved collectors' pieces. Don't think they are only objects of beauty," he explained. " Not at all. I smoke every one of them."

I was impressed—and I really was. At the same time I was a bit worried. I thought of the rows of pipes gazing reproachfully at their owner when he came to make his daily choice. I had a vision of hundreds, and started dividing them into the number of days of the year and waking hours not occupied with meals, bathing and other activities that made pipe-smoking really out of the question. I found my fancy transporting me to realms of madness.

" I have brought a large selection with me, and amongst it—a Dunhill ! " he added with enormous pride and considerable dampness.

I thought it would be too unkind to withhold my admiration any longer. We embarked on an apotheosis of the pipe, and I lied in my teeth when I conveyed the impression that I was never without one. I was too exhausted to explain that I was an habitual cigarette smoker, and that to me a pipe was an unmanageable mystery that always discharged nicotine down my throat, would never keep itself alight and gave me a form of lockjaw. We became undying friends when I

told him that Cooper and I had brought some English
tobacco with us and that we would be very happy if he
would accept a tin ; this went very well, for Sarazinski
was an acquisitive person. At the end of the
conversation I found myself the possessor of one of his
collection, not as a gift but as a sort of indefinite loan.
There was a technical description of its virtues and
shortcomings, and I had a vague impression that I was
meant to smoke it in.

The *Médecin-chef* looked tired and preoccupied as he
made his way across the courtyard to the reception
ward, but he smiled and stopped when he saw us.
" Thank God this hospital is at last running more or
less smoothly," he said, " two days to re-equip a place
this size, and then to be caught by yesterday's rush was a
bit too much for anybody. However, things have sorted
themselves out and we are ready for anything now."

He asked us if we knew the short cut to Pavilion 1.
We confessed that, apart from the main drive down to
the *château*, we were very confused by the whole lay-out
of the place and especially by the little clinkered inter-
secting tracks, which seemed to run about in a most
inconsequential way. He proceeded to show us the
short cut, and launched into a long description of the
hospital and how it came to be built.

I did not pay a great deal of attention to his discourse,
although from time to time I nodded and said " Ah ! "
at what I hoped were appropriate moments. I was
really wondering all the time how on earth one could
drive an ambulance down the ghastly pot-holed little
track without pitching the wounded out of the stretchers.

He brought us back a different way, for he explained
that inside the grounds all the traffic was one-way,
though how one was supposed to recognise the circuits goodness only knows, for there certainly were no
indications anywhere.

He paused for a moment to look at the country

below ; one could see for miles. The early morning haze was still quivering in the valleys ; it was all so placid and unperturbed. Silently he pointed to the road from the north which, like a long grey gash, cut through the little woods and fields where animals were grazing. It bore an irregular but endless flow of ambulances making their way to the hospital. I made no comment ; there was really nothing to say. Gone was the time when one could talk of the futility and pointlessness of it all. We were living in a moment of action ; work and not talk was the only reply to anything now.

The *Médecin-chef* could control himself no longer and blurted out his darkest secret : " Hundreds of them, hundreds of them ! However big this place is, whatever arrangements we make, we cannot cope with this ! Here we are, supposed to be a relief hospital, and we are being turned into a front-line dressing-station. Why, half the men we are getting come straight from the battlefield, with nothing but the bandage tied on by themselves. The whole thing is out of hand—what the devil is to be done ? " It was a revelation ; we had no idea that things were quite so bad.

In the bright hard sunlight he suddenly looked old and weary. The very way he stood, his shoulders drooping, his hands crushed into his pockets and his receding chin sloping away down his neck, gave him a defeatist air. His blue, staring, watery eyes seemed to search out each ambulance, as if he would peer inside, sort and docket each case even before it arrived at the *château* gates. " Nobody visualised this advance. Who could have thought it would take this turn ? "—this almost as if he expected the trees round us to answer. " And what is the result ? Every single hospital for miles has been thrown out of gear, and goodness knows where I am supposed to send half these wounded men on to."

He got a little more purpose back into his shoulders

as he shrugged them : " Oh well, it is lucky you are
here. But it means a great deal of work for you."

Sarazinski had been unusually silent for quite a long
time. Nevertheless, I could willingly have knocked him
to the ground when I heard him embark on a long
conversation on the origin and causes of the war. As
we walked back to Pavilion 2, they went at it hammer
and tongs : the same old arguments—the Saar, the
Ruhr, Munich, and all the rest—Sarazinski spluttering
loudly, the *Médecin-chef* quiet and defeatist, his shoulders
shrugging up and down with a ceaseless, hopeless
regularity.

' Snow-White's Grandmother ' was outside the
reception ward.

" I heard there was a call for cars." He seemed to
bristle with efficiency.

I was heavily polite : " Two are wanted and two are
here." I was too pompous and felt silly.

" I know, but I thought you would like some help."

Considering the insulting remark which Cooper had
justifiably made to him on our joint behalf the night
before, I realised he was being extremely kind ; so I
thanked him and contorted my face into what I hoped
was a friendly smile. I think it was the smile that
drove him off for a bit.

It was not long before the *infirmiers* started filling up
my car, and during the next hour and a half I made the
journey between the two pavilions many times.

The little road turned out to be as bad as it looked,
but after the first journey I knew how to get my charges
down the hill with the minimum of discomfort. They
were an odd collection—Chasseurs Alpins, *poilus* from
no regiment in particular, Légionnaires and Spahis.
These last were always very grand. There were
stretcher cases (some very bad), others were " sitting,"
which meant they could just about get along by
themselves. Some were quite gay and talkative, but

most of them pretty silent ; they were a strange mixture of every possible type.

One load of " sitting " seemed to be more dour and silent than the rest. I had packed them in as best I could on the two little seats inside, on the floor, and one in front. As I moved them about to make room for each other, it was like arranging furniture ; they had that unhelpful, pathetic look that furniture has when it first arrives in a strange room. I knew they wanted to help, but I knew they could not.

When I had packed them in I offered them some cigarettes. There was an awkward silence. They seemed incapable of grasping the simplest statement ; I was not quite sure whether to thrust the packet at one of them, shut the door and hope for the best, or just give up. Then, suddenly I heard a young and charming voice thanking me, and saw a beautifully shaped but excessively dirty hand stretching out from among the muddle of bodies and baggage on the floor. I passed the cigarettes over and drove down the hill. I had not been able to see the man himself, but I could not help thinking how odd it was that anything as delicate as that hand should be mixed up with that half-human collection.

When eventually they stood in a huddled, lost, little group outside the door of Pavilion 1, I was trying to guess which one of them it could possibly have been. But with their dirty, unshaven faces and their ragged clothes, they were indistinguishable from each other. One of them disengaged himself from the group and came up to me. I recognised the voice and the hand that he stretched out towards me. He was the youngest and smallest soldier I had ever seen in my life. Very gravely, and with that natural poise that never deserts a Frenchman, he thanked me on behalf of his comrades. As he turned to go he smiled for a second. I got into the car and looked back at the forlorn collection. The

little soldier had become part of it again, and I could
no more distinguish him from the others than I could
sheep in a pen.

In another load there was a Spaniard from the
Foreign Legion. Nothing could stop him talking, he
had a fine natural gift of the gab. He told me that he
had been through the Spanish Civil War, fighting on
the Government side ; that he had managed to escape
to North Africa at the end of it, and with several of his
friends had joined the Legion. He said it was a fine
life, with plenty of fighting, and he was furious that he
had been knocked out just when the fun was starting
in France. Although he told me the same stories as the
men the night before, of the tanks, the endless line of
advancing Germans, and the ceaseless machine-
gunning from the air, he did not seem discouraged
either. He assured me, like so many of the others,
that he would get back soon " to have another go
at them."

The morning was well advanced when I returned to
Pavilion 2 after one of my trips and found the Colonel
looking for me. There were some men with bad
head-wounds whom he wanted taken to Sézanne ; at
that particular hospital they were dealing with head
and eye cases, and quite a number of big specialists
and surgeons were working there. In addition the
Pharmacien-chef had to collect a consignment of drugs
from the depot there, and it was necessary for somebody
to drive him over and transport his supplies back.

I cursed my luck. Although Sézanne was only some
60 km. away and I was by now very much awake, the
thought of driving wounded down those long straight
French roads in the heat of the midday sun, feeling I
might inadvertently fall asleep, was rather alarming.
However, there was nothing to be done about it.

First, I had to collect the wounded from Pavilion 1.
The head *infirmier* came with me to see that the men

were properly arranged for the journey. There were two, both straight from the operating table.

It was difficult to believe that anything human could be concealed under the mass of bandages and blankets that came out on the first stretcher.

" You will have no difficulty with him on the journey. He will not move," the head *infirmier* remarked. Then he added, " I hope they will be able to do something for him."

As they brought the second man through the door, he shouted at the shock of his sudden encounter with the bright sunshine : " My God ! My eyes. . . ." The rest of his cry was lost in the corner of the blanket which was quickly thrown over his face. We hurried him into the ambulance, and when his face was uncovered I could see that his right eye was bandaged.

" Why are you sending me to Sézanne ? " I could sense something was on his mind.

" They can do more for you there than we can here, *mon vieux*."

" But it is my legs and not my eyes, isn't it ? " He was almost pleading with the head *infirmier*.

" Why yes, of course. Don't worry so much."

" Then why Sézanne ? I know what they do there."

That shook the head *infirmier*, but he lied magnificently. " Who has been telling you a lot of nonsense ? They do everything there. You will be on your feet in a few days, after they have attended to you."

The soldier seemed reassured ; he lay back on his stretcher and loosened his grip on the bars at the side. The head *infirmier* quickly changed the conversation before there was time for another question.

" Is there anything you want ? Would you like something to drink ? "

" Lemonade."

" I am afraid I can only give you water," was the reply. And then an odd remark : " We do

C

not have lemonade here. You see this is only a relief hospital."

The water was brought, the door shut at the back of the ambulance, and I drove the head *infirmier* back to Pavilion 2, where I had to collect the medical certificate. I could see he was upset.

" He is bad," he said.

" Eyes ? " I asked. He nodded. " Very bad ? "

" I'm afraid very bad."

As he got out of the car, I asked him a question : " Does one ever get used to all this ? "

He turned to me with a wry smile : " Unfortunately, never."

He was a splendid man, that head *infirmier*, strong as a lion : I have seen him lift enormous badly wounded men in his arms, tenderly and gently. He was calm and patient and I never remember him being cross or losing his head at any time during those few difficult days that we observed him at work.

They were a fine lot, those French *infirmiers*.

I found Sarazinski waiting for me in his car in front of the *château*. He had three men to drive to Sézanne, and offered to take the *Pharmacien-chef* and lead the way. Nothing could have suited me better. I had not been looking forward to the prospect of a formal conversation with a superior officer during the journey.

I reported at the office in the *château* and collected the necessary authorisation for the journey. I was given a document of enormous length, which I completed with the aid of the clerk, who spoke excellent English but took an undue length of time airing it for the benefit of his colleagues. Eventually, I got away by promising to drink with him in the village that evening.

Alas, I never kept our rendezvous ; but making " dates " that are never really meant to be kept is part of war, it is part of a hope that to-morrow must come. I often said " See you to-morrow," " See you next week," when everyone knew that there was no chance, no possibility of the meeting taking place. It is a form of consolation, for parting seems so final when destinations are so vague.

Once we had passed Charly the road was not too bad, and Sarazinski led quite slowly. Taking the *Pharmacien-chef* turned out to be a great blessing, for at the bridge over the Marne at Nogent, and at other points on the road, the sentries let us by with scarcely a cursory glance at our papers.

As we went through the little villages, people would lean out of the windows or run from the doorways into the street to watch us pass. We were an unfamiliar sight, for ambulances were still comparative rarities in that part of the country. I noticed that their expressions were the same as those of the people in the streets of Paris the day we had left—serious and a little frightened.

After about 20 km. we got to Viels-Maisons, where we joined the main Paris–Châlons-sur-Marne road ; up till now there had been practically no traffic, but from this point on to Montmirail, another 15 km., there were endless vast petrol lorries dashing along at great speed. They swayed from side to side in the most dangerous-looking way ; they were camouflaged with boughs and shrubs and sometimes whole trees ; as they charged down the road there was little question as to which of us had to get out of the way. It was not always very easy, for at times there was a considerable camber on the road, and I tried as much as possible to avoid driving the wounded along at a perilous angle.

Suddenly I became conscious that I was being stared at. I turned my head and glanced in through the window that divided the driver's seat from the main body of the ambulance. I found that the man with the bandage over his right eye had turned over on his side and was looking at me. He smiled in a friendly way and seemed to want to talk, so I asked him if he was all right and if he wanted anything. He said no, he had everything. Then I asked if his companion was moving at all—it was difficult for me to see without stopping, for the other man was immediately behind me—but he said that he was still unconscious.

I could not think how to begin a conversation. The obvious topics were out of the question, for I hesitated to talk to the wounded of war unless they started it themselves. Then he asked me if we had far to go ; I lied and said a very little further, for the thought of a long journey in an ambulance always unnerved them.

My awful French accent gave me away, and he asked if I was English. He was delighted when I said : " Of course—roast beef and plum pudding ! "

" Roast beef and plum pudding ! " he repeated, and we both laughed a great deal at my poor joke.

" I like your accent," he said, " it is very funny. All comics on the stage talk with an English accent ; it always makes us laugh."

He wanted to know what I was doing in the French army. I said I was a little surprised myself, and explained how Cooper and I had joined. Were we the only English with the French ? I said that, apart from a few with the American Field Service, I thought we were. He laughed a great deal at that.

And so we went on, past Montmirail and on to the road which leads to Sézanne, talking and laughing and smoking cigarettes. We became enormous friends. I think we both knew that if our meeting had been in different times we might have seen each other again.

Every now and then he would turn his head away and I could see he was in considerable pain. Great tears would slowly drop down his face. It was the only sign he made. Then he would fumble and try to brush them away and quickly look at me again and laugh. Sometimes as we talked they would start again, but we both pretended that nothing was happening and went on with the conversation.

He came from Bordeaux, and was pleased when I said it was one of my favourite towns. We talked of its restaurants, of its wines, and of the good times we had each had there.

Then he started on the topic I had been dreading. " Why are you taking me to Sézanne ? Sézanne is for eyes, and there is nothing much wrong with my eyes."

I countered, " There are some very good doctors there."

" Yes, but for eyes," he persisted.

" They are good for everything there."

He paid no attention to my remark. " My legs are bad, but not as bad as all that, they told me so at Villiers." And then back to the thing he obviously dreaded most : " But my eyes—why there is less than nothing wrong with them ! "

I think he must have known : of course, he knew. But he was not going to admit it. I knew, for the bandage had slipped, and where once his right eye had been there was now only a socket.

It was so important that he should get well quickly, he explained, it was a matter of the family honour. His father was a regular army officer and he was a regular soldier too, but in the ranks. His family had always been in the army. He had worked, done well, and now in one month he was due for his commission. After all, a slight leg wound was not serious, he would get over that in a minute. He stared at me very hard, as if to force the truth from me, but I kept my eyes on the road and drove straight on.

I confessed that I had lied about the distance to Sézanne, but we seemed to arrive quite quickly and drew up outside the old hospital of Henry I, which was just off the centre of the town. Sarazinski drove in, and when he had discharged his cases I followed. There was a little bridge at the end of the garden, which ran between the main buildings, and I went over this into an orchard where there were some tents. Stretcher-bearers hurried the unconscious man into one of them and I followed with my friend.

It was a long, low-pitched tent, with several stretchers placed at intervals on the right. On the left there were some odd stretchers and tables with bandages and instruments on them. One man was delirious, and repeated everything we said. He made the most commonplace remark sound macabre and meaningless. "Two cases from Villiers-sur-Marne, *mon capitaine*," he screamed as I reported. "Is that the lot?" he repeated after the doctor.

In the far corner a group of white-coated figures were bending over a stretcher, and there was a strong smell of anæsthetic everywhere. I realised that they were operating then and there. My friend looked nervous and hung on to my hand with a vice-like grip, but I disengaged it and moved away while several doctors and some nurses gathered round him.

I stood outside the tent and waited, regretting that the whole thing had been so quick and that I had not had a chance to say goodbye. After a minute one of the doctors came out and called me in. "He wants to talk to you," he said ; he seemed faintly surprised.

As I saw my friend lying there, I realised that he was a tall man. His hair was a reddish-gold, and his face, beneath the awful mess where his tears and blood had run among the dust and dirt, was strong and well shaped. The doctors made way for me and, as they waited for him to speak, they too seemed a little surprised.

He did not say much, just "Thanks" and "Goodbye," and if I came back would I come and see him. Then we shook hands. The white-coated figures gathered round him again, and I went out into the sunshine.

I am afraid I made rather a fool of myself, but quite quietly, and I do not believe anybody noticed, for I went for a quick walk round the orchard. When I got back and started to move my ambulance to the court-yard in front of the hospital, I had quite recovered.

I found Sarazinski and ' Snow-White's Grand-mother ' talking to the *Pharmacien-chef*. We were to lunch at the hospital, he said, and go with him after-wards to collect his supplies. I was very surprised to discover that ' Snow-White's Grandmother ' was with us. He had come without authorisation, travelling in the back of Sarazinski's ambulance and looking after the three cases who were in a serious condition. Sarazinski told me that he had been invaluable and that without him it would have been very difficult.

The feeding of us presented a nice problem in military etiquette. We had not been invited to lunch with the officers : on the other hand, we were of commissioned rank and could not be put with the soldiers. But a com-promise was effected, for we lunched at a table alone, and had the advantage of the choice of both menus. The meal was a memorable one for the reason that I ate " army bread " for the first time. The first loaf we began on turned out to be rather a failure, for it had gone green, but the second was excellent.

In a moment of weakness I became friendly with ' Snow-White's Grandmother,' and to my surprise found him very pleasant—I wondered how easily I would be able to persuade Cooper about this—but after that meal we became firm friends. Certainly there were moments when he was very irritating, but on the whole we got on well together. I think the whole thing was cemented when, after lunch, I took him and Sarazinski into the town and gave them coffee and cognac. We also bought a National Lottery ticket between us, on the back of which, at the suggestion of ' Grandma,' we solemnly inscribed our names—I presume to prevent any one of us running away with the proceeds in the event of our winning a prize. This was entrusted to Sarazinski, as the *avocat* among us, for safe keeping.

Back at the hospital I found that one of the nurses was looking for me. " A soldier who came in this morning has been asking for the man with the glass in his eye," she said. " That must be you, I suppose." I said it must be, and asked if she wanted me to go to him. She explained that it was impossible at that moment because he needed quiet, but that if I would still be there later I might be very helpful. " A familiar voice can make a great deal of difference." She assumed that we were old friends. It was too complicated to explain to her, so I simply said that my orders were to leave at once. I gave her a message for him, and said that I would probably be back within the next few days.

The rest of the afternoon was taken up with collecting the *Pharmacien-chef's* supplies, listening to his stories, and as far as I was concerned, keeping awake. I made a bargain with one of the attendants in the drug department, and in exchange for a packet of cigarettes he gave me a potion which he guaranteed would keep me awake for three hours. I was very careful to stipulate three hours only, for I knew that I would just about be back at Villiers by then.

On the way back the *Pharmacien-chef* insisted on stopping outside Montmirail at the column erected by Napoleon III to commemorate Napoleon I's great victory of 1814. As we looked over the valley of the Petit Morin, he gave me a short lecture on the column and the battles which had been fought on this spot.

Then, from his heart, the true Frenchman spoke : " Look at this stretch of country, you must agree it is beautiful ; yet for centuries it has been the battlefield of Europe. Oh, my poor France ! No matter how you are scarred and wounded, you always rise again richer and more beautiful than before. Look at these peaceful woods and fields ! Who would believe that in the last hundred years, three times a battle has been fought here ? Napoleon I, Napoleon III, then the Great War. And again to-day the enemies of France march towards this very spot. Again this beauty must be destroyed : but again France will rise."

As we got into the cars, he turned to me and added : " Napoleon was a very great man, but I know you do not think much of him in England."

I assured him that he was mistaken, but he was not convinced, and I do not believe, even if I had been able to talk to him for a long time, that he would have altered his notion.

We stopped this time outside Viels-Maisons, where with great ceremony he invited us to drink with him in a little *bistro*. Sarazinski rather blotted his copybook by leaving us waiting in the road while he spent hours in the lavatory. I agreed with the *Pharmacien-chef* that for someone who was not ill it was an unnecessary length of time. When Sarazinski did appear, he did not help much by explaining in comic-bogus medical language something about the necessity of attending to the major gut. An ill-timed joke.

I just remember arriving back at the *château*, helping to unload the supplies, and realising that three hours had passed and the effect of the potion was wearing off. More faintly still I remember Cooper bringing me some food ; but after that I remember nothing.

(ii)

(*Cooper's narrative.*)

LIKE THE OTHERS, I had spent more or less the whole day on my bed, sleeping, reading, or trying to collect my thoughts. In a burst of energy, when I could stand my own smell no longer, I had set out to explore the

amenities of the barrack which was housing us, determined to find some form of bath. I wandered upstairs
and down, along corridor after corridor, but either the
baths I found were broken or the water would not run.
At last I had met with success and hurriedly torn off
my clothes. There was a hand-shower which presented
a curious problem. It was a perforated metal hoop
attached to a piece of rubber tubing. I tried to grasp
the inventor's intention, but in despair wore it like a
horse-collar. As the water trickled down my body I
felt like any Triton at Versailles. But the effect was
immediate, and I had returned to my duties lighter in
body and mind and considerably strengthened.

After Freeman's return the first thing to do was to
overhaul the ambulance, fill the petrol tank and check
the oil and water. Then the interior had to be cleaned.
We were still on guard, so the car had to be at the door,
and it was my turn to leave when the call came. I
quickly did what was necessary and returned to hear
what Freeman had to tell. I found him exhausted and
preparing to sleep, so I refreshed him with the news of
my bathroom and went downstairs to fetch him some
food, which was now ready. One of the many con-
veniences of a *gamelle* is that one can carry about a
whole meal in one dish.

After I had eaten I sat outside in the evening sunlight, hoping indeed, if there was work to be done,
that the call would come sooner rather than later,
especially not in the middle of the night. I was not
disappointed. Presently the order came for two
ambulances to go to Pavilion 1 instantly. I called
for Raymond, the other driver on guard, and we drove
round and reported to the doctor in charge. For me
there were two stretcher cases there, and a third to be
fetched from Pavilion 2 ; for Raymond, four wounded
who could travel " sitting."

The operating theatres of Pavilion 1 were on ground

level and as I looked in through one window, I saw a surgeon at work on an amputation. The entrance hall, at the top of a flight of steps, was crowded with doctors and nurses, and on every balcony were crowds of wounded lounging around. In front was the usual crowd of ambulances. One gathered at once from the now familiar evidences of activity that the battle must still be raging as intensely as ever.

There was a wireless set in the entrance hall round which people were starting to gather. I joined them, hoping to hear the news. One had no confidence, even at this time, in the news as published in the press, but on the whole there was an idea that more was to be learnt from the radio. In fact one learnt nothing from either, but when the portentous voice began " *Ici Radio-Journal de France* " a hush fell ; it was official, therefore it must be speaking the truth.

To-night the news was preceded by another of Reynaud's surprise speeches ; he had re-shuffled his Cabinet and Daladier had at last disappeared, but there was the sinister inclusion of Prouvost. I no longer had time to follow the intricacies of political jugglery—perhaps it was only because I had come from Paris so recently that I felt any surprise or interest at all. I could not help speculating on the meaning of it all ; the others only registered lack of interest or mute disgust. They believed in Weygand ; all they asked was firm military leadership until the enemy had been exterminated.

A few moments later two stretchers were brought out and I found myself loading an Algerian and a Chasseur Alpin. They were both fairly seriously wounded, and the Chasseur seemed in considerable pain. The men whom Raymond had to take were also Colonial troops. This was the first indication we had that any of these regiments had been brought up to the north.

I told Raymond I would meet him in front of the *château*, and drove up to Pavilion 2. Here the rush was still continuing. I went to the reception ward to report and get the medical papers. The third case was still on the operating table, they told me, and I would have to wait. But this was not all. He was in such a serious condition that it would be necessary for me to take two *infirmiers* as well. Moreover, I should drive with the utmost caution as it was probable that he would die during the journey. This was not a cheering prospect, especially as I would be driving by night.

Eventually the door of the operating theatre opened and a stretcher was carried out. On it was a figure swathed from the head downwards in bandages, wound tightly round and round like a mummy. He was wrapped in blankets, and only his naked feet were visible at the bottom. He was unconscious. The stretcher was attended by a nurse and two surgeons, still in their white caps and overalls with masks, which they had not bothered to remove, over their mouths. Someone else carried all that remained of the wounded man's belongings, a water-bottle, two boots and a steel helmet with an enormous gash in the left side.

The stretcher was fixed on the floor of the ambulance, and then room had to be found for one *infirmier*. Somehow he managed to fit himself into a corner, but in a crouching position : there was no possibility of sitting. Before I shut the doors a nurse leant over and placed a spittoon on the man's chest, then she gave the *infirmier* a hypodermic syringe and a small glass tube of morphia.

The surgeon then took me aside and explained that I was to go to Sézanne. The man had a bullet in his head, as well as some shrapnel in the lung, and they had just finished amputating one arm. " Be very careful," he said, " but I don't think he will ever come round from the anæsthetic."

I got into the driver's seat, and the second *infirmier* came and sat beside me. We began the descent down the long hill to the *château*. I drove as slowly as I could, but the road had never seemed so bad as it did to-night. I was already nervous, feeling every bump, every stone as acutely as the men behind. Knowing the distance, I wondered how they could survive.

Raymond had reached the *château* before me, and I found him waiting on the lawn with Bouveret who, as usual when we were working, was in an excited condition. When the *ordres de mission* were completed, we were ready to take the road, and with myself leading, at Raymond's request, we drove through the gates at about 9.30 p.m. It was the most difficult hour of the day to start. It was still more or less light, but just sufficiently dark for the element of surprise to be at its strongest. It was the time of day when distant trees look like advancing lorries and bicyclists appear like Flying Dutchmen from the ground in front of one's wheels. It was the weird moment when forms dissolve and disembodied voices work their devilry.

We drove as usual across the Marne to Nogent. All was still, dark and deserted. From here we climbed the ridge of hills on the south side until on the top we reached a large wood, through the centre of which the road ran straight. Convoys of enormous camouflaged and hooded lorries were drawn up in irregular groups on both sides of the road, and a great many figures were moving among the trees. Here and there were piles of cases, standing in front of cuttings which seemed only to lead into the undergrowth. I asked the *infirmier* what was happening, and he explained that it was one of the main ammunition dumps of the region. Some of the groups of lorries were those that came down by day from Paris with more supplies, while others were the military ones which, under cover of night, drove what was needed up to the front line. They had already started the work of loading and unloading, and it would obviously not be long before it would be safe for them to start moving.

We were on a narrow dusty side road, which at least had the merit of being free from traffic, but our progress was terribly slow ; the *infirmier* was horrified when I estimated that we would be lucky indeed if we covered the 60 km. to Sézanne in three hours. He told me that he knew the road well, so I gave him my torch and entrusted him with the responsibility of watching the sign-posts.

The *infirmier* behind told us that he was already in difficulties. His unconscious charge was beginning to stir. He was restless and began to mutter ; he became quite active with his feet ; then almost instinctively with his remaining arm he started to scratch at the bandages and feel for the one that had just been amputated. There was nothing for it but to take hold of his hand and restrain him.

The sickly fumes of ether which were wafted through the windows behind my head started to nauseate me, and I realised what it must be like for the men inside. It is a smell which I find both odious and fascinating, it revives too many memories. I was frightened of falling asleep anyhow and now doubly so. I started to smoke one cigarette after another. I wanted to talk, but my neighbour was drowsy and the people behind were now silent.

We were stopped by the sentries at the main road. I waited to see that Raymond was still behind, and calculated that in the first hour we had only covered fifteen kilometres ; it looked as though I had over-estimated the speed at which we could travel, so I said nothing to the *infirmiers*. The road was now perfect and I settled down to the grim business of getting to Sézanne as quickly as the improved surface and the

final descent of night would permit. Among other
indications by which to steer a straight course, there
were at last white bands painted on the trees.

The human senses are often at their most acute in
the darkness, and to-night I discovered that my eyes
might have been those of a cat. There was no moon, but
it was cloudless and one could see the stars ; the sky
appeared transparent and the landscape luminous
with that suffused glow which is part of a summer night.
I remembered how often I had commented on the new
beauty of Paris at night. It is the only pleasure of the
black-out that it has restored to the towns their
silhouette, and to the streets their air of mystery and
mischief which is proper to them. In my imagination
I was walking again through my favourite streets by
night—I thought of my friends, of what happens by
night, of individual nights. My thoughts were
beginning to wander.

My reverie ended with a shock when suddenly I
heard a great noise ahead and realised that out of the
darkness a large lorry was charging towards me. I
hooted in fright ; the lorry was in the centre of the
road. To my relief the driver reacted and we passed
each other unscratched. But this was by no means the
end of my alarm ; it turned out to be the leader of a
whole convoy, which occupied the centre of the road
and was charging along blindly, like all heavyweights.
Nor was this all. The convoy was naturally accompanied by at least two small touring cars, drably
camouflaged and even less visible, containing the
officers in charge, whose prerogative it seemed was to
drive in a separate outer column and therefore completely on my side of the road. Strictly against all
orders, I ventured momentarily in self-defence to flick
on one very subdued blue sidelight, but the screams of
" *Lumière !* " as the cars passed were so hysterical that
I had no option but to turn it out. I cheered myself

with the thought that until a few weeks previously the casualties on the road had been much greater than those at the front, and wondered why the army was so economical with white paint.

We eventually arrived at Montmirail, having successfully avoided contact with any form of motor vehicle, lorry or ambulance, or any of the daring despatch riders whose diversion was to dodge desperately between the columns. Montmirail had become another relief hospital since the afternoon, and was very much awake under cover of the black-out. Ambulances and cars were parked everywhere ; a large Red Cross flag fluttered outside the church, and a big reception tent was pitched on the other side of the road. Figures were dashing about, some in white, some with torches. Convoys were going up to the lines, and the road was heavily policed. I rang my bell with the determination of a fireman, and its warning was heeded.

We were now half-way on our journey and we all needed a few minutes break. I thought it would be quieter outside the town after we had left the main road. I was held up at the cross-road by the military police, who had cleared the road for another convoy, and, anyhow, was obliged to wait for Raymond. We drove on a few yards, then stopped. First of all there were things to be done for the wounded, whose physical needs were the same as ours. This time, too, I had brought some hot coffee as well as water. The poor *infirmier* was greatly relieved to be able to walk around for a few minutes in the fresh air. He had no hesitation about grumbling at the discomfort, and I could not help sympathising. His companion evidently had no intention of changing places, so we continued the journey as before.

Everybody seemed to have woken up except the unconscious man ; the smell of ether still hung about, and the *infirmier* expected him to start vomiting at any moment. The Chasseur asked where he was being taken, and then the conversation began.

His story was horrifying. He had been wounded almost twenty-four hours earlier on the Chemin des Dames. During the night the Germans had dropped parachute troops behind their lines, and when day broke his regiment had been attacked with machine-guns in the rear as well as in front. Most of his comrades had been wiped out ; he himself had been badly wounded in the back and head. " The pick of the French Army is being destroyed," he murmured.

The Algerian had been in the same sector, but he had been wounded later. In his curious accent he described the thousands of tanks which he had seen being thrown into the attack, and one could almost hear him shudder with terror as he thought of them. He had actually seen these monstrous machines spitting out sheets of flame.

I encouraged them to talk while they were in the mood. The Germans, it seemed, must have advanced considerably. The Canal de l'Ailette was crossed and their troops were at the gates of Soissons. The men talked of the carnage, of victory, but they had no illusions about the seriousness of the situation. Both of them had only been in the north a short while, having been rushed up as reinforcements.

The *infirmier* added to the picture with his own story. " Well, I think I have made enough sacrifice to Hitler for this war. I had a nice little farm between Lille and the Belgian frontier on which we all lived. I have been mobilised since September and have only been back once. Now, of course, my wife and two children have fled, I do not know where. The Boche has got the farm and all my seventy-five cattle. That is all I have to give."

Sézanne was very dark, but I knew my way—from earlier and more pleasant visits—to the centre of the town. I found a sentry who led me from there to the hospital. We turned off the main street, down an avenue of trees and along a little lane to the narrow entrance of the old hospital. With the aid of a red torch I was shown the way—it was more or less an obstacle race—and finally halted in front of the long low tent which was acting as reception ward. I offered to turn on a small light inside the ambulance while unloading the stretchers, but this was forbidden ; it had been a night of air-raids and there were still 'planes about. We carried the stretchers into the tent and set them down on the ground. I looked at my watch ; it was almost 1 a.m.

Inside there was just room to stand upright. The only source of light was a hurricane lamp swinging from a cord in the centre of the roof. There were several doctors and surgeons kneeling on the ground and bending over stretchers. In one corner there was a soldier having his head completely shaved by a nurse. The ground, which earlier in the day had been the grass of the field, was now covered with hair and straw.

Raymond came in with his four passengers, all Algerians, who mutely retired to benches at the opposite end and huddled together like lost sheep.

I was thankful to have arrived and find that my man was not only not dead, but that he had not even vomited. He was semi-conscious and I realised that something had to be done for him quickly. The *infirmiers* had lost interest. I walked over to the surgeon-in-chief, gave him the papers of the case and the X-ray photographs, and pointed out the urgency. He came at once, examined the man, and decided to operate immediately.

Meanwhile, the other surgeons were examining the remaining new arrivals. They had more work than it was possible for them to attend to, and all the hospitals in the town were full. It was wonderful to watch the

gentle and sympathetic manner with which, even at
this late hour, they handled the wounded. They were
all immensely modest and sensible, able to put everyone immediately at his ease, and not at all the sort of
doctor who freezes one with his silence and professional
look.

Those men who were in a condition to stand a
longer journey were now being sent further south. My
Algerian, they decided, could perfectly well continue
his travels. Then they turned their attention to the four
who had come with Raymond. They were more or less
inarticulate, not so much from fright or pain as simply
from an insufficient knowledge of French. They, too,
were not serious enough cases to be allowed to remain.
They were each given a cigarette and a drink to
encourage them. It was decided that Raymond would
take my man as well and go on to Troyes, which was
their new destination. They were cowed but uncomplaining when the news was broken to them. No one
could have failed to see that they were simply longing
for a bed and someone to attend to their wounds.
But there literally was no bed available, and precedence
had to be granted to the more serious cases.

Raymond filled his ambulance, collected the necessary papers, and left. I was asked to stay behind and
help carry some stretchers, as they were short-handed.

At the end of the tent was a flap through which I
had observed nurses and surgeons passing in and out.
I thought it led back into the fresh air. Now I was told
to carry my unconscious man through there. I discovered that it led to a second and similar tent which
was serving as an operating theatre. I had hardly had
time to realise what was happening when I saw in one
half of the interior a group of white-coated figures all
at work around a table, and heard a curious high-
pitched dead sound which I knew to be that of a saw
on bone. I longed to walk over and look inside a

human head while the skull was open—for I knew they must be trepanning—but there was an empty table waiting for our burden. He had to be lifted off the stretcher and put in place.

I found out at once that my first-aid rules learnt in a Paris garage were no help now. I followed the instructions of a very efficient nurse and somehow we managed it. The poor man was drowsy and groaning ; I hoped that he would forgive the errors of a pair of inexperienced arms. I hoped, too, that he would not be upset by the operation already in progress.

I looked closer at the other table, and saw that it was the man whose head I had seen being shaved a little earlier. Even under these conditions an operation is a beautiful sight for a lay spectator.

As I came back through the tent, my little Chasseur, who still had to wait his turn, called out goodbye and we shook hands as I wished him a good and quick recovery. Outside by my ambulance the two *infirmiers* were waiting. I gave them something to eat and drink, and we started out for home. I felt sure this might not be easy as there were so many turnings to memorise. Besides, I was certain my companion had not been watching.

The road was straight at first, and we bowled along a little faster than before, now that my charges had left us. I looked for a turning which I remembered we should take to the right, but somehow we missed it, and as the road was temptingly straight we continued.

Eventually I came to a fork, and as neither road was sign-posted to Montmirail I knew we must be wrong.

I had already protested to Bouveret as we left that the only map which had been issued to us was of no use for the journey to Sézanne. Now I cursed him for his retort : "Oh, that's not important !" Seeing that one road went to La Ferté-Gaucher, I decided to risk it.

I knew that there must be a way across country from there, as my own map covered about half of it.

La Ferté was dead ; I brazenly switched on several lights in an attempt to attract someone's attention. There was nothing but a few cats. " You want to go to the right," I told myself, and sent the *infirmier* out with a torch to read a sign-post. He looked at one on the left. I had made up my mind already that he was a stupid man, now I was annoyed with him.

At last we found the road : Bellot, Verdelot, Viels-Maisons, it read. It looked easy. But the countryside was full of obstacles, barbed wire entanglements, tanks, ditches, policemen and sentries. If I was held up once I was held up fifteen times in not as many kilometres and made to show my papers. Admittedly there was an aerodrome nearby, as I could see from the revolving yellow searchlight which threw a small beam over the fields every few seconds. Once or twice I no doubt deserved to be stopped for shining a bright torch on the sign-posts. The *infirmier* was either myopic or illiterate. I spent a great deal of time getting in and out of the car myself. I was always losing the way, and none of the sentries had been long enough in the district to know the roads.

When we arrived at Viels-Maisons it was more or less daylight. This was our home stretch at last, and I was thankful to be able to travel a little faster in safety. Soon we came to the ammunition wood, which was now quite deserted : no sign of either man or machine.

When we reached the top of the hill dominating the river, there was a series of violent explosions behind one of the hills facing us. We felt the shock and saw bursts of red flame, followed by a cloud of smoke and dust rising like a fire-balloon upwards. We knew it could only be a bombing raid and so we stopped. We were just working out the objective when there were three or four more explosions, this time nearer still, perhaps eight kilometres away. It was clear now that the bombs had been meant for the railway, which ran along beside the Marne, so we guessed that the first salvo of bombs had been dropped on Château-Thierry. When we could neither see nor hear aeroplanes we decided to hurry on home.

When we arrived, the gate-keeper came up suspiciously and tried to turn us away.

" We are not taking any more wounded here," he protested.

" It is all right, I'm only coming home empty. Why no more wounded ? "

" Oh, I do not know, but the *Médecin-chef* is talking of evacuation." Puzzled, we drove on.

I left the two *infirmiers* outside Pavilion 2, which they were very happy to see, having been on duty for thirty-six hours, and then parked again in front of our building. It was 4 a.m. : we were still on guard for another four hours. I crept upstairs with that feeling of satisfaction which one has at the end of a difficult job successfully carried out alone. Uniform and all, I crawled into my sleeping sack and relaxed, hoping that the telephone that was used to summon those on guard would not ring before 8 o'clock.

Friday, 7th June.

PIERRE D . . . and Ido M . . . obviously had a grievance ; there was none of the light-hearted chatter with which most mornings began. They drank their tea without enthusiasm. When we compared notes on our experiences of the previous day, they showed no interest and would not be drawn into the conversation, and when we asked them what they had been doing, both replied bitterly : " Absolutely nothing ! " For one awful moment we thought we had made a *gaffe*. What could it be ? Had we broken one of the rules of " the

game " ? We racked our brains, but for the first hour
of that morning the mystery of their sulks remained.

Our guard was over at 8 o'clock. After a glass of
whisky, our companions became human and fired off
their troubles : " We came here to work, not lead a
barracks existence—we want to go to the front." The
mystery was explained.

Caillemer took the morning parade. We had two
suggestions to voice after our previous day's experiences : the need for adequate maps and the advantages
of white paint at night. Caillemer said in a final sort of
way that there were no maps available, but agreed that
white paint here and there on the cars might be a good
idea. We went off to do our daily job of cleaning.

Nobody seemed inclined to do very much work as
there was very little for them to do. It was very hot,
and some of the more ingenious ones constructed a
shower-bath under the water tower. We fetched a pot
of white paint, and while one of us cleaned the car the
other began to paint. In front we painted the ends of
the bumpers and the tips of the wings, a strip on each
of the outer edges of the doors behind and a large
square in the centre. We were just admiring it when
Bouveret and Caillemer appeared. They were surprised at our audacity in taking a decision and carrying it out alone, and Bouveret in particular was
predisposed to find fault. He walked all round with
a critical eye, longing to find an objection, but his
logical French mind told him that a regulation pattern
had been followed and that he had no real grounds
for complaint.

However, his prestige had to be maintained, and so
he had to think hard and quickly. The square on the
back gave him his opportunity. He looked at it intently, took a step back, put his thumb up and squinted
at it like an art-master correcting a pupil's work. We
watched in silence and waited for his judgment.

" Why a square ? It is such a common emblem, all
the military cars use it. I want something distinctive,
so that we can always pick out our own cars in a
crowd."

He looked at it again, and then as if inspired called
for a rag and some turpentine. With a few magic
strokes he turned it into a rough circle. We pointed
out with great deference that this was just as common,
and proposed, as a compromise, a hexagon. We
quickly painted a trial one.

" Very well," he said grudgingly, " let us decide on
that. But since you have taken on yourselves the
responsibility of starting to paint, you had better continue to do all the cars of the Section. I cannot have
every car painted as its driver feels inclined, I must at
least have uniformity." We did not know whether this
was meant as punishment or recognition of talent, but
as he moved off he showed his friendliness by adding :
" At least you have made a good job of it." We painted
hard for the rest of the morning ; the others were
delighted to have something done for them.

About 1 o'clock the whole building shook. There was
a series of colossal explosions. Most of us were on the
fifth floor at the time. In our excitement we rushed to
the windows in the passage. There was a terrific air
battle in progress over Château-Thierry. There was
intense anti-aircraft fire. We saw the bombs fall and
explode in great numbers, and expected that at any
moment the remaining bits of glass in our windows
would clatter to the ground. Then we heard the bursts
of machine-gun fire and the zoom of the French fighters
as they engaged the Boche in combat. We were thrilled
and forgot the elementary precautions which had been
so carefully drilled into us. Our spectacle was inter-
rupted by a ferocious blowing of the whistle, and we
galloped downstairs, for the most part as we were,
without helmets. Bouveret was waiting at the bottom,

dressed as if for action. " You hear what is going on,
don't you ? I would rather have you appear without
your trousers than without your *casques et masques.*
Never forget this in future."

There was another raid during the afternoon, but
as we were dressed for the occasion this time we went
on with our work of painting the cars.

In the evening there was an atmosphere of excitement. There was a rumour that more cars were to be
sent to the front. Caillemer arrived in the middle of
dinner and made a speech. He had been to the front
line dressing-station that afternoon to visit the group
of our ambulances which had gone up there three days
previously. The attack was going on ruthlessly, and
they had been working day and night. He had brought
one of the drivers home, as he had been severely
bombed and was in a state of nervous collapse. The
rest were returning in the early hours of the morning.
" We will be sending fresh ambulances up in relays at
intervals of three days ; you will all have your turn.
We cannot send too many at once, as the *Médecin-chef*
here needs us. The first group will leave to-morrow
morning at 7 o'clock : ambulances 12, 13 and 19, will
you please be ready to start at that hour. Only one
driver on each, as the other must be kept in reserve for
emergencies."

We sought him out later and asked if we could go
together, pointing out the obvious advantages of having
two people on the job. But he was adamant, and said
that the work was extremely nerve-racking and that,
rather than use up two people at once, he considered
it more useful to have one fresh and always ready at the
base. So we realised that there was no point in arguing
further.

As it meant leaving early the next morning, there was
a certain amount of work to be done on the car that
night. There were tyres to be inflated, the tank to be

filled, and a hundred and one little attentions a car needs before a long journey. Worst of all, the oil had to be changed ; a tedious job at the best of times. We bribed our mechanic with some cigarettes to do this for us ; it was a fair exchange, for even at this time cigarettes were difficult to get. Then we walked down to the village to have a drink with Ido M . . . and René de S . . . .

We found them with Caillemer in the café. It was a sober little party this time, and the conversation was heavy going. We were thankful when 9 o'clock came and we had to go back.

Outside the Control Office was a group of ambulance drivers gathered round a car. They seemed excited and were pointing at something. As we passed we asked what it was all about.

" He has a good aim, the Boche "—and one driver pointed to a bullet-hole in the windscreen.

" You see where it is ? " he said. " Luckily I had got out in time or it would have hit me full in the face."

" Were you with other military cars ? " Caillemer asked.

" No, we were just a group of ambulances alone."

" The swine ! The swine ! " the men muttered.

We were all silent as we walked back home ; we bid the others good night and went upstairs. As we had agreed to take it in turns when we worked alone, it was obvious which of us should go.

The night was broken by occasional calls for ambulances.

Saturday, 8th June

(i)

(Freeman's narrative)

WHEN I DISCOVERED ' Jack-and-Jim ' under the trees, snooping round the cars, and found that he was in charge of our expedition, I did not feel at all happy. It was bad enough leaving Cooper behind, but to be landed with the " old troll " in command was too much. It was not a question of likes and dislikes, it was the fact that I had no confidence in him that depressed me. It was certainly a consolation to know that Erwtemans was coming with us ; as we got ready for the departure, we both agreed that we would have felt more confident had Raymond been our No. 1.

I did a bit of white painting on Erwtemans' car— he had been out on a mission the day before—then we drove down to our Pavilion to get our parting instructions from Bouveret.

We found that the men we were relieving had just returned, and were waiting outside the door to see us off. They looked tired and dirty and were unshaven, but they seemed in good spirits. It was hard work, they told us, " bloody noisy, but on the whole not too bad."

Bouveret and Caillemer did a fine display of " *Bonne chance*," " *Courage* " and " *Bon retour*," which embarrassed me considerably and left me at a complete loss for a reply. I was trying to make up my mind whether I should say " Thank you very much " or something on those lines, when mercifully ' Jack-and-Jim ' blew a whistle and we started.

No. 19, driven by the lean old Norwegian—the " Tipperary " one—with ' Jack-and-Jim ' as his passenger, led ; I followed, and Erwtemans, with one of the transport orderlies from the dressing-station to which we were going, followed me.

I had no idea of our destination, it had been kept a secret. The men who had just returned had obviously been told to say nothing about it, and ' Jack-and-Jim,' whom I had seen poring over a map with Bouveret and the transport orderly just before we left, had given no indication.

As I drove down to the *château* gates, conducted between two cars, both of which knew exactly where they were going, I felt rather like a child being sur-reptitiously whisked off to the dentist. I knew we were going north, I supposed towards Soissons, but that was all, and as I did not like the idea of being led blindly by 'Jack-and-Jim,' I made up my mind to extract our destination from the transport orderly at the first stop. In the meantime, I thought it more tactful to ask no questions and let " the frozen North " go on playing at soldiers for a bit. When we turned right, on to the main road, and immediately took a little lane which ran round the back of the hospital, then due west, I was extremely surprised, gave up all speculation, and hoped for the best.

The Norwegian car was a Ford, and bowled up and down the hills at a terrific pace. Erwtemans and I had Citroëns, which were not so powerful. I only managed to keep up at all at the expense of my second gear. Erwtemans' car was not running nearly so well as mine, but knowing that he knew the way I did not wait for him, and made a mad dash along the lanes in an attempt to catch up with my leader. On some of the long stretches, with neither of the cars in sight, only an inadequate map and an unknown destination, I felt miserably lost. Fortunately, I made correct guesses at the cross-roads, for eventually I found the Ford waiting for me.

I explained the differences in horse-power and num-ber of cylinders between our cars to the old Norwegian, and asked him to take it easy on the hills. He agreed, and I set off again feeling a little reassured. But nothing could restrain him, and in a few minutes I saw him dashing away over the horizon.

It seemed extremely stupid to break up my car in such an unworthy cause, so I set myself in the middle of the next cross-road and waited for Erwtemans. When he came, I explained the madness going on ahead, and insisted upon knowing where we were going.

I found our destination was Oigny, a little village in the middle of the forest of Villers-Cotteret, about twenty kilometres south-west of Soissons. Looking at my map, I found we were taking a cross-country route, running more or less parallel to the main road from Villiers-sur-Marne to La Ferté-Milon and Villers-Cotteret. " Curious," commented the transport orderly, " for there is no traffic to speak of on the main road. But they would go this way." Playing at soldiers, I thought to myself again.

At last I knew where we were going; my map showed the whole route, which was a miracle; but to make quite sure that at least Erwtemans and I should keep together, I suggested that, as his car was slower than mine, he should lead. So we set off again with myself behind.

We found car No. 19 on the outskirts of a little village. Here we met Estevez, the lieutenant in charge of the men we had replaced. We exchanged a few words with him and moved on: he back to Villiers, we on to Oigny.

His news had not been very cheering: the German advance was rapid, and the situation was not looking at all good. Moreover, he did not think that we should be in Oigny very long. " I believe they will have to evacuate Oigny very soon, whether they want to or not," had been his parting words.

There was considerable air activity from now on, and we stopped twice to take cover: once when there was some bombing nearby, and another time when there was an aerial battle overhead.

Eventually we reached Oigny and parked our cars under the trees on a sort of minute village green. There were many other *Service de Santé* cars around, tucked under every available tree, bush, or wall that could possibly serve as a shelter. The little village looked not unlike a gigantic garage.

The place itself was charming. It amounted to little more than a few cottages on either side of the road; at the north end, where we were parked and where the road led off to Villers-Cotteret, there was a church on the left and a small sixteenth century *château* on the right. Behind the church was a little lane, with a few more houses and what looked like a school building. And that, as far as I could see, was Oigny.

The villagers could not have left so very long before, for the little gardens looked well tended and there was an air of orderliness and well-being about the place. It was difficult to reconcile the ceaseless thunder of the distant guns and the busy movement of the doctors, *infirmiers* and stretcher-bearers with the rural scene.

As I looked up the village street I could see that the cottages had been transformed into dressing-stations. The simpler operations were performed in the forge. There were a great number of wounded about, and more were coming in all the time.

When I got out of my car, I spoke to Erwtemans in English. A crowd of ambulance-drivers who were nearby and had been watching us with idle curiosity, gathered round me as if I was some strange creature from another world. " You're English," they said, " that is interesting, you're the first we have seen since the war."

" There are plenty about, but further north," I explained.

" A pity that they are not down here," was the general comment. They were not criticising, but expressing their need for help.

I did not go any further with my explanation; it meant touching on the subject of Holland and Belgium, and I did not particularly want to embark on that with Erwtemans by my side. The men could not have been nicer or more friendly. In a way it was as if they were giving me a welcome from one Ally to another.

Some of them knew an English word or two, and they tried them on me like a lot of excited children. One of them told me his lieutenant lived in London and was a hairdresser from a very big, very important *maison*. We were all getting on very well, my accent as usual amusing them enormously. Erwtemans kept them in fits of laughter with a number of jokes he always seemed to have up his sleeve. Then the Colonel in charge appeared and led us off to the kitchen for a meal.

"The great thing here," he said, "is always to eat when you can, one never quite knows when the next meal is coming." Then he turned to me and added with considerable pride: "We are not so uncivilised here as you might think, for there is always tea if you would care for it."

The cook also added his bit to this demonstration of the Entente by showing me a large cauldron of boiling potatoes: "Engleesh—like—potato!" he said, and I returned the compliment by eating one, which at about 9.30 in the morning was, I consider, fairly patriotic.

We started work quite soon. I was given the first load—four "sitting"—and told to take them to Villiers. It seemed rather an anti-climax going back again, but I felt a bit better when the doctor who was helping me load up told me to hurry back to Oigny as quickly as possible. I asked about the main road and was told to avoid La Ferté-Milon, which was blocked by army convoys; as everybody seemed to agree that anything might be happening on any of the roads, I decided to take a chance through Neuilly-Saint-Front.

It worked out quite well. From Neuilly I cut across country and joined the road to Villiers.

Once I turned a corner and passed about three metres from an anti-aircraft gun which was blazing away at a Boche overhead. The gunners and I were equally surprised to see each other, and I moved on pretty quickly, for I realised that if there was an air-raid that was not the place to take cover. So I put my foot on the accelerator, told the chaps in the back to hang on, and hoped for the best. I had not gone far before it was all quiet again; I stopped and had a look in the back to see how my charges were. But they were none the worse—in fact they were beaming with delight, only regretting that, as far as we could see, the Boche had not been brought down.

Another time, when I was making enquiries from a military policeman (who, as usual, did not know) to make sure that I was on the right road, a nice, friendly ' drunk ' came rolling up. He became curious beyond words when he finally managed to focus his gaze on the ambulance, and as he made a thorough examination of the car, myself and finally the wounded inside, he kept up a running commentary. Unfortunately, his conversation was entirely to himself, and it took a long time to find the direction from him. However, when his curiosity was finally satisfied, he made a sweeping gesture, which took in the whole countryside, and said: " That is your way."

Once again that morning I trusted to luck and the road I chose turned out to be all right. I was back at Villiers by about 11.30.

I did a couple of quick jobs between Pavilions 1 and 2. I learnt with horror from one of the *infirmiers* that the first victims of a gas attack had been brought in the day before. It was only " tear gas " but in a new and more virulent form. At first the doctors had mistaken it for a new kind of gas, but now, after three days, the effects were wearing off and the men recovering their sight.

I went back to Oigny by the way I had come; it seemed a good road, not quite as direct as going by La Ferté-Milon, but I now knew it and thought it better not to take any risks. The ' drunk ' was still at the cross-road, and we waved affectionately as I passed; the anti-aircraft men were eating and did not see me.

I was halted for a minute by a flock of sheep in a little village just before Neuilly-Saint-Front. As I drew up to let them pass, a young medical lieutenant dashed out of a nearby house. " Thank God you have come," he shouted.

He could see from my look of surprise that I was not his man. " Aren't you stopping here ? " he queried. I explained that I was stationed at Oigny, that I had just completed a mission and was returning. " Oh, sorry! " and he turned away.

He seemed so terribly disappointed that I called after him, and asked if there was anything I could do. " I have sent for cars everywhere and none have come— it is desperate. I have got some men up at the front and I must get them here. Could you stay with me just two hours ? "

I remembered my strict instructions to accept no orders under any consideration from a section with which I was not working. I explained this to him: " Give me a note to take to the Colonel at Oigny. Ask him to send me back. It may work, and if he is willing I can return in half-an-hour." He was grateful for the suggestion, and asked me to come with him while he got a superior officer to write the note.

He took me across a courtyard into the house. I supposed it was a farm. In the big room I was surprised to find about eight officers sitting round the remains of lunch. I could see they were doctors from the Aescula-pian serpent embroidered in gold on their red velvet tabs.

The note was written, the official stamp put on it, I bid them goodbye and set off again.

Back at Oigny they were as busy as ever. The Colonel read the note, seemed very embarrassed, shook his

D

head in despair and said: " I will see what I can do later; in the meantime I want you here." So with a passing regret at the apparent failure of my attempt to help the section at Neuilly, I sat myself down and waited for further instructions.

I was sitting on a low wall by my car when I heard a voice say in my own language: " Are you the Englishman ? " It was a young lieutenant; he sat down by my side and started to talk. He was a slightly built man, with a round, cheerful, friendly face. He looked extremely young, about twenty. But I realised after a bit that he must have been at least eight or ten years more than that. He told me that he was the transport officer. He worked normally in England and had lived there many years. He was married, and Twickenham was, I think, his home, where he had left his wife. He had tried to get home on one of his leaves; permission and everything had been granted, but he had had no luck, for as he got to Calais all leave had been cancelled. We talked for a long time about many things; I liked him and hoped I would see more of him at Oigny. I realised that he must have been the hairdresser, though we never referred to the subject, and I wondered to myself as we talked if any of his smart *clientes* would have recognised him now. There was none of the wavy-headed hairdresser about him; he certainly gave the lie to that overworked joke. Here was a soldier.

When he was called away, I sat in the car and read for a bit. There were aeroplanes overhead all the time. Occasionally there would be bursts of anti-aircraft fire and then everybody walking along the road would take cover under the trees until it stopped.

Finally, my next call came, and two stretchers were hung on the upper rails in my ambulance. " The third case will not be long," they told me, " we are trying to patch him up for the journey."

When they brought him out he looked very bad, and

as the stretcher-bearers were fixing him in I asked the doctor how serious he was. " Losing blood all the time. Get him there as quickly as you can—he may last out." I looked into the ambulance quickly to see if the man had overheard. I knew by the look of horror on his face that he had, so as I shut the door I said: " Don't worry, I will get you there all right."

" Risk it and go through La Ferté-Milon," I was told. " It is quicker and the road is better. You will have to trust to luck with the traffic."

As one goes south from Oigny, the road, which is little better than a track, leads through the forest for about four kilometres before reaching the little village of Silly-la-Poterie and the open country. With the most beautifully sprung car in the world it would be a nightmare; with a lightly constructed ambulance it was a journey that defied description. At this moment, with a more serious load than before, the prospect of that short but seemingly endless stretch ahead left me speechless. I crawled along the first three hundred metres, wondering how soon I would have a complaint from my passengers in the back.

I had noticed some men by the side of the road making gestures with their hands in the air; but as my thoughts were only of the road ahead I had paid no attention and gone on. Now again I saw more men making the same signs, so I thought I had better stop and see what it was all about. The moment I stopped I knew what their signs meant. The noise of my car groaning along in first gear had prevented me from hearing anything before, but now I could hear only too distinctly that there were many aeroplanes over-head, and that Oigny itself was being bombed. The men who had signalled to me disappeared into a little hut by the side of the road, and as I took a quick look back at the village, there was not a soul to be seen; everybody had taken cover.

Quickly, I tried to think what I should do. My latest instructions on such occasions had been quite definite: " Put the car by the side of the road in such cover as possible and preferably under trees. If the wounded are in a state to be moved, get them out. If not, leave them and take cover yourself." The principle was sound; after all, it is more important to preserve one able-bodied individual than three disabled ones should the ambulance be hit. It was impossible to move my men, so I thought it would be wiser to drive on a few hundred metres to where the trees were thicker, but an anti-aircraft battery down the road started firing and I realised that this was out of the question.

Suddenly one of the men in the back let out a blood-curdling yell: " It is those aeroplanes again. Oh God, the aeroplanes! "

I tried to quieten him: " It is nothing serious, they are a long way off. God knows what the anti-aircraft think they are doing."

" I can hear them—those engines—I know the sound." He was getting hysterical.

In desperation I made up some story of a convoy passing and said that the lorries were back-firing. But it was no use, for as I spoke my words were drowned by the crash of a bomb. It seemed unbelievable that they should really be attacking Oigny, where I knew that there was no military objective, but I was beginning to learn by now that the Red Cross was more of an attraction than a warning.

The next quarter-of-an-hour was undiluted hell. The bombs seemed to rain down, and the car rocked about like a dinghy in a rough sea. It was no good pretending I was not frightened; I was. I was terrified out of my wits. Anybody who says that he is not frightened at such times is either a liar or has something wrong with his glands. I think the scream of the shells was the nastiest sound, but there was little to choose between that and the screaming man.

Then the worst happened: the two other men started. The dying one below kept pleading: " Drive on, for God's sake, drive on. Do you want to kill me ? You know I can't last long. Please, please, *please* get me to the hospital."

I threw my instructions to the winds; I could not possibly get out of the car and leave them, so I stayed where I was and shouted back to them through the din. Poor devils, it was awful; they could bear the un-believable pain of their wounds, they could bear any hardships, any privations, but the terrifying memories of the aeroplane attacks had completely broken their nerve.

One aeroplane zoomed louder than the rest; I could hear it getting nearer. As I looked through the back windows of the car, I could see its black shadow coming along the road from the village; lower, lower it came. I could see the beastly thing now, flying not much higher than the houses. Then the rat-tat-tat of its machine-gun started. Instinctively I crouched, but as it passed I saw the little pools of dust that the bullets were making on the road. It had missed us. As the battery further down fired at it, it flew up and off.

It seemed hours before the sound of the aeroplanes died away, then slowly one by one the guns stopped firing. A man came out of the hut and lounged against the door, smoking a cigarette. Further back some men were strolling down the road towards the village. Over the village itself there was a pall of smoke. My soldier below was moaning slightly, the others were silent—exhausted. " It is all right now," I said; but they did not reply, and I drove on through the forest.

The moment I got on to the La Ferté-Milon road I regretted it. The lines of convoys seemed endless. They were mostly horse-drawn gun-carriages and carts, and the going was very difficult.

The little town itself was in chaos, and Racine on his pedestal looked down with a puzzled look on his home and the confusion of lorries, carts, horses, and sweating, swearing soldiers that were swirling round him. I forced my way through it all, ringing my bell without ceasing, and especially loudly when I saw any officer who looked like holding me up.

Outside the town I breathed a sigh of relief. It was clear on the road, and I thought I had passed the heavy traffic; but not at all. Almost at once I ran into more convoys. In desperation I took a side road which I knew must lead me in the right direction. I cut through a convoy as it stopped to take shelter from aeroplanes overhead. Someone shouted a warning to me, thinking that perhaps I had not noticed the 'planes, but I could see a wood down the side road, and the moaning of the man behind me made me more determined than ever to get away from the traffic.

Again it was not long before I met another convoy, and I cursed myself for being such a fool as to take this route at all. I had got about half-way past the long column when for the second time that afternoon I heard the anti-aircraft guns at work. At all costs, I thought, I must get away from this convoy.

The road ran through a thick wood, and I knew that for a bit anyway I was as safe moving as standing still. Then suddenly the back part of the column coming towards me swung across the road, in front of my car, and started disappearing down a track into the wood. It was impossible to go on, impossible to go back—a hopeless situation. I begged the officer who was directing the lorries into the wood to hold them up for a moment and let me pass. " Out of the question," he shouted back, " anyhow, if you go on, you are mad— if the Boche do not get you when you come out into the open, the anti-aircraft will. You had better take cover with us."

I thought of the pools of dust on the road at Oigny; I thought of the windscreen at the hospital the night before; then I heard the shouting and hooting of some cars behind me, whose way to shelter I was blocking. So I turned and drove abreast the lorries into the wood.

I asked one of the drivers what the enemy's objective could be. As far as I knew, there was nothing of importance this side of La Ferté-Milon for some long way. Perhaps they were after the convoys, I suggested.

" They would not mind getting us," he replied, " we are carrying ammunition, but I suppose they are after these woods principally." Then he added: " Why, every clump of trees for miles around is an ammunition dump! This wood is full of it."

I laughed despairingly at the irony of the whole thing. He asked what was wrong with me.

" Oh, nothing much," I replied, " only that it seems a bit absurd, when you think of this little ambulance taking cover with a whole lot of ammunition lorries in a high explosive dump."

We were not there long, and thank goodness my charges were quiet. Perhaps they were reassured by the sight of other soldiers round them, or perhaps they had just given up. One of them kept looking out of the window to see if he could find a friend: " Oh look, there's a man I know," he would say, " please call him over." But it always turned out to be a mistake. He was like a lonely dog shut up in a closed car, pressing its nose to the window, searching, searching for a familiar face.

I asked the officer in charge if he would let me get out of the wood first. When I explained the urgency of my mission, he agreed at once. I had already manœuvred my car to the edge of the track. It was only a question of seconds to get on the road again. I was off before the attack had completely died down, but I could not see any difference between being blown sky-high in a wood or being machine-gunned on a road.

The relief of getting to the hospital at last turned to black despair when I found that the queue of cars waiting to unload their wounded at Pavilion 2 stretched half-way down to the *château* gates. I arrived about 8 o'clock, but it was a good hour and a half before I eventually crawled into the courtyard in front of the Pavilion.

" It is no good, we cannot attend to any more for the moment," the doctors kept saying. I ran up and down from one to the other, with the medical report of the man at the bottom of my car. " Please look at this case," I kept repeating. " I have been hours on the road and it is desperate."

At last one of the surgeons took pity on me: " What is it ? " he said.

" He is losing blood and needs immediate attention," I replied, as I pressed the report into his hands.

He read it. " My God, get him out at once," he shouted. " Stretcher-bearers quickly! Bring this man in."

The man did not move when they carried him away, and I did not look too closely to see if he was only unconscious. I had an awful feeling that perhaps if I had taken a different route . . . ? I did my best to stop any self-recriminations. We were lucky to be at Villiers at all.

I went to see what I could do for my two remaining men; water, a little food, a cigarette—I gave them what they wanted. It was hot and oppressive, so I left the door open at the back.

" Do we have to stay here long ? " I was asked.

" Not long, they will move you out soon."

" I wonder," was the faint, hopeless reply. " Are you sure we will not be moved on ? " I was not sure; I did not know what to say, I pretended not to hear.

Next to me was an army lorry. The driver and another soldier were lifting a wounded man out of it.

" I don't care what they say," the driver said defiantly to me, " we are going to take him inside." As they moved away to the reception ward, I heard a faint whimper of a dog from inside the lorry. It rose to a melancholy howl. The man they were carrying turned his head and called out: ' Quiet, quiet." The howling stopped. " Look after him," I heard him say to the driver, " he is a good dog."

One man with his arm in a sling sat on my running-board. He looked just about all out. " Why don't you sit in front on the seat ? " I asked him, " it is much more comfortable." He thanked me and moved inside.

The head *infirmier* came up and told me that there was a hospital train due at Nogent very soon: " We have got to get everybody we can on to it," he said.

" Will I have to take my two men ? " I asked. " They need attention here before moving on."

He looked doubtful. " Run them down to Pavilion 1, you may get somebody to see them there. Anyhow, you will have more chance of finding out what are the orders."

I took his advice, turned my car round and started to go down the clinker track. Then I thought of the man by my side. " I do not think you ought to come with me," I said, " they will look after you up here." He clutched me with his free arm.

" Please do not leave me, please let me come with you. There are so many so much worse than me here, and I am so tired of sitting, and sitting all alone. I'm no worry, am I ? I don't take up any space that matters ? Let me stay with you, please; I won't be a nuisance, I promise. If there is a train, take me with you there, but please don't leave me here."

What could I do ? I began faintly—unconvincingly: " But orders. . . ."

" What are orders ? . . . I crawled off the battlefield this morning—I had gone on until I had no more ammunition left. There was no point in staying, I could not fight with my arms, one was useless. I sat in a ditch and put this bandage on myself. An army lorry picked me up and brought me here with a lot of others. What would have happened to any of us if that driver had obeyed orders ? Please take me with you."

We went on down to Pavilion 1.

A doctor gave a quick look at the men behind: " For the train," he said. " You have room for one more, I will send another case out."

" What about the man in front ? " My new man looked at me pleadingly. " For the train ? " I asked casually. The doctor shrugged his shoulders. " All right." He hurried away.

" Well ? " I looked at the man.

" Thank you, Englishman," he said.

On the stone steps by the door were about half-a-dozen men sitting on the low wall and lying on the ground. I passed some cigarettes round. I said to one of them, who looked particularly miserable: " Cheer up ! It can't be as bad as all that."

In a dull, flat voice, he replied: " We are lost."

" No, no, we will stop them in a day or two."

" We are lost," he insisted.

Another man took it up: " It is the truth. They have got us this time. We are lost all right."

And the first man repeated like the voice of doom: " We are lost."

I was thankful to get away from the mournful little group by the door. It was dispiriting; I had not heard the wounded talk like that before. They had always been so confident till now. Was it possible that the morale was breaking ?

It was about 10.30 p.m. when I finally got away, and about 11 p.m. when I arrived at the station at Nogent. I got the men on the train almost at once, and the man with the bad arm, who got on last, said: " Goodbye,

Englishman . . ." and then something I did not catch.

A stretcher-bearer by my side laughed: " You have had a success."

Across the bridge over the Marne there was a block of traffic. An officer was sorting it out. I asked if I could move on, and he came up to the car and peered at me through the darkness. " Ah, English! " he exclaimed. My accent had given me away again. " It is a great pleasure to talk with an Englishman. I am very fond of England, I know it well. I spend a lot of my time there and I am very happy to meet you, sir." And then, as if he were a parting guest: " You must forgive me if I leave you now—I have things to attend to." He insisted upon giving me detailed directions to Villiers, and although by now I knew the way backwards, I felt it would have been churlish of me to stop him. I thanked him, and as I drove away I heard him call out: " *Vive l'Angleterre*." I shouted back: " *Vive la France*." Men like that officer make the Entente a real and living thing.

I knew that I ought to go straight back to Oigny, but as I got to the hospital I realised that I needed more petrol, so I drove through the gates and went into a yard on the left where the petrol supply was kept. The custodian of the pump was in great form. I think he must have made several attempts to get to bed and taken a stiff nightcap at each attempt, for he filled up my tank with great vivacity and displayed at the same time enormous *bonhomie*.

I think perhaps it was his unnaturally high spirits that made me suddenly feel extremely tired and started my mind working out the pros and cons of going to Oigny then and there, or staying until daybreak. It was now midnight, I argued to myself : at 3 it would begin to be dawn. Then I could make the journey in daylight, when it would take a quarter of the time; also, by staying I could sleep for nearly three hours and be fresh for another day's work. Whereas if I started now I should only get there at the most half an hour earlier and without sleep. . . . I did not listen to the rest of my argument, but drove straight up the hill to Pavilion 3 and my bed.

I put the car at the back by the coal heap—perhaps it was a slightly guilty feeling that prompted me to do this, but I avoided discussing the subject—and dragged myself up those five flights.

When I reached the top, somebody flashed a torch in my face. " Who's there ? "

" Freeman," I answered.

It was Bouveret. " What are you doing here ? "

I explained that I had brought a load of wounded from Oigny, had put them on the train, and was going to wait for dawn before returning. He agreed it was a good idea.

" Sleep well," he said. Then he whispered: " How are things at Oigny ? "

" All right—plenty of bombardments and a hell of a lot of convoys on the road."

" Which way are the convoys going ? To the front, or away from it ? "

I was surprised. " To the front," I whispered back. I felt we were like conspirators.

" And the morale of the men ? Did they appear calm ? " I said that I thought so.

" Good, good." He seemed relieved. " Sleep well."

I was very puzzled. What on earth did all that mean ? I set Ido M . . .'s alarm clock for 2.45, took off my tunic, and fell asleep.

(ii)

(*Cooper's Narrative.*)

I HAD THE CHANCE to spend a peaceful morning, as I was again without a car. Most of the Section had gone off on missions and the place was very quiet. I had time to read and write some letters, and to wash some clothes. I was dispirited, probably because I had too much time to think and war can only be thought about calmly by those whose advanced age, respectability and sincere naïveté seem to have qualified them for positions of authority.

Here we were, living from minute to minute, suspended as it were between two existences, the past and the future, the past seeming almost further away just then than the future.

Weygand had asked the French to hold on for four weeks, at the end of which time victory should be in sight.

The third week was ending. What was the position ? We knew nothing except that the battle was at its turning point, the Germans apparently continuing their advance; and we were stationed with our backs to the Marne, the scene of their defeat in the last war, and likely, so we thought, to be the scene of a new French victory in the not too distant future. The soldiers we had seen were all more or less confident, though the first signs of doubt had perhaps crept in during the last twenty-four hours. They knew that they could kill far more Germans than were killed of their own number, but they were helpless against the massacring monsters of metal and machinery. " *On les aura* " had given way to " *Il faut les arrêter.*"

I heard a commotion and voices outside, and went to see what was happening. There was a series of dull thuds not far away, and the ground and air quivered; it was a new bombing attack. Aeroplanes had been flying overhead all the morning making a great deal of noise, but there had been no firing. A second and more violent series of explosions followed, this time only a very few kilometres away. Everything shook. We speculated on the objective.

One of the *infirmiers* gave us a newspaper. The news was vague, as usual. One paragraph attracted my attention: " All Italian ships," it ran, " have been ordered to proceed at once to neutral ports." There did not seem to be much doubt now that Italy had decided to join in. Perhaps, after all, the Germans' situation was desperate. We discussed it for a few minutes eagerly, until on the confident note of Allied supremacy the conversation dropped.

An instant later Caillemer appeared. I was to take a small car belonging to ' Jack-and-Jim ' which was at the door, and go at once to Troyes to fetch a mechanic. I dressed as quickly as I could—for I was only in dungarees, our working dress—and came back downstairs. This time I explained I must have a map, and Caillemer lent me his own.

The car was a Citroën. After the heavy ambulance, it responded beautifully to a touch on the accelerator, and I was down at the *château* in a few seconds. Bouveret was waiting on the steps, he was obviously impatient.

" You have been a long time."

" Only ten minutes, sir, just time to put on my clothes and fill the tank."

"When did you get the order ? I telephoned half an hour ago. It is urgent."

I was led to the Colonel's room for fuller instructions, a letter, and the usual *ordre de mission*. I was to go to Troyes and fetch a radiological mechanic to dismantle the X-ray apparatus of the hospital.

It was wonderful to be driving a normal car again, and I sped along at a good rate. There was some excitement in Nogent : people were standing in their door-ways, the single street was crowded with cars and carts.

" What is it ? " I called out in passing.

" Oh, Monsieur, the bombs. They are after the rail-way and the bridges. They dropped three on us just now."

I drove on, wondering what I should find on my return, but at the same time laughing at myself for my fears. Admittedly, as I turned a corner and caught a last glimpse of our hospital, standing large and white on top of its hill, I could not help thinking how conspicuous it really was.

My attention was soon caught by a series of sad little processions straggling along the road. Refugees. There were children running on foot, driving a few obstinate goats; some, luckier, had bicycles. The father of the family—in most cases the grandfather, to judge from his looks—would be at the side, leading a team of noble percherons which were harnessed to the large farm waggon. This was filled to capacity with chairs, tables, pots and pans, wardrobes—I had no time to analyse the contents. On top of it all were the mattresses, which offered the softest seat to the women and babies who travelled like kings on top of their castle.

I looked at their faces; one or two were crying, but the rest had a grim, set look. Something had happened which they did not understand, and they were too surprised to cry. I felt alternately hot and cold. It is war, I thought to myself, trying to be detached, there is nothing else for them to do but move away to safety. Safety—the word seemed strange that day, but after all France is a very large country, I reflected. Then I found myself slowing down. I was at a fork in the road where two carts had drawn up, and there was a signpost which would serve as an excuse for stopping.

" Where have you come from ? " I picked a group at random.

" Soissons."

" Really ? When did you leave ? "

" Last night."

" Are the Germans there—did you see them ? "

" Oh yes, *mon lieutenant*, it is terrible, the bombardment; the whole town is in flames. We fled immediately."

" Where are you going now ? "

" South, to some friends."

" Bon voyage."

I got back into my car and hurried on, feeling miserable and disgusted at what I had just seen, remembering that for many of them it was probably the second time in their life that they had been driven from their homes by the same invaders.

My hunger, and the hope of being able to sit down again to a normal meal, got the better of me at Sézanne, and I stopped in front of the Hotel de France. It was 1.30 p.m. and I had not eaten. M. Boucheron, the *patron*, whom I knew, was delighted. Of course he was open and could feed me. I explained my hurry, and as I ate his delicious *plat du jour* he insisted on offering me one of his best bottles of wine, which we drank together in the courtyard. The hotel was crowded with officers, practically all of them doctors and surgeons. One I had met two nights before, and we exchanged a few friendly words. M. Boucheron was full of praise for all of them, and the brilliant work which they were doing at the hospital.

There was, indeed, an unusual amount of activity for such a peaceful country town, but it was no more than one would expect to find round a base hospital well behind the lines.

It was as much a relief as a surprise to find shops open and an air of disregard still prevailing. I ran to the bookshop to try and buy a map, but I was informed that they had been sold out for several months. So I thanked M. Boucheron for my meal, told him I would be back later, and in a fit of extravagance, decided to buy three bottles of champagne to take home in the evening. He promised to ice them in the interval.

Traffic was not heavy and driving was a relative pleasure. A convoy of fifty ambulances, spaced out over two or three kilometres, took some time to negotiate, and I was just contemplating the open road again when my eye was caught by an English number-plate on a lorry just ahead. As I passed it, I saw that it belonged to the R.A.F. and could not help feeling satisfaction at seeing that some members of this great force were in our sector. In Anglure, the next village I came to, I suddenly saw a crowd of soldiers whom I recognised from their uniform as English. Perhaps after all there are some English troops still in France, I thought as I hurried past; these were the first I had seen. I made a mental note for the return journey that they probably had a canteen where I could buy cigarettes.

I drove faster and faster, playing with the car like a child with a toy, and chuckling to myself at a mischievous idea which had just entered my head: if I drive all out all the way to Troyes, I said to myself, I shall have gained sufficient time to justify another stop. But in that annoying way that cars have when one really needs their co-operation, this one decided to defeat me. It was a punctured back tyre. I wondered for a moment whether to crawl into the village of Méry-sur-Seine, one kilometre ahead, and have the repair done instantly, since I knew nothing about the condition of the spare tyre, but then decided to gamble on getting to Troyes, where I knew that I would certainly be delayed by formalities. So I drew up under the trees beside the road and sweated away in the heat.

"Would you like a hand?" I turned round and found a kindly old French peasant standing over me. He was driving his cartload of hay home from the fields, and impelled by that simple generosity so characteristic of his class, he had stopped. I protested my competence, but he set to work. All of a sudden I heard the increasing roar of approaching aircraft, and looked up.

"We are used to those," he said, "there are several

airfields just over there. We have been bombed, too, three or four times."

I just had time to recognise the peculiar rhythm of the engines as German when the battery of anti-aircraft guns opened up. The peasant ran to his frightened horse and patted it. We were glad to be under the shelter of the trees. It was only a question of seconds before we saw three 'planes swoop down and release their bombs one after another. There were a few terrifying explosions, the guns kept up their rattle of fire—and then we saw the raiders disappear.

Having changed the wheel, I drove on, trusting to my luck to get me to Troyes without further mis-adventure. At Méry I was held up by the sentry, who did not seem to think that the danger was yet over. So I waited a while and we talked. A great number of French 'planes had been destroyed on the ground in a series of such raids, both there and at Romilly, some 10 km. away, he told me; the one we had just witnessed was apparently quite a small affair. After five minutes I felt it was safe, and he agreed to let me pass.

I still had 30 km. to go, but they were rapidly put behind me as I indulged in a glorious race down the long straight road with some senior officer of the Air Force.

Arrived at Troyes, I left my tyre to be repaired at the first large garage I saw and drove round to the *Régulatrice* (medical headquarters), which was in the Lycée. I was sent on to the Supply Depot outside the town to fetch the mechanic. As I drove through the streets, the town seemed to be in every way functioning normally. It was a hot Saturday afternoon, and there were crowds of people everywhere, shopping and sitting at the cafés; people poured in and out of the cinemas. Admittedly there was a larger number of uniforms than usual among the crowd, and a smaller number of cars, and even the shop windows had a monotonous military display of khaki and dark blue.

Behind barbed wire and sentries, among stacks of artificial limbs and bed-pans, cases of chemicals and bottles of distilled water, in a former goods yard with the railway running through it, I found the man I had come to fetch. He was an item to be supplied like the rest. He gathered together his gas-mask and a bundle of clothes, and we left.

I still wanted maps, but again I was unlucky in three or four different shops. Then, as I was buying a newspaper, I found myself standing beside two R.A.F. men. There was an English canteen in the town, they said, and showed me the way. I presented myself to the sergeant in charge—who was surprised to see an Englishman in French uniform—and came out a few minutes later with some bottles of whisky, tins of Players' cigarettes, chocolate, and—most valuable of all—Lifebuoy soap. I felt immensely pleased with myself, hurriedly collected my tyre, and left again for home.

The mechanic was excited at being fetched in a car and took an immense interest in the countryside, which, he said, was new to him. He seemed to spend his whole time making similar journeys to repair X-ray apparatus; not long before, he had been in Alsace, and two days previously had returned from Verdun. In fact, he never spent more than two or three days at a time in Troyes between journeys. He had applied for a small car for himself, as he wasted so much time in trains; journeys which ordinarily would have taken five or six hours would now take nearer twenty-four.

As if by fate, I had a second puncture as we reached Anglure. But this time it happened at the doors of a garage. The temptation was too great, so I drove in and decided to have the repair done at once. I had the worst misgivings now, and almost expected the whole car to fall to pieces before I reached home. Outside in the street I found several English soldiers. They turned out to be members of the Pioneer Corps, whose duty it was to follow the R.A.F. around making landing-grounds for them, and digging reservoirs for the supplies of petrol. There had been many more of them until quite recently, they admitted, but now that most of the English airmen had left they themselves were expecting to be moved any day.

I was pleased to find that they liked being in France and found it " really a jolly good country." As this seemed quite a large concession for an ordinary English-man to make, I tried to arouse their enthusiasm a little more by talking to them about the Champagne country in which they actually were. It had always seemed to me unfair, especially in a war where two great nations—England and France—were practically fused, to expect soldiers to fight and give their lives in defence of a nation about whose history, soil and traditions they were most probably ignorant. If the Entente was to be effective, I argued, it would have to come through real contact and understanding between the two peoples.

It was 7 p.m. when we reached Sézanne.

M. Boucheron was depressed : the news had just been published that the Germans had reached Forges-les-Eaux and were pressing on towards Rouen and the Seine. They seemed to be advancing everywhere. Weygand had issued a proclamation. " *Nous sommes au dernier quart d'heure,*" adding that victory was in sight. The public was inclined to be sceptical, but not yet without hope.

Nearer home the roads were horribly congested; the stream of refugees had swollen to considerable proportions in the short space of an afternoon, and there were not only lines of people on foot, but in addition a large assortment of barking dogs of all sizes, goats, cattle and poultry. Heavy military vehicles, too, were on the move, and when I looked closer I saw petrol lorries, radio cars and the ground staff of air-fields going south. It was an alarming sight, and I wondered what it might mean.

At Nogent there had been another air-raid in the afternoon. The bridge was closed as it had been necessary to start one-way traffic to deal with the refugees. We were sent round by a long detour to Charly.

Back at the *château* ambulances were pouring in and out of the gates, and everyone seemed in a state of agitation. I found Bouveret and reported my return: he told me to report for instructions about the mechanic to the *Médecin-chef*. The latter seemed lost in the middle of so much commotion; perhaps he really was as calm as he pretended. At all events I was instructed to drive the mechanic to our Pavilion 3, have him fed, find him a bed and tell him to report at Pavilion 2 at 8 o'clock the following morning. I was reassured, and so, I think, was the mechanic, who was inclined to fear that he had inadvertently been transported right to the front.

Our drive up the hill seemed endless. Where the circuits divided, there was a queue of ambulances coming down from Pavilions 1 and 2, while all the way ahead of us, going up, was another queue stretching as far as we could see. We took our place and moved gradually forwards until we arrived at a small clinker track which I knew led to the back door of Pavilion 3. It was now almost 9 p.m. The building was empty, as far as I could make out; there was even no one on guard in the office. Then I found Lenoir who undertook to provide us with food. I carried my purchases upstairs, found a *chaise-longue* for the mechanic and told him to meet me downstairs. Then I went over to the kitchen to help Lenoir fetch the meal.

The scene in the courtyard outside Pavilion 2 was almost incredible. There was a moving chain of ambulances arriving empty at one end and leaving full at the other. Bouveret caught sight of me.

"There is still one of our ambulances without a driver. Go and fetch it from under the trees. We need all we can get." So I left Lenoir to deal with the mechanic, and his food, and took my place in the chain.

Twice I was loaded with wounded and made the round trip to Nogent station, where a large hospital train was being filled. It was a terrible drive. By now tanks and heavy artillery had arrived to add to the milling mass of mankind and motors moving behind the Marne.

The strain of keeping calm was not relieved by the mood of the wounded. They were gloomy for the first time. One of them said he would sooner be dead, while others, in the intervals of protesting that there were no French 'planes to defend them, carried their pessimism to the length of adding: "We are lost."

One little episode, a contrast in human natures, cut through the routine of it all and made me feel the horror. As one man, who had lost both legs, was carried out and laid on a stretcher, I saw him reach out with his hand and feel the stumps: "*Merde!* They have taken off both of them," he ejaculated, and lay back laughing. A few moments later, on another stretcher, I saw a figure quivering and yelling: "My leg—they have cut it off. What shall I do?" His only thought must have been of the future and of his disability.

It was almost 10 o'clock by the time I had finished my work. As I went upstairs to bed, I met Caillemer. I gave him back his map and we exchanged a few words about the events of the day. As I left him, I added: "I suppose we will have some rest for a few hours now, the hospital must be almost empty."

"I wish I thought so," he replied dejectedly, "but I am afraid we will be lucky if we get through the night without having to leave here ourselves."

I went to my room. To my surprise I found Freeman asleep on his bed; I wondered why he should be there. Pierre D . . . and Ido M . . . had still not come in; I supposed they must have been sent on special missions, as I had not seen them at the train. I started to take off my boots. Suddenly a torch was flashed through the window on the passage, and then I heard a gentle tap at the door. A head came round: it was ' Jack-and-Jim,' who beckoned me.

" Is Freeman there ? " he whispered.

" Yes, why ? "

" Do you know what his orders are ? Is he going back to Oigny ? "

" I have no idea, I have only just found him. Do you want to talk to him ? Shall I wake him ? "

" No, do not disturb him. It is only that Oigny has been taken and there is no need for him to go back."

I was amazed at his nonchalance, as I realised that Freeman might well leave while I was asleep. " Oh, but really I had better wake him; you must tell him yourself."

He seemed surprised, but before he had time to protest I was already shaking Freeman. Then he said rather tamely: " What are your plans ? "

Freeman told him that he was leaving for Oigny at 3 o'clock. " Well, there is no more point in your going, the Germans are already there. Goodnight "— and he vanished as mysteriously as he had come.

" That was a piece of luck! " I said, and we both started to laugh. " You know that he really was not going to wake you."

I opened one of the bottles of champagne, and we celebrated Freeman's escape before going to sleep.

RETREAT

Sunday, 9th June

PERHAPS WE SLEPT for half an hour before we were awakened by the whistle. Somebody was running along the passage.

" Pack everything. We leave at once. The hospital is being evacuated." It was Caillemer giving the order. At last it had come. Although it had been talked of for two days, it was still a shock. Speed was essential : it was a question of minutes, we were told. From the other rooms we could hear sounds of beds being pushed aside, boots dropping, and the babble of voices.

Dressing in the dark, with only the light of one or two torches, was a small problem compared with collecting our belongings from among the confusion of chairs and mattresses. Saucepans, half-eaten tins of food, packets of tea and bottles appeared from every corner of the room. We bundled them all into sacks and a canteen with our few clothes, determined not to leave anything for the Germans. Then came the tedious business of carrying everything downstairs.

In the middle of all this we came across the radiological mechanic, looking completely lost. We hesitated between asking him to help us and sending him straight to Pavilion 2 to report, but finally decided on the latter, feeling that he might at least try to dismantle the machine even if he had to do it alone.

One of us then went to fetch the ambulance, which had to be extricated from the coal-heap, while the other wearily lagged the first load to the door. We were all only half-awake, and to anyone looking on it must have seemed like a procession of sleep-walkers groping their way up and down the five flights in the darkness. Tempers were short and voices loud. Why could not the

order have been given either earlier or later ? Why did it have to be at this most difficult hour ? We were all querulous and unreasonable.

We struggled with our baggage, and eventually had it all loaded inside our car. The belongings of Pierre D . . . and Ido M . . . were still lying about the bedroom; they had not yet returned, so we felt that we ought to pack for them, and take their canteens, assuming that they would find us wherever we might go.

They were not the only absentees. Several others of the Section were not present, and nobody seemed to know whether they had been delayed at the station or whether they were still at work transporting wounded. At all events, their absence was pleasant in so far as it reduced the confusion, though a curse in so far as it meant plenty of extra work. Nevertheless, we were a little apprehensive and hoped that they would reappear soon.

Somehow we managed to get it all done. Our car then looked more like a luggage van than an ambulance. We presumed that we should now drive down to the *château*, which was the meeting-place. But Bouveret suddenly appeared and called for people to help bring down the Section's archives and stores.

Bouveret had kept his store chamber richly stocked. There were extra stretchers, blankets, mackintosh capes and nine demijohns of Vittel water, all of which had to be loaded. Only one ambulance could be spared. As ours was nearest to the door and already the most full of luggage, it seemed the one most indicated. There were still a few remaining wounded in Pavilion 2 who had to be taken to the station; the other ambulances were told to fetch them on the way down to the *château*.

By now the first glimmer of daybreak made it possible to work without torches. Other members of the Section had not shown themselves so kindly disposed as ourselves to absent comrades; there was more packing to be done, and bundles of possessions had hastily to be tied up in blankets, and thrown into the car. We quickly ran through all the rooms searching for anything that had been overlooked. As we came down Bouveret was waiting at the bottom of the stairs.

"Have you got everything? Are you sure nothing has been left behind?"

"Only the hospital mattresses and blankets, and the mountains of cotton wool on every landing."

"Take them, take them! Do not leave anything for the Germans."

Rather than waste time and energy by carrying them downstairs singly—mattresses are heavy objects—the simplest solution seemed to be to throw them from the windows. For a short space, mattresses and blankets rained down from the fifth floor on to the heads of the people and the roofs of the cars below. We had very little room left, but we took what we could.

The cotton wool presented a separate problem; there was enough to fill several lorries. We had no room for more than a few rolls. In the dispensary a chemist was at work packing up his bottles of drugs; we thought that perhaps the responsible officer would remember the rest of his wool.

When everything was ready, about 4 a.m., we started on our way down to the *château*. There was still a queue of cars.

We ended up in the midst of an extraordinary scene. On the lawns, hundreds of people were standing around, expectant and rather bleary-eyed. On both sides and on the grass, ambulances and cars of every size were parked, most of them loaded with wounded. There were buses too, full of seated figures with some part of them tied up in a bandage. Nurses clustered together under the trees, officers ran about briskly organising one knew not what. We found several others of our Section and grouped ourselves around Bouveret and Caillemer, frightened of losing them in the crowd.

Where were we going ? What did we have to do ?

The *Médecin-chef*, appalled, hurried through the crowd muttering: " *C'est une pagaïe organisée.*"

Bouveret could be heard murmuring that we were supposed to attach ourselves to the new front line dressing-station at Jouarre, just south of the Marne. Someone asked what we were waiting for. Then someone else casually pointed out the folly of this extremely vulnerable conglomeration of Red Cross workers and suggested that a bomber could hardly find a more perfect target. There was a moment of cold terror. Were there already aeroplanes overhead ? At least we were all in our steel helmets. But what of the wounded who had been left in the various ambulances ?

Panic took hold of Bouveret at that moment, and he led us round and round behind the *château* and on all sides looking for gates which we should use as ways of escape and trees to hide under in the event of a bombing attack.

Against such a rabble there was little chance of our prior claims being established in a rush. Should the ambulances full of wounded perhaps leave at once for Nogent ? When would the bridge be blown up ? What would they do once they had crossed the Marne ? Should we split up into groups ? He walked and walked, hurrying from gates to trees and trees to gates, taking off his helmet and hoping that the chill morning air would clear his head.

" Are there any big woods near here ? "

" Yes, sir, on the top of the hill behind the Marne."

" Is there good cover there, Cooper ? "

" Yes, sir."

" Could we hide there until we receive our orders ? "

" Yes, sir, but it is the main ammunition dump."

Then we came across the mechanic again, by now a

very forlorn figure. " How did you get on ? " we asked him.

" They said there was nothing to be done about it; the whole installation has simply been abandoned."

" What are you going to do now ? "

" I have to get to Troyes somehow, I am looking for a car to give me a lift anywhere in that direction."

We shook hands and said goodbye; it was beyond our power to help him. What became of him we never knew.

Under one group of trees which we went to inspect, we found an orderly line of cars labelled " *Ambulance Américaine*." We were staring in amazement when we saw a girl driver whom we had met in Paris. She was English, in the uniform of the Mechanised Transport Corps, and attached to a formation whose headquarters were in the Château de Blois. We exchanged a few hurried words; she had arrived on the previous evening, and had no idea where she was going now. We were unable to find out more before we were carried off to some other shrubbery.

By now we were forming into little groups of grumblers. The situation was intolerable and something had to be done to end it. It was a dejected, hopeless horde that hung around waiting for orders. Allard, with us, was determined to persuade Bouveret to make a move. If the congestion was to be dispersed someone had to start, and there seemed no reason why it should not be ourselves.

Then an improvised ambulance—in reality a delivery van—broke out of the heavy stream of traffic on the road, and drove in at the gate. It brought three or four wounded men on stretchers, who begged to have their dressings attended to. They might have committed a crime of unheard-of daring to judge by the reception they received. Could not the driver see we were evacuating ? Of course there were no dressings to hand,

nor anyone to attend to them. The driver looked round
at the gathering of doctors and nurses and pleaded.
Again it was Allard who showed himself equal to the
situation. He simply fetched a nurse, sent for some
water and any bandages available, and set to work
himself.

At about 5.30 a.m. Bouveret must have made up his
mind, for we took the initiative, detached ourselves
from the rest, and set out in a long line for the station.
We said a few hurried goodbyes to those of the staff
whom we knew. This sudden atmosphere of chaos and
uncertainty, with the unspoken word " Retreat " in our
minds, left us wondering if and when we would see
any of them again. We took a last look at the *château*,
which by now we had come to regard as such a per-
manent base. It seemed hardly possible to imagine
ourselves being replaced in, as we supposed, a few
hours by the Germans.

Our line of cars did not remain unbroken for more
than a few moments. The stream of vehicles and
refugees on the road outside was, if anything, even more
intense than it had been at midnight. We were too
bewildered and ignorant of what was really happening
to feel the full poignancy of what we were witnessing.
It was a hideous spectacle. We had to observe it; for,
having no business at the train, we were left to wait on
the main road outside the station yard for at least an
hour and a half.

Just in front of us was the level crossing, and looking
across to the left we could see the station platforms.
They were both crowded with civilians, massed together, looking for trains to come and take them away.
Half of them seemed to be oblivious of the fact that
they were on the platform for trains going north. We
did not know whether their departure had been
organised in this way, or whether they naïvely supposed
that any train would carry them to safety. It must be

remembered that these were simple villagers, the great majority of whom knew nothing of the world beyond a few kilometres around the homes where they had been born and brought up. Paris was as remote as Timbuctoo; they had very little sense of direction.

There they stood, almost overflowing from the platforms on to the rails, many without coats and hats, each with his little bundle; the women wore their best summer dresses, the children's hair was tied with the inevitable bow of ribbon, the men were in their Sunday black. They might have been going for an excursion.

Carts with creaking wheels lumbered continuously by. Figures pushing perambulators, wheel-barrows or hand-carts full of belongings were among the vehicles, others carrying bursting suit-cases in each hand kept to the side of the road. From time to time the gates of the level-crossing would close and cut off the endless stream. Those on the road would stop and wait patiently; on the platform, eyes were strained looking for the train; but it never came, and after a few minutes the gates would swing back again and the stream continue its course.

It was a silent crowd; the only sounds one heard were the creak of the wheels, the clatter of the hoofs, the crack of the whips, and the occasional crowing of a cock from its coop suspended between the wheels.

Down each side of the main village street was a line of any and every sort of vehicle, into which the remaining inhabitants were emptying the contents of their dwellings. As each family finished, it would draw out and join the main stream. Eventually the only people left in the houses were the soldiers who had been stationed there to defend the bridge. They came out and started to wash at the few pumps in the street. Their unhurried movements seemed almost casual by contrast with the animation of the departing villagers. The sight of them washing, and the smell of their breakfast coffee, reminded us of our own needs. We looked for a café, but the proprietors were not opening. Everyone was determined to get away before the Boche came.

There was no panic, no chaos. It had the appearance of a careful and timely evacuation of both banks of the Marne, leaving the terrain free for the great battle which would be fought. We had seen the preparatory moves. The Air Force, we knew, had withdrawn its advance bases in order to set up their new positions; we had noticed the material and staffs passing several hours earlier. A great deal of heavy armament had been moved, too. Now the medical services were retiring. In its turn the civilian population had to leave, and as we saw it at this moment the departure was perfectly orderly. The Army had not yet appeared; it was still holding positions further north and fighting hard.

The Retreat was on.

It was after 7 o'clock when our column, headed by Bouveret, drove out of the station yard. We fell into line and followed where we were led. When we came to the main road we turned to the right in the direction of Paris. Now we were away from the stream of refugees, and the only traffic we met was military lorries coming from Paris towards the Marne. At several important points the road was being mined.

We halted in a little village beyond La Ferté-sous-Jouarre for about two hours. We washed and shaved at the village pump outside the Mairie, and made ourselves the inevitable cup of tea. The theological student, who had been nicknamed ' Mustapha,' moped around whining for his possessions, which were buried somewhere in the confusion inside our car. Expecting to move on at any moment, it was out of the question to start unloading.

When the missing members of our Section had all caught us up, we set off again, still heading west. After a few kilometres we took a side road to the right and halted under cover of a wood. With a look of amused surprise we had read the sign-post: Armentières 2 km. That was the last place in which we expected to find ourselves.

In the haste of our departure, no arrangements had been made for feeding us, and for the first time we were confronted with our iron rations. Fortunately the *pinard* had not been forgotten.

Pierre D . . . was not very friendly disposed towards us; we had overlooked his suit-case, but luckily he had been back to Villiers and found it himself. Our carelessness was in a way excusable, for he was one of those methodically tidy people who always find the most elaborate hiding-places for their belongings. Our oversight was as nothing beside the major disaster for which François, the accountant, was responsible; he had omitted to bring with him both the petty cash and his accounts. Bouveret was enraged, and ordered the trembling man to go back at once. He was more frightened of Bouveret than of the Germans, and left quickly. Bouveret then disappeared for the afternoon in quest of our new headquarters and the General's orders.

It was a beautiful Sunday afternoon: very hot, and the sun shining from a cloudless blue sky. We retired to a field to sleep. We were on a ridge above the Marne, and as we lay in the shade, our rest was broken by frequent aerial battles, the sound of bombs in the distance, and the constant rumble of artillery.

It was about 6 o'clock when François reappeared, his mission successfully accomplished. The Germans, he said, had still not reached Villiers, but the whole place was deserted except for a few cats and the enormous quantity of hospital equipment that had been abandoned. Then Bouveret returned. We were hastily served with the remains of our bully beef, and once again our line of cars took the road.

E

We went back to La Ferté and turned south through Jouarre to Rebais. Rebais was full of soldiers, especially Air Force men. Columns were forming, the square in the centre of the town was full of lorries, and convoys were pouring through. We, too, passed through, and just as dusk was falling, turned in at the gates of a large farm a few kilometres beyond. We found ourselves in the rick-yard. Facing us was a Dutch barn, under which the first cars were parked; on the right were the farm buildings. We drove between the two into the large orchard beyond and distributed ourselves under the trees. In the half-light it was impossible to see very clearly, but we realised that there was already a number of lorries and horses about the place.

Some of our comrades slept in the hay, others on the stretchers inside their ambulances. But we were in a quandary. We could not leave our car because of the stores, nor could we put up stretchers inside. We seemed to be faced with no other alternative than to sleep on the grass, an unattractive proposition with so many stray animals wandering about. Then we had a brain-wave. Having got rid of all the luggage belonging to others, the most bulky part of our load left was the mattresses and blankets. Half of these we lent out for the night, and with the rest constructed for ourselves a precarious divan on top of the demijohns and other baggage. It was a curious and not altogether uncomfortable arrangement, rather like a travelling seraglio. At least we were safe from the animals in the orchard and in the hay.

Monday, 10*th June*
OUR FIRST SURPRISE on waking was to find ourselves parked beside a mobile anti-aircraft unit. We looked around to see what other strange neighbours we might have. Into the confined space of about two acres, which was roughly the size of the orchard, every type of

vehicle seemed to have been crowded. There were large lorries, touring cars, *Section de Santé* ambulances, buses full of *infirmiers* and stretcher-bearers, horse-drawn medical supply waggons, and, in the far corner, a forlorn conglomeration of farm carts and refugees. In the early morning sunlight, as each little group came to life and a general movement started, it was like the scene in the gypsy encampment from any operetta.

It was an unusual orchard; the trees were very big, very old and mostly dead. Those that showed any signs of life showed no promise of fruit. At the end furthest from the farm, the ground fell away down to a tiny stream where there was a wash-house. The stream's slight movement prevented it from being completely stagnant; it was a victim of the drought.

At the farm end was a wall, and through a gate one entered a large yard, which was enclosed on all sides by farm buildings. It was the usual sort of spacious French farmyard, full of mud, dung, and hens. Now it was peopled with hundreds of soldiers, washing, shaving, watering their horses or filling cans and buckets. On one side were two enormous horse-troughs, with a pump between them. We filled our water bottles and, deciding there was less of a crowd in the orchard, washed and shaved there as best we could from a saucepan.

Just beyond the anti-aircraft guns by our side was a very large bus, which seemed to be the home of a group of soldiers standing beside it. The driver of it caught our eye first. He was nonchalantly sitting in his seat smoking a cigarette and, with a look of satisfaction, obviously receiving the congratulations of this crowd. We thought he must at least have won the National Lottery or captured a dozen Germans. We wandered over, and then we heard him say: " It was no trouble at all. Of course, I knew it was imminent, and when I woke up this morning there they were." There was laughter, and some newcomers, urged on by the others, pressed forward and peered into the car. We were equally inquisitive, and peered in ourselves; there was the cause of the excitement. A mongrel bitch, with a heritage of every dog known to man, lay at the driver's feet with a look of supreme satisfaction, nursing six black puppies. Like hundreds of other dogs, she had been picked up, homeless and starving, in a little village in the evacuated area where she had remained after her owner's departure.

There is a legend that the Latin peoples treat their animals unkindly. Nothing could be more untrue. The kindness and care which the French peasants in flight showed for their domestic animals was astounding. It is true that large numbers of dogs were found by the soldiers in the evacuated areas, but these had, for the most part, lost their masters in the confusion and returned to the only home they knew; few had actually been abandoned. To the peasants the loss of a favourite dog was a matter of serious concern, but they need not have worried, for many a lorry-driver or other soldier was only too happy to adopt a faithful companion.

The atmosphere at the midday meal was tense. Food seemed to be the cause, but as there was plenty and it was quite good, we did not immediately grasp the grounds for complaint. We soon knew; Horiot, one of the volunteers, exploded: " How can I be expected to eat a meal without bread ? "

We offered him some army bread: " It is green." We offered him some of our biscuits: " It is not the same." We expressed surprise that bread had not been fetched from Rebais: " Ah, but one car went into town this morning to fetch the bread, and what have they done, the *salauds* ? Why, they are gorging in a restaurant while our meal is ruined! "

Bread is as essential to a Frenchman's meal as a potato is to an Englishman's; we understood his resentment. We suggested that, if permission were

granted, the three of us should go into Rebais after the
meal, he to get his bread, we to have our car greased.
Our car was new, the work hard and exacting on the
chassis, the pressure of a manual grease-gun insufficient
to penetrate the paint-clogged points, and automatic
greasing in the early stages was essential. When we
explained this to Bouveret he agreed to let us go, but
told us to be back at 3 o'clock, when he proposed to
distribute the stores which we were carrying.

Before we left, Bouveret announced our new postal
address, it was:—

S.A.T.S. 5412/19,
Service de Santé 17ème C.A.,
S.P. 13,441.

This was the first indication we had that we were now
attached to the 17th Army Corps. For two days everybody had been very preoccupied with the fate of letters
addressed to them at Villiers; now they felt happier,
and a great orgy of letter-writing began.

We took with us in addition Jean P . . . , one of our
Belgian comrades. We drove first to the garage attached
to the hotel in the main square, but it was before 2
o'clock and the mechanics had not returned from their
dinner. So the four of us sat down in the hotel parlour
to enjoy the luxury of a post-prandial coffee and liqueur.

Horiot was still moderately incensed over his ruined
meal, but under the mellowing influence of alcohol his
indignation subsided. He was a dark, middle-aged,
stocky little man, with twinkling eyes and a mild, un-
assuming appearance. He was sensitive and had a
quick temper, occasionally to the point of ungovernable
rage, but with a little tact and understanding he could
be easily handled. He had been in the Foreign Legion
and was thoroughly rough and ready. In fact, he was
quite out of his element in our corps, but no one could
have been more genuinely kind-hearted. Through the
missing bread, we made a new friend.

Jean P . . . we had known and liked from the beginning. He was a friend of Raymond's, and they shared
ambulance No. 11. He, too, was an actor, and was
half Swiss. He was dark and handsome, with a look of
gentle melancholy. There was no mistaking the actor,
and we were not surprised to learn that his success
had been immediate in his first part. He was very
modest about his work, but Raymond told us that he
had a considerable reputation in the theatre. He was
pensive and detached, friendly and unforthcoming.

When we had finished our drinks, there was still no
sign of the mechanic. The personnel of the hotel was
unhelpful. It was hopelessly under-staffed and they
were serving lunches in wild confusion to a large
number of officers. So we went to look for other garages
in the town.

There were two. The first was friendly but could do
nothing for us. The proprietor was mobilised, and his
wife was in charge. She could not work the automatic
greaser herself, and the only person she would allow to
do so was a soldier stationed in the town, but he was on
sentry-go at the moment. If we liked to call him away
from his guard he would no doubt help us. We felt
that was a little too complicated, and moved on.

The second one was at the back of the town. Fortunately Horiot had gone off in the interval with Jean P . . .
to look for a baker, otherwise there might have been a
scene, for there we found the bread-defaulters and
Allard with their two ambulances. We had all had the
same idea about greasing.

Allard was in the middle of a fierce and acrimonious
argument with the proprietress. Her husband, too, was
mobilised; she, however, had mechanics, two minute
little boys, but they no longer had a machine. Having
decided that the situation was getting rapidly worse
and that she must leave Rebais, she had disconnected
the apparatus that morning. Allard was furious; we

were all furious; it must be connected again at once.
" What would happen if everybody ran away like
this ? " he asked. The Germans were still miles away,
she was quite safe, and if essential services like garages
closed down, panic was bound to follow. If evacuation
became necessary, the decision would be taken by the
proper authorities and orders given accordingly; until
that time it was the duty of everybody to remain where
they were. Under the flow of Allard's just rebukes, the
woman burst into tears, retired inside her shop and left
it to us to do the best we could.

We tried, but failed; the terminals were in a hopeless
muddle and it would have taken hours to disentangle
and connect them. While the others were still trying
hopefully, we looked for maps in the shop. The proprietress burst into tears again at the sight of us, and we
had to console her. But she had no maps. We gave our
tyres some air; this machine was still working.

When we had finished we found that three or four
exceedingly old harridans had gathered round us.
They were very inquisitive, and asked in turn who we
were, what we were, where we came from, what we
were doing, and what the news was. They were assisted
in their questions by neighbours who leant out of
windows or stood in their open doorways and shouted
at us across the road. They were all delighted that we
had attacked the proprietress of the garage, for they
did not intend to leave. They had enormous confidence
in the Allied armies, and were certain of ultimate
victory. But when would it be ? Meaning only to encourage them we said: " Don't worry—soon."

The oldest harridan, who was quite toothless and
had a fine beard, beamed and said: " Messieurs, when
it is all over you must come back and I will give you a
bottle of champagne to celebrate. Now, don't forget.
That is the house, across the road: number 13."

Then the anti-aircraft guns suddenly opened fire,

and with hasty goodbyes they ran to their houses and disappeared. We took shelter in a house while the 'planes fought overhead. The raid was soon over, and, as our companions had finally given up wrestling with the greaser, we returned to the centre of the town to pick up Horiot and Jean P. . . .

We had remarked earlier that the crowds of soldiers of the night before had vanished; but passing the Town Hall on our way to the square, we noticed that their place had been taken by refugees. On the grass in front, on the steps and in the courtyard, hundreds were squatting. There were others standing and sitting by their cars and carts in the streets, and every approach to it was congested. They were waiting for bread, which was being distributed by the officials. They were bovine and had the look of disinterested cattle in a market-place; it was a patient and orderly crowd.

Our two companions were on the square. Horiot had been successful in his search for bread; although everybody had directed him to the Town Hall, he had found one baker with a few loaves left, which he had agreed to sell.

A brush in a shop window caught our eye, and so did an enamel basin; we needed both very badly, the first to clean the inside of our car, the second for every purpose. Then we hurried back to our orchard.

At 3 o'clock punctually we reported to Bouveret, and the distribution of stores commenced. He and Merckx stood by our side while we carefully and methodically unloaded and checked the things as we handed them over. They were sorted into neat piles on the ground.

Grouped round Bouveret in a semi-circle were the members of the Section, and as we unloaded, our labours were accompanied by a chorus of voices eagerly allocating to themselves each object. It might have been " Remnant Day." They practically snatched

things from our hands, but with stolid English persever-
ance we kept them at bay. We laughed to ourselves at
our characteristic display, and true to the tag of
"*perfide Albion*" we had, of course, managed to keep
hidden all that we needed for ourselves. If the French
had their "*Système D,*" so had we.

Bouveret was very amused at us, and the others took
it in very good part when they realised that we could
not be rushed. It was from that moment that we earned
the title of "*les vraies vaches anglaises.*" Bouveret divided
the material, and we were officially given a demijohn
of Vittel, a mattress and two blankets. With an empty
ambulance at last we had plenty of dirt to clean up,
and we set to work with our new brush.

By the time we had finished we were sweating hard,
as the heat was still intense. We debated whether we
should wash at the pump or take a risk in the stream
below. But the stream won.

All thought of splashing in a clear woodland stream
vanished as, armed with our new bowl and Lifebuoy
soap, we advanced towards the wash-house. The little
stream looked most uninviting. There was a rich green
scum on top, and through the patches of floating vege-
tation, the water was a pale shade of mud. However, a
running stream, no matter how sluggish and reluctant
its movement, was not to be lightly disregarded. So we
set to work. We had meant to sit on the wooden platform that formed the floor of the wash-house and put
our feet in the stream as a preliminary; but the clouds
of impertinent dragonflies made that impossible, so we
filled the bowl, sat on the bank, and proceeded to wash
on the "up as far as possible and down as far as
possible" principle.

We were doing quite well when we saw a soldier
advancing towards us carrying a collection of dishes
and saucepans. He was obviously a cook coming to
clean his kitchen utensils ready for the evening meal.

The prospect of a little more grease and refuse being added to that already overworked stream left us unmoved, but we felt that it would have been much nicer if he had waited for another quarter of an hour. The cook evidently felt the same, as he offered to fill us a second bowl before he scoured his dishes. During our respective ablutions we carried on a conversation, and hearing us talk English he ventured to suggest that of course we knew Le Touquet. He was really a *maître d'hôtel* at the Hotel Hermitage, but was now a cook in a *Section de Santé*. He was very friendly, and offered to supplement our rations should food ever run short.

We were naked when the whistle blew. Looking up to the orchard, we saw everybody running about searching for their steel helmets and taking cover under the trees. The anti-aircraft gun crew were standing by, ready for action, and we could hear the sound of aeroplanes. We had neither *casques* nor *masques*, but without saying a word to the other we each continued our washing. Everybody was much too busy watching a dog-fight overhead to notice two naked bodies sitting beside the stream. When we returned the alarm was over.

We felt wonderful, and the mention of Le Touquet reminded us of times that no longer existed. It was 6 o'clock—we remembered the champagne. Solemnly we escorted one bottle to the horse-trough, which proved an excellent cooler.

The evening meal was now ready, so we fetched it from the kitchen lorry and, not wishing to appear too ostentatious, sat ourselves beside our ambulance to wash it down with our special bottle. We were quite a centre of interest to the soldiers in nearby lorries, and soon had a lively group around us, chattering, drinking and laughing. One man came up and added his voice to the others: " Italy has declared war on us."

' How do you know ? "

" Since when ? "

" What for ? On what pretext ? "

" The swine! "

It took a few minutes before the cross-questioning was over and he was able to reply that he had just heard the news over the wireless. There is no hiding the fact that it came to us at that moment as a blow, although we had half-expected it for several days. But the French press had led one to believe that the attack would be on Jugoslavia, and once again people had been lulled into a sense of false security.

Some of the soldiers in our group were Corsicans, we discovered, others from Marseilles and the south. Discussions became heated as old hatreds showed themselves. We agreed that it was typical of the Italians to choose this moment for such a decision, but at the same time there was a feeling of relief. Now the issue was clarified. We knew that the south of France was well protected and full of troops, especially Colonial regiments, but hitherto they had been immobilised, guarding the frontier. Now all the armies of France could operate together. It looked like a confession of German weakness to call on the half-hearted ally just then. And what of the attitude of Russia ? Turkey ? The Balkan countries ? We covered the whole field of international politics. There was no missing the pleasure they felt at being able, at last, to have a smack at " the macaroni."

We broke the news to the other members of our Section, but they were inclined to be incredulous.

It was about 8 o'clock when the whistle blew and we gathered round Bouveret. A detachment of six cars, under Caillemer, was to go at once to Coulommiers and transport some men to Melun. The rest of us would be leaving in another direction in a few minutes.

" Lastly, I want to deny a rumour," he went on. " There is a story that Italy has declared war: this is totally untrue. This rumour has been started by a member of the Fifth Column in Rebais, who has already been discovered by the Police."

There was a sigh of relief and looks of scorn for us.

" But, sir, the news comes from a soldier who heard it announced over the wireless."

" Where is he ? Send him to me at once."

He was found and brought over. Then Bouveret began: " What you have done—spreading false news—is immensely serious, coming as it does from a man in uniform. . . ."

" But, sir, I heard it myself over the wireless in the farmhouse."

Bouveret's face fell. He looked less convinced of what he was saying. " I tell you it is totally untrue, and the man who started the story has been arrested in Rebais."

The man was sent away protesting that he knew it was true.

Each driver was then handed a little slip of paper with the names of the villages on our route, and we were told to get ready to move to Beton-Bazoches. In about half an hour we left.

In time we halted at the side of the road in an open piece of country. There seemed no obvious reason for stopping, but we stopped. We could hear the noise of guns firing; it was the persistent sound of artillery in action. We wondered where the battle could be. We thought it might not be far away. Over the whole stretch of country to our left was a heavy pall of dark grey smoke. Bouveret came up to us casually and said in a grudging way: " It is quite true: Italy is against us. I have just heard it myself on the wireless."

It was pitch dark the next time we stopped, but we were conscious that there were high trees all round. By the light of a torch we were shepherded down a forest ride which seemed to have obstacles on both sides. We came out into a clearing but were then

backed into a glade which led off it. Here we were
told that we would spend the night.

With our allotted mattress and the three that we had
hidden we reconstructed our divan. It was drizzling
slightly; after the intense heat of the day this was a
comfort. It was the first rain we had seen.

Tuesday, 11th June

THE WOOD had filled up during the night. As we walked
down the ride in search of Bouveret and our orders for
the day, we found that the cars and waggons had
followed us from the orchard and were also hidden
among the trees. There was a perpetual rustle in the
undergrowth; men and horses were everywhere. The
men looked solemn and depressed. We were all rather
lost.

There was a surprise awaiting us at the end of the
ride. On a log by the kitchen lorry sat Caillemer, his
head swathed in bandages. He looked " flaccid and
drained " and a cup of coffee was trembling in his hand.
We thought that at least he must have been hit by
shrapnel. But not at all. He had fallen asleep while
driving in the night, and had run into the back of one
of the ambulances. He confessed that, hot and tired, he
had taken off his steel helmet. The ambulance was unscratched, but his own car had been quite badly
damaged and his head had been thrown against the
windscreen. Although he was badly cut, it was a
miracle that he was not worse. Like its owner, the car
was on exhibit as a sort of cautionary tale, but we were
all rather callous and felt that a road accident in the
middle of a war hardly merited our attention.

The mission to Coulommiers had been full of incident. There had been soldiers with contagious diseases
to transport to Melun, always a disagreeable job. Afterwards the ambulances had been sent on to Fontaine-
bleau and the drivers disinfected. A fumigator had been

put in each ambulance and lighted; then, in the dark and rain, the column had set forth to find Beton-Bazoches. The ' Grandmother of Snow-White ' led the way, and, as if pursued by the devil, had hurled himself down the road. The others, following at break-neck speed in an effort to keep up with him, had slithered along, cannoning off the grass verge, bumping into trees, like balls in a game of snooker. The while, they had been blinded and asphyxiated by the fumes from the fumigator behind and terrified lest at any minute it should be overturned and set the ambulance on fire. The expedition had not been a success, and nobody was speaking to ' Snow-White.' The net gain to the Section seemed to be one map, which Ido M . . . waved triumphantly, saying: " The Duchesse d'Uzès gave me this herself."

There were still no orders, and Bouveret had dis-appeared. There was talk of a large *château* not far away in whose park we were now said to be. The officers were supposed to be inspecting it with the intention of setting up a new base hospital, and we expected to move in during the afternoon. It was all very vague, and we could get no confirmation, so we decided that these suppositions were probably ground-less.

Lunch was a dismal affair. We were all in rather low spirits except Erwtemans and van B . . . , who were infuriatingly funny with some egg-laying trick they had invented. They crowed, one louder than the other, until we could have kicked them.

Lenoir had brought a newspaper from the village when he had fetched the provisions. Italy's declaration of war was the chief item of news, and we all sympa-thised with the bitter sentiments of Reynaud's speech: " This very moment when France, wounded but valiant and undaunted, is fighting against the hegemony of Germany . . . has been chosen by Signor Mussolini to declare war on us." We also read that Narvik had been abandoned and that King Haakon and his Government had arrived in London. Did this mean that the English were coming back to France, where they were desperately needed ? But if they did come, where would they land ? We learnt at the same time the worst news: Rouen had fallen, and the Germans had crossed the Seine.

Bouveret told us that once again we were moving. We packed our belongings and drove out of the wood.

Retreat: we could not get the word out of our minds. The lack of coherence at Villiers and a seemingly aimless departure: our long delay in the wood near Armentières: the orchard at Rebais: the wood in which we had just spent the night: and now another move. It had all been so vague, so purposeless. Were we going anywhere, or were we just wandering about ?

We had come out to work, and just at the moment when there must have been plenty to do we were unoccupied. Everybody was growing restless, apprehensive. What had gone wrong ? It was curious how Lenoir had to improvise each meal with no central depot from which to draw provisions. For three days now we had lived on scrap meals as if he had no time to get anything ready and was always prepared to leave at a moment's notice. It was curious how the mechanics, with so much time on their hands, would never undertake any but essential repairs. It was curious, too, how Bouveret would disappear for hours on end and then return and sit about, nervous and fidgety. If the line of resistance was re-forming on the Marne, it ought to have been completed by now, with ourselves in position at the front line dressing-station, or at least at the relief hospital.

Our new destination was not far. It was a pleasant country house with a large farm attached, belonging to the Belgian novelist, Charles Plisnier. A Dutch barn afforded good cover for our cars, and the house, though uninhabited, looked inviting. Everybody was pleased at the thought of being billeted there and began to inspect the house and grounds, even going so far as to work out the sleeping accommodation. Bouveret was less optimistic: " I don't think we shall be here long." That was all he would say.

The stable yard became a bath-house and there were queues at every tap. We, with our bowl and two borrowed buckets, crept away to the marble-paved terrace at the back of the house, looking on to the lawn.

The kitchen garden proved an irresistible attraction. The unpicked ripe fruit was not allowed to hang on the bushes for long, and finally even the unripe goose-berries had disappeared. These were mostly consumed by ' Mustapha,' though whether as penance or from sheer greed we were not quite certain. Others of our Section, more industrious, went into the fields to help turn the hay. Some worked on their cars, changing the oil. We were all busy in one way or another. The general uneasiness had spread, and no one could keep still. The atmosphere was not helped by the continual presence of large formations of German 'planes in the sky, and we were irritated by the ineffectual popping of a machine-gun close at hand.

Mindful of the unsuccessful feeding of the past few days, we bought milk and eggs from the farm. How-ever, this evening, Lenoir had excelled himself on the large kitchen range in the *château* and we sat down to feed at a long table. We were delighted to be under cover, as it started to rain.

After the meal we inspected the interior of the house ; it was the typical setting for a literary celebrity. There was a large number of books, a certain amount of art, and a great deal of atmosphere. We opened one book ; it was inscribed :

to Charles Plisnier
with all my sympathy
G.... de C....
P.S. I no longer receive *your* books.

Suddenly Pierre D ..., from the next room, called
out in surprise. We ran to see what he wanted and
found him pointing to a bronze head. " Look what I
have found ! It is one of my father's works."

We were all told to wait in the kitchen as orders were
about to be given. After a while, Bouveret, accompanied by Caillemer, with a paper in his hand, appeared.
He read out a list of six cars : these were to proceed
immediately to G.S.D. (*Groupe Sanitaire Divisionnaire*, a
front line dressing-station) at Jouarre. Then a list of
four others including ourselves : we were to go to
G.A.C.A. (*Groupe d'Ambulances du Corps d'Armée*, the
Casualty Clearing Station) at the Château des Minimes,
Champcenest. The rest of the Section was to be held in
reserve to replace or reinforce us.

Confidence was immediately restored. There was a
front again, and, as we had expected, it was the Marne.

As we were about to drive off, the disillusioned
Norwegian journalist stood in our path. He was red with
rage and defiant. He obviously had another grudge.

" How long have you been in France ? "

We were so taken aback that we laughed as we told
him that we knew the country very well and had spent
a great deal of time there. That seemed to upset his
plan, for he continued rather lamely : " Oh, that's
different. I thought you had only just arrived. I could
not understand why you always get work to do, when I,
who know France well, get nothing." Then he became
confiding : " There is a plot ! My chief hates me. He
must have told Bouveret that I am no good. But I am
going to get to the bottom of it. I must go to the front.
I must get ' copy ' for my book."

We formed our line. There was one Norwegian ambulance with ' Jack-and-Jim,' one driven by René de S ... and Sarazinski, another by Mazella, a Corsican, who owned an hotel in Paris, and our own.

After about five kilometres we arrived at the ugliest red-brick *château* imaginable. It was quite large and had a touch of that outward Gothicism which was so popular at the end of the last century from Aberdeen to Amalfi. It must always have been sad, even when it was new, but now, unfurnished and untenanted, it was dank, decaying and desperate. The rain had stopped by the time we got there ; drops were falling off the trees and steam was rising from the ground. The house seemed to thrive on the grey sky and the wetness, and would probably have been much happier harbouring a Scots industrialist in a glen.

Once again we found ourselves in a wood, this time a very wet one. It amounted to little more than a thick covert round the ornamental water at the side of the *château*. At the end furthest from the road there was a little bridge, which led across a pond to the stables. When we had parked, we went across to inspect our new headquarters.

The first person we saw was Miss Bennet, the English girl driver whom we had left at Villiers. She introduced us to the other members of her unit, including their leader, Miss Marjorie Juta, a tall South African, who concealed her capabilities with charm. We found that their unit consisted of five ambulances fitted with oxygen apparatus. There were seven English girl drivers, two French military doctors to administer the oxygen, and a middle-aged American (who called himself Commandant) who had organised the unit and gone to the war with his Labrador retriever.

There was a group of French nurses who gave us some coffee and immediately made us feel at home. We talked for a while and they asked if we would be stationed with them for long. They were charming, intelligent women, and most of them spoke excellent English. They, too, were complaining of their inactivity during the last few days, but here was a house again, and in an hour or two it would be completely equipped as a hospital.

We had joined the *Service Sanitaire* of the 17th Army Corps, recruited from Toulouse. The *Médecin-chef* greeted us. With him was a lieutenant, the chief surgeon, whose noble, pale, ascetic face was made even more spiritual by his black chin-beard. Speaking with a broad Toulousain accent, he informed the nurses that he was starting duty at midnight, from when on he expected casualties to start arriving. His advice to us was to follow his example and get some sleep right away, as we would certainly be called on during the night.

Wednesday, 12th June
EXPECTING to be called at any minute, we hardly slept at all. Our excitement was unnecessary as everything over at the *château* was still. Our wood might have been a tropical forest in the rainy season. We hated it long before morning came. The air was hot and fœtid, the rain poured down, the mosquitoes were as large as bats and the frogs croaked without ceasing. When finally we went over to the stables to get our morning coffee, we found all the personnel of the hospital in a dejected state. There was still no sign of any wounded. What had happened?

Shortly afterwards a Norwegian car arrived from Paris bringing the organiser of the Norwegian section with letters and food for 'Jack-and-Jim.' His news was startling. The Germans had captured Pontoise. They had crossed the Seine. Parachutists had been seen in the forest of St. Germain. German troops were certain to be in Paris in a day or two. The Parisians

were fleeing in all directions. Food was practically unobtainable ; everything was shut. We asked whether
Paris would be defended. He thought so. A special
decree had been passed enabling English residents to
carry firearms without a licence. The ring was closing
in, but the Government was still in Paris. At all events
he was returning that afternoon.

He painted a desperate picture, and we were alarmed.
Then we talked to the French officers and started to
reason. Of course Paris would be defended, it was the
capital. It might be necessary for the Government to
withdraw and continue its deliberations in a provincial
town, removed from danger, threats and pressure.
Other provisional capitals were available. By tradition,
French governments moved to Bordeaux in times of
crisis. Paris would be armed and it would look after
itself.

At last the first casualties appeared, brought by our
drivers from Jouarre. Their wounds were examined.
Most of them were sent on immediately to the big
hospital at Provins, a matter of 10 km. One man, a
captain in the artillery, had to be taken to Sézanne ;
this was our mission. But we no longer had to go to the
hospital we knew ; a second one had been opened at
Frécul, just outside the town, to replace those of
Montmirail and Villiers.

We had not gone very far before we realised that the
captain was in great pain. He had a bullet in the left
arm which was in a sling. He made no fuss, but through
our little window we could see that he was ashen grey
and doubled up on the seat. We stopped to see if anything could be done for him, but most of all he needed
a stimulant. He felt better after a glass of whisky.

As we continued our journey, he told us that he had
come straight from the south bank of the Marne, where
the battle was fierce. The troops were fighting bravely
but he was gloomy because, he said, the organisation

had broken down. The news that the Germans had crossed the river at Château-Thierry was the worst of all. It had happened that morning when, under cover of a heavy smoke-screen, they had thrown across a pontoon. It was disastrous news ; the line on which we had been relying had been broken, and if the organisation of the forces had collapsed there seemed very little left for hope.

As we sped down the road, passing long lines of convoys and buses full of troops heading for the Marne, we wondered if they would get there in time. All the Paris buses, camouflaged, were being used for transport, but the troops they were carrying were obviously not fresh.

Approaching Sézanne the traffic became thicker, and the town itself was in a hubbub ; convoys and troops were converging from every side. The military police were unable to deal with it, and we had great difficulty in forcing a passage. Nobody seemed able to direct us to Frécul ; the police had only just arrived and the townspeople were too stunned by the sight of so many troops to be able to reply coherently. Even when we did find a tradesman to direct us, he was too preoccupied to say more than : " You mean Sans-Souci " —and with a vague wave of the hand, " It is up there and to the left."

We drove on, up a steep hill, for about two kilometres, and there, on the highest spot for miles around, we found a large *château* in a park. We immediately compared it in our minds to Villiers. Was it essential for hospitals to be so exposed ? Had the hospital authorities still a blind faith in German respect for the Red Cross ? Or were suitable houses so difficult to find ?

The scene at the hospital was as busy as we would have expected : lines of ambulances, stretcher-bearers, *infirmiers*, doctors and surgeons. There were rows of tents round the *château*, and when his turn came we accompanied our captain into one of them, where he lay down on a stretcher among the other wounded and waited for the doctors to come to him. The hospital had only just been opened, but it had an air of great efficiency.

Back in Sézanne we at last found a garage that could grease our car, so we left it with the mechanic and went to look for food. The Hôtel de France was crammed with soldiers. Every table, every chair was occupied. Madame Boucheron was in the kitchen. She could just manage to give us a plain omelette, but that was all ; she had not even any bread. There was no table at the moment, but if we liked to go out and buy ourselves some bread, she would put the eggs aside until our return. It was the best she could do ; there was no food left in the town. Her husband had gone off that morning to take their few objects of value to a place of safety. It looked as though they might have to leave at any minute.

Leave Sézanne ? The idea had never occurred to us. The Boucherons were solid people and not likely to be scared unless there was real danger. We felt like backwoodsmen.

Our search for bread was by no means as easy as we had thought. Every baker's shop we went to was besieged by hungry soldiers. There was not even any bread to buy, it was the hope of a new baking which made them wait.

Suddenly there was an air-raid warning and fierce firing. The streets emptied quickly, but we ignored the shouts from the police to take cover, and went miserably on in our quest. Down a side street we came at last upon a little shop that was deserted except for the baker at his oven. He protested that his loaves were all reserved. One of us argued with him while the other pulled a loaf straight out of the oven. The air-raid and the sight of a few francs quickly broke down his resistance.

Our short sprint from the baker's shop back to the Hôtel de France must have been extremely funny. But as the raid was still on there was nobody to observe it except a few military police, who kept shouting to us to take cover. The promised omelette and our new bread made us determined that the only place where we would take cover was the hotel itself.

The loaf was extremely large and also extremely hot. It was quite impossible for either of us to hold for more than a few seconds at a time. As we ran down the road, we threw it backwards and forwards to each other. It must have looked as if we were either playing a curious form of rugger or, like Keystone comedy policemen, were trying to get an incendiary bomb to the nearest bucket of sand. The military police certainly looked surprised, but it was nothing to the amazement of the people in the hotel courtyard when we rushed in and threw our red-hot prize, with triumph, on to the only free table on the terrace.

We cut off a bit of the loaf for our lunch, carefully wrapped the rest in a raincoat and hid it under the table, safe from prying eyes and anxious hands. We were beginning to learn that food, especially bread, was becoming a major problem in everybody's life, and possession was indeed nine points of the law.

Our strange behaviour had been noticed by three soldiers at the next table. They were greatly amused. We must have had a very furtive look, rather like a couple of children hiding stolen jam. They laughed heartily as we caught their eye. We laughed with them and got into conversation. It was not long before we had joined our tables together and a spirited party was in progress.

They had done themselves proud—at least as proud as Madame Boucheron's limited *cuisine* would permit. But Monsieur Boucheron's cellar had made up for his wife's defection, and the proof of it was to be seen in the splendid collection of empty bottles. But more spectacular still, decorating the table in the most imposing and generous manner, sat a rich unopened magnum of Cordon Rouge. All three men smoked cigars as they lay back in their chairs meditating on the vast bottle of champagne, through a haze of repletion and smoke.

It was an odd party. They were Chasseurs Alpins, all from the *Midi*. There was no mistaking that ; their accent, their looks, their spontaneous friendliness, their easy and charming manners, all bore witness to it. The sun was in their natures, their very bones. They were as dirty, ragged and unkempt as three men could possibly be, but they might have been three *seigneurs* entertaining their guests in a remote Provençal *château*. Their fine disregard for their appearance contrasted oddly with that of the officers at the neighbouring tables.

Quite leisurely and almost casually, they began to tell their story. Yes, they had just reached Sézanne : it had taken three days. From where ? Oh, Chemin des Dames. They had walked. It had not been pleasant, but what else could they have done ? They were the only three left of their company.

It had been a terrific battle, but an unequal one. They had watched their comrades being slaughtered, but fighting to the end. The ammunition had run out— bayonets and bare fists were of no avail against tanks, aeroplanes and surging waves of well-equipped infantry. They had to flee—the only three left. Yes, it was a long trudge from Chemin des Dames, but they were Chasseurs and knew how to walk. They had come as best they could, following the sign-posts. They had no map and did not know the region. They swam the Marne. Eighty-five kilometres in three days—and no food. Now they were feasting to forget.

Where were they going next ? Oh, south. They

would find some part of their regiment somewhere, somehow. They had hoped to find a central depot in Sézanne at which to report, but the confusion was too great. The depot had already moved back to Sens ; they would have to take to the road again. Of course, it would be all right in the end.

In the meantime—and they brushed away the cigar smoke—here was the magnum waiting to be drunk. It had seemed too majestic to open for just the three of them—it would be almost unreasonable to drink it all alone. It was fate that had made them hesitate—here were the Allies. Now was clearly the moment for the wine to justify itself.

We protested : we had supplemented our frugal meal with Monsieur Boucheron's best *nature*—we had to drive our car home—it was wrong not to save the bottle for their journey. Our protestation was feeble ; before we had finished speaking, the cork had popped.

We had a glorious party. The rest of the company looked on enviously. As the champagne flowed, there was more and more talk—at least from two of our friends. The third sat back, mostly silent, with the look of a man basking in the sun well content with the world.

The last glass was drunk, the last toast given. It was time for us to go. We bid them goodbye, and with due solemnity presented our Allies, on behalf of the English, with a bottle of Armagnac.

Immediately they called for a corkscrew. We must go, we explained, the bottle was to encourage them on the road. We had made a *gaffe*, and we realised it very quickly. If we would not drink with them, then they could not accept our gift. This time, however, our protestations were firm. It was impossible, really impossible. We were already late and still had things to do in the town before starting for home. But they refused to accept any excuse. We must drink with them or they would not accept the bottle. They insisted on a compromise. We should do our business in the town and then call back on our way to the garage. They would wait, there was no hurry.

The raid had been over some time and the streets were full again. Now we could see more closely what was happening. It was astounding. The place was teeming with soldiers of different regiments in small groups, in pairs, alone. They seemed to be wandering round and round aimlessly, helplessly searching for something. It was like a town peopled by ghosts. In every shop a figure would come up and demand despairingly if we had seen the so-and-so regiment. We were stopped dozens of times in the street and questioned, and questioned again. It was awful to have no reply. Was there any other way in which we could help? Cigarettes? Food and drink? A little money? They were mostly destitute. But it was not any of these things that they wanted. It was their regiment, their friends they were seeking.

We felt indescribably powerless in that chaotic town full of soldiers in flight, of lost men.

Then came a second raid, this time much fiercer than before. We ran from shop to shop, more eager to complete our purchases and leave this despairing maelstrom than to take cover. In one shop we found the old proprietress hiding beneath the counter. Her voice quavered as she repeated : " We are lost, messieurs, we are lost."

" In England there is a saying that if the women of France lose heart, then—and only then—France is lost," we replied.

" You are right, messieurs, I had forgotten myself for a moment. The women of France will not lose heart." She showed us to the door when we had made our purchase, and bid us goodbye as if it were an ordinary June afternoon in Sézanne. The little door-bell rang a defiant challenge to the bombs and shells. She disappeared back into the shadows of her store.

We returned to the hotel as we had promised. Our three soldiers were still there. They were very silent now, industriously writing letters, oblivious of the ghastly noise about them and of the rain pouring down.

The Armagnac was opened. We drank a glass to the *Entente*, this time adamantly and successfully refusing to be tempted further. We exchanged addresses ; to what purpose we none of us knew, when our addresses were as temporary as our existence. But it was a signal of friendship.

In the garage we found the car ready for us, greased and oiled, distilled water in the batteries ; it had had every attention a car could ask for. The back door of the garage opened on to a small road which led to the outskirts of the town ; we waited for a lull in the raid and then slipped away.

We did not speak for some kilometres. It had been an awful experience ; not the raids—we were used to those by now—but the men, those haunted, lost faces. Here was a proud people on the retreat, realising that each step they took was a foot more of French soil for the invader. Retreating, not with a regiment—knowing that somewhere they would turn and face the enemy again with renewed courage—but, each one alone.

Just outside Esternay we were stopped by soldiers guarding the road. A few yards ahead was an enormous crater where the road should have been. It was steaming ; the bomb had been dropped only a few minutes before, and with singular accuracy. There was no way for us to pass except by mounting the grass verge. Men were already hard at work shovelling back the earth, but the crater was immense and it would be several hours before any convoy could pass. Just ahead the road crossed the railway by a bridge. The station was on our right ; it was quite an important junction, and there were several pairs of lines. Another bomb had been dropped in the centre of this junction on a train which must have been passing through. The engine and carriages had been overturned and the wreckage was in flames. On the left was another train which had met a similar fate. The rails everywhere were tangled like streamers at a carnival. Still more craters could be seen in the fields beside the cutting. There was no questioning the deadly accuracy of the German aim.

Immediately we drove up to the station to see if our services were needed, but there were few casualties and they were being dealt with.

At the little village of Montceaux, where the road forked, we were stopped by another soldier. Bombs had been dropped there also and two houses were in flames. Villiers-Saint-Georges, too, we gathered, had been damaged. The Boche were obviously determined to destroy both the main road and the railway. The villagers were trying to leave, and we were asked to take two sick children from a farm. The parents were in a terrible state ; it did not matter where we took the children, but they must go. They were infectious, and the doctor had said that morning that they were in no condition to move ; but they must go. We explained that it was not our business to go against doctors' orders. As a matter of fact we were not entitled to carry either infectious cases or civilians without a special permit. With regret we hurried on.

Back at the Château des Minimes the situation was unchanged. The staff were all waiting about for work ; there were still no casualties arriving. We went directly in search of the *Médecin-chef* to report on our mission. He was in the mess with most of the other officers, listening to the wireless news bulletin. We told him of the bombing raids and of the crater at Esternay ; it might be dangerous at night for drivers who had not been warned. His pocket, as always, was bulging with maps. He pulled one out and as he unfolded it his hand was clammy and trembling. The map was spread on a table, and we studied the geography of the region. We described the situation in Sézanne and the new hospital. The officers were clearly worried. How great was our danger ? They began to question nervously.

The more the *Médecin-chef* looked at the map the more shaky he became. Were there many convoys on the road ? Had we seen many troops ? Were they moving up to the front or away from it ? Were they fresh troops or not ? Our answers did nothing to reassure him. The conclusions to be drawn from our observations, in addition to what he knew already, merely emphasised the catastrophe. The advance was much too rapid. With the Marne already crossed in one place, the rest of the line was bound to break. We ourselves realised that our renewed hopes of yesterday had been vain. But there was still the Seine and, if necessary, the Loire. We left the room knowing that we must retreat again.

We parked our car on the grass at the edge of the covert, close to the front door of the *château*. We saw other cars there, and were determined not to return to our tropical swamp.

Our manœuvre was watched by a very young lieutenant, who was standing in the doorway of the reception ward. He was short, very dark and chubby, with a smile vacant as that of the Cheshire Cat and equally broad. He was obviously bored with the lack of work, for he leant against the door with his hands in his pockets. He came over and introduced himself to us : " I am James of ' Old England '—you know the shop, of course. All Englishmen do. My father owns ' Old England ' in Nice, Cannes and Monte Carlo." We offered him a cigarette. He was delighted to find it was a Players, and asked if we had any more. We produced a packet, intending to give it to him ; but he insisted on being allowed to pay for it.

René de S ... and Sarazinski joined us. They, too, had moved their ambulance from the swamp for the same reason as ourselves. A few minutes later some of the English girls appeared, then de S . . . , who fancied himself with the girls, produced a bottle of brandy. The girls had done no work for days, and confessed to being thoroughly bored. The Commandant spent his time listening to the wireless news, and they had just heard that the Italians' first warlike gesture was to blow up the bridge at Ventimiglia.

Our party lasted till the evening meal was ready. There was nothing else to do but sit about and talk. Everyone was nervous; everyone was bored. Even the sane, calm nurses had caught the feeling, but they were angry at the waste of time. Under an outward appearance of calm, it was perfectly clear that every person in the Château des Minimes that evening was in despair. If there was a battle, where were the wounded? If there was no battle, what had happened to the Army ?

PANIC

THE CARPENTER was making a rough cross out of
two thick branches of laurel. The padre was hovering
around. A wounded man brought in during the night
had died. He was to be buried in the grounds.

The scene in the stable-yard was the same as it had
been on the previous morning: men creeping out of
every dog-kennel and hay-loft where they had spent the
night, food being distributed from the mobile kitchen,
nurses and doctors eating at tables in the coach-house.
Where were the wounded? Everyone was mystified.
Certainly a few ambulances had arrived during the
night, but they had brought unimportant cases and
had all been sent on to Provins.

'Snow-White,' Pierre D . . . , Ido M . . . : three of
our ambulances suddenly drew up in front of the
reception ward. There was a scurry; everyone seemed
to be on duty. Even those who were not actually on
duty were unable to restrain their curiosity and stood
around gaping. One after another the stretchers were
carried into the ward for an examination of the men's
wounds. One after another they were carried out again
and put back into the ambulances; they could go on
to Provins. One case only was sufficiently serious to be
kept; he had to have an immediate blood-transfusion.

Our friends' arrival was a welcome opportunity for
getting some information straight from the front. We
questioned them eagerly. Things were not going well.
There was fighting at La Ferté, but the river had not
yet been crossed there. The French resistance was
strong considering that ammunition was lacking and
the reserve troops had not appeared. The organisation
of the army had collapsed, but no one could find the

reason. Of course there were wounded, but they were
already being sent further south. The bombardment
was fierce and it was only a question of hours before
Jouarre would have to be abandoned. The line of the
Marne was cracking. The inference was obvious; even
our position was insecure.

'James of Old England' came up confidentially.
"We are going to move. The order to pack has just
been given. I promised to let you know as soon as
I heard anything." This time it was no longer a shock;
it seemed almost a matter of routine. The advance
would stop one day, we reasoned; until then we must
go on retreating. Weygand, after all, must have a plan
—or had his plans been defeated? For the first time
the thought came to us seriously.

There was a crowd in the officers' mess that morning
to listen to the wireless news bulletin. It was not simply
an interest in the news which made each person inter-
rupt the work he was doing and assemble round the
loud-speaker. It was in great part a desire to have
official confirmation that the situation was not really
as critical as we secretly believed. Normally, the Ministry of Information fulfilled this desire admirably, but
to-day it had a bitter blow in store for us at the very
moment when the order for a new retreat had been
given.

Paris had been declared an open city; the military
governor, General Héring, had asked to be relieved of
his post in order to take up command of an army; the
Government had left the capital.

It was no ordinary crowd of gloomy and depressed
officers who left that room to carry on with their
duties. It was a group of broken men. If Paris was to be
given up so lightly, without even a gun being fired
in its defence, then where would the German advance
be held? The French were on the run and they knew
it. But they still did not know why.

For two days we had heard nothing of Bouveret and that part of our Section which he had kept with him. If the Château des Minimes was to be abandoned it was important for us to get some orders. We consulted at once with the few others who were with us and then we learnt that Bouveret had been at the Château during our absence the day before, fetched ' Jack-and-Jim ' and told E . . . , the other Norwegian driver, where he could be found. He was at a farmhouse some five kilometres away. We felt it was our duty to make contact with Bouveret immediately. As E . . . knew where he was, it was agreed that he should go and find him and at the same time we asked him to bring back the few bits of baggage which we had left behind.

In the meantime we reported to the *Médecin-chef* and asked what his orders were. G.A.C.A. had been instructed to move south of the river Yonne. He pulled a map out of his pocket and traced a route with his pencil. They were going to St. Valérien. If we had no instructions from our own lieutenant by the time they left we were to accept his orders and follow G.A.C.A. We studied the map for a few minutes and wrote out our route.

We realised the move was drastic and this encouraged us; it was over sixty kilometres. We felt that with-drawal on such a scale must mean that definite decisions had been taken. At St. Valérien we would be so far from the front that we would have time to establish ourselves before being overtaken by the German advance—always supposing that the Germans could advance so far.

Having nothing to pack ourselves, we watched the others feverishly at work. We filled in a considerable amount of time attending to the wants of the English girls, such as cleaning their shoes and boiling quantities of shaving-water for their Commandant. They were really very feminine and inadept at fending for themselves.

In time E . . . returned with orders, having seen
Bouveret. He and Mazella were to leave at once for
Jouarre, where more help was needed; we and the
other ambulance were to stay with our present unit.
E . . . had forgotten to bring our baggage with him;
this was most annoying, for our tinned food was among
it and the mobile kitchen had closed. Fortunately an
officer appeared who said that there were still some
tins of bully beef in the stables and that we had better go
and eat quickly. With Sarazinski and René de S . . . we
sat down in the coach-house to a hasty meal. Someone
had discovered a cask of cider in a neighbouring farmhouse and this was a welcome addition. Two of the
English girls passed by; seeing us eating they went to
get some food for themselves. Others followed, then
the nurses joined us with some officers and soon the
small stock of bully-beef was exhausted.

For appearance's sake Miss Juta had expertly
marshalled her girls to a separate table, and a prim
little party they were. Our French companions were
much impressed that even in the stress and chaos of
a retreat, the *convenances* were not forgotten by the
English. The American Commandant, with his dog,
added himself to our party. He was bad-tempered and
queasy. He suggested that we ought to retire to
Vichy; it was a long way from the front. It was
certainly the right place for him.

In the middle of the meal the General arrived,
accompanied by the Colonel. Everyone immediately
sprang to their feet. He consulted with the officers and
then left. The General had been calm and smiling; it
was encouraging to know that we were still in contact
with headquarters.

The moment of departure came; we walked back to
our car to await the signal. In the centre of the lawn we
found Bouveret, who asked why we were still there. He
seemed very surprised to see us; then we discovered

that he had given orders for us to go to Jouarre, but that in a burst of heroic enthusiasm, E . . . had secretly substituted himself.

" You will come with me at once then," he went on, " Drive out on to the road and I will lead the way."

We explained that we had already been given orders and a route by the *Médecin-chef*; we thought that we had better inform him of our departure.

" That is quite unnecessary," said Bouveret. " We shall all meet again in half an hour."

Puzzled, but obedient, we followed him down a series of country lanes. Soon we stopped in front of a cottage whose occupants were busy loading their belongings on to a farm waggon. Bouveret went inside and reappeared with an armful of washing. We drove on again for about a kilometre to St. Hilliers and drew up in front of a large farmhouse where we found the remnants of our Section. The kitchen and breakdown lorries were there, so were Caillemer and Estevez; there were four ambulances besides our own and we found our baggage in Erwtemans'. We were told to leave it there as we were now going to Provins, where the hospital had to be evacuated, and his car was the temporary transport-waggon.

The farmer and his family were busy emptying the house and packing up. They were leaving. In the large farm-yard were two big waggons already practically full of the family's possessions. The horses were harnessed; one could see he was a prosperous farmer for they were fine, well-kept animals. The chickens and ducks had been gathered into coops which were ranged beside the waggons, ready to be hung on at the last moment. The children were carrying out chairs and the wife was carefully loading the precious linen. They seemed unruffled and calm as they went deliberately about their business.

The interior of the house was a sad sight; drawers

left open, cupboards bare, bedsteads without either mattress or bedding, piles of discarded rubbish in every corner. Even the pots and pans had disappeared from the kitchen range, and all the china had been taken. Although the members of the family still moved from room to room, picking up a last object of value or sentimental interest, the house already had an air of desolation. Truly it had been looted, but by its owners.

" Take every bottle you can find," the farmer said. " Fill your cars. I would rather give all I have to the soldiers of my own country than leave so much as a crumb for those filthy Germans. It breaks my heart to leave them my flock of sheep—three hundred of them—and my fine young crops. But what can I do ? "

His wife looked tragically round at her home. " We know what evacuation means in my family; we have lived here for almost a hundred years. My grand-mother owned the place first and in 1870, when my mother was two years old, they left for the first time. In 1914, when I was a child, we left again. And now to-day, I must leave with my children."

We had no time to ask them where they were going, nor on whose orders they were leaving. Probably it was instinct which drove them away, the fear of being caught by the Germans. At this moment it never occurred to us that they would be leaving except on the orders of a higher authority. We remembered the old women in Rebais and thought that the stolid peasant would never move on his own initiative.

Bouveret was impatient to leave, but Caillemer and the rest of us realised the importance of collecting any provisions we could in case food became scarce. Lenoir was prepared to slaughter two sheep on the spot, but that would have caused too long a delay. As it was, we persuaded him to roll out a fine barrel of *pinard* while we carried as many bottles as possible. We loaded the

kitchen lorry with a choice selection of bottles of
burgundy, peaches in brandy, pickled onions, bottled
plums, pears and cherries. Nevertheless each of us
had enough cunning to pack a few bottles into our own
cars. It seemed a pity to risk everything being consumed in our absence.

Bouveret's persistent blasts on the whistle prevented
us from taking any more. But we stopped with the
satisfaction of knowing that nothing of importance
remained. The great gates of the farm-yard were
ceremoniously closed, the bolts shot and the padlocks
put in place. The farmer was weeping by now at the
thought of the enormous sums of money, in the form
of flocks and crops, which he was presenting to the
Germans. Bouveret blew a final and penetrating
blast; we jumped into our cars, started the engines
and drove away from that farmhouse. As we looked
back we saw the farmer and his family setting out on
their lumbering course. We were both almost in tears.

As we drove the last few kilometres through the flat
countryside into Provins we could see that the whole
population was in flight. From every farm and hamlet
across the fields and down every lane, came sad little
processions. We wondered how the news could have
spread so quickly. We thought it must have been
organised, it was so deliberate.

It was a brilliant sunny afternoon and as we
approached Provins the mediæval ramparts round the
upper town stood out bold and brave against the blue
sky. Cæsar's Tower and St. Quiriace beside it shim-
mered in the sunlight. The town seemed to float in the
clouds as if indifferent to the new invader. Who was
Hitler compared to Bismarck, Henry IV, the Black
Prince and Charlemagne? It seemed supremely
conscious of its history.

Bouveret had timed things well. As we reached the
entrance to the town we joined the column from the

Château des Minimes which had come by another
road.

The scene in the main street was chaotic, belying
the town's outward appearance of calm and the orderly
little processions that we had seen earlier. Everybody
was fighting to get through the narrow streets first.
There were endless military convoys, cars driven by
white-faced refugees covered with mattresses against
machine-gunning from the air, and lastly our own
column. Lost in the middle of so much mechanisation
were the terrified peasants with their unwieldy waggons,
their horses rearing and shying at the strange smell of
petrol fumes and the hooting of cars. The noise and
heat were terrific; the congestion almost impenetrable.

There was only room for a single line of traffic. On
both sides, parked against the curb, were stationary
vehicles of every size and shape; farm waggons,
delivery vans, bicycles, touring cars, pony carts.
Each of these was being loaded by the inhabitants
of the house in front of which it stood. Dazed groups
of townspeople stared in amazement at the stream
of strangers pouring through their streets. They were
jostled, pushed, thrown back against the walls by
impatient passers-by. Most of the shops were open,
but as we passed the proprietors were putting up their
shutters and shovelling their wares into the vehicles
outside. Their haste was feverish. Every wasted second,
one felt, brought them nearer to death or captivity;
uncontrollable panic had gripped the town.

Our convoy stopped for minutes at a time in this
frenzied traffic. It was hopeless, bewildering. We felt
like helpless logs blocked in some rapids; each pause
was no relief, but an awful strain waiting for the jam
to break. We gathered that the object of our leader
was to get us up to the square at the very top of the
town, turn us, and then bring us down to the hospital

which lay at the foot of the steep hill where the road turned towards Sens and Nogent-sur-Seine.

At one of our enforced halts in the main street, we stopped in front of a grocer's shop. Through the milling crowds which streamed between us and the open door we could see an inviting bunch of bananas staring at us from the counter. " How much ? " we called to the grocer. He peered at us from the shop, looked at our ambulance and our eager faces, then smiled. " They'll cost you nothing, my friends. You can have them," he shouted back, " I'm leaving. Come and take them." We accepted his invitation with lightning speed and shouted our thanks from the car as we jerked on again.

Once past the cross-road it was a simple matter to climb the hill, turn and range our cars down the precipitous cobbled lane. We were a considerable detachment, with the cars from the Château des Minimes and the English girls. The nurses, who had arrived in a charabanc, which was their travelling home, hurried into the hospital to help the monstrously over-worked staff prepare the wounded for their journey. The doctors accompanied them, while the rest of us waited by our cars.

We were some way back in the line, perched high on the hill. As we looked down we could see the mass of traffic, which we had left some minutes before, slowly forcing its tortuous way along the road. Occasionally we could see a space being cleared and an enormous lorry pushing its way through, but it was usually only a single lorry piled high with pontoon boats. No convoy, however skilfully led, ever managed to keep in formation in that swirling mass. The single military police-man swore, gesticulated and cajoled, but all to no purpose; no human agency could have brought order out of that chaos unless—prepared to use a revolver. But *use* it; threats, however frightening, were of no avail, the terrified people were unmoved by the barrel

of a gun. Nothing but a fearful example could have
shaken them back to sanity and discipline.

We turned away from watching the sickening confusion below and began to take stock of our surroundings. The houses on either side of us were enchanting;
every period was represented in their architecture, as
varied as the history of Provins itself. One particularly
graceful and melancholy house caught our eye. It had
an eighteenth century façade with elegant double
bow-windows. It wore an air of reserved tragedy—
Werther might have known it; aloof, disdainful, it
seemed dissociate from the noisy officers of the Medical
Corps who had established themselves there. On the
wall which screened its miniature courtyard and
garden from the passers-by was a plaque, which bore
the legend: " In this house was held the first meeting
of the Jacobin Club." Pale, tortured ghosts of those
revolutionaries must have stood at the bow-windows
on that afternoon watching, as we did, the crowds
below throwing away the heritage for which they had
fought so hard.

Very little traffic passed up our road; an occasional
despatch rider, taking the short cut to Paris, would
charge the cobbles, but for the most part there were
only our own people sauntering up and down. 'James
of Old England' was very active and popped up now
and then to exchange a quick pleasantry. At regular
intervals Caillemer panted up and down from the
hospital to see if they were yet ready for us. Erwtemans
became excruciatingly funny and unbearable. It was
not his moment; the heat, the scene at the cross-road,
the tension, all conspired to divest his wildest capers of
their point. Only van B . . . seemed to appreciate
his outbursts; we observed, with some bitterness, that
he had the makings of an apt pupil.

We sank into a hot, sticky, lethargic gloom. At one
moment we were pulled out of it by an extraordinary

sight. A despatch rider passed us at the usual ferocious
speed; perched precariously on his pillion, erect and
dignified as if on a charge on parade, was the most
formidable Colonel we had ever seen. With none of the
usual trappings of a motor-cyclist, goggles, crash-
helmet or gauntlets, he sat there staring straight ahead
at the road before him, his long grey beard flowing in
the wind on either side of his determined face. He did
not look at all comic, he rose above the ridiculous
situation with supreme dignity ; the popping motor-
bike " became " him and he " became " it.

Next we saw a small funeral procession detach itself
from the stream below and slowly wind its way up our
hill. The solitary horse, with no proud black plumes,
strained and stumbled with its load. The undertaker,
as he led his horse, looked a little ashamed, as though he
would explain that this apology for funerary pomp was
the best that such times would permit. The coffin was
not small enough for a child and yet it was white. " A
young girl," someone whispered, " a virgin." On it
there was no wreath, only a bunch of flowers already
slightly withered in the terrific heat. Behind, on foot,
were three mourners, a middle-aged woman, an old
woman and an old man ; dry-eyed, but unseeing, they
followed to the cemetery beyond the square.

We wandered down to the town. We could not have
been in Provins for more than an hour, but the shops
were now completely closed and many shuttered
houses showed that the inhabitants had already left.
The traffic was still pouring through and we hurried
back to our car.

The passing funeral had brought some women out
from their houses and when we got back we found
them gathered in a little group round a doorway by
the side of our car. One was embroidering busily and
her little daughter was similarly employed. The
others stood, arms folded or akimbo, talking and

gossiping. A small boy played in between them, getting, from time to time, an odd cuff on the head or a passing caress.

Suddenly they pointed to the sky and drew back into the doorway ; there was an aerial battle overhead. It was short and sharp ; a quick burst of anti-aircraft fire, the rapid rat-tat-tat of machine-guns, then, as quickly as it had started, it was finished. We could see one aeroplane left suspended in mid-air, it hovered for a few seconds quivering slightly ; then, like a star from a rocket, it burst into flames and fell.

A parachute floated slowly down to earth almost dead straight, for there was no breeze that day. It looked as though it would land just beyond the town, over the hill. We watched it idly ; it was very beautiful against the bright blue sky. One of the women gasped out the word " Parachutist ! " and we turned in surprise. Had she not seen the aeroplane fall ? we wondered. Almost at once, the cry was taken up and everybody seemed to go quite mad—three, four, seven, a dozen—there were parachutists everywhere. Everyone gaped, stared, peered into the sky, jumped about and shouted to each other. Motor-cycles and cars, with soldiers armed to the teeth, hurtled up the hill ; people ran after them. It was a splendid scene of excitement. The poor English pilot, who had baled out just in time, must have had a surprising reception when he landed !

No excitement lasts for long when town gossips get together and the women were very soon back in their doorway, at it hammer and tongs. But now their talk was of departure.

We learned for the first time that no official orders had been given and that the local exodus was quite impromptu on the part of the farmers and townsfolk. It was appalling ; a whole countryside moving without orders—this was something we had not

visualised. Unorganised, undisciplined hordes flooding
and cluttering up the roads !

As we listened to the women we realised how this
dreadful thing had come to pass. At first their talk had
been of trivial nothings, with no hint of scare. Casually
and only occasionally, even a little disdainfully, they
had watched the mob below, but they had given no
sign of taking any part in it. Now, only half an hour or
so later, the air raid, the excitement of the parachute
and finally the news, brought by an excited newcomer,
of their townspeople fleeing, had changed their whole
attitude. They agreed that the air raids had been
getting worse and worse ; at first they had been an
excitement, then a nuisance—now it was serious. They
click-clacked on ; each one looked preoccupied. The
woman with the embroidery jabbed her needle in
more firmly and pulled her cotton more tightly ; the
little boy got fewer caresses and was cuffed more rapidly
and frequently. Their chatter was more staccato.

An old, dried-up, wise-looking woman was the first to
say *it*—" I shall take my bottles of liqueurs ; I have a
fine *marc* and nothing will persuade me to leave that
behind. But I shall have to leave my chicory and that is
a great pity ; it will be a fine crop in a few weeks." At
first the others looked at her in surprise—surprise at her
daring to be the first to express their unspoken
thoughts. Then they started. Without hesitation they
enumerated the objects each intended to take. It came
plumb out ; each choice had been made quite
deliberately. We realised then that each woman had
come to a premeditated, not to a hasty decision.

We had no time to hear the development of their
conversation but we knew the inevitable end. Flight !
Here was a group of women who had woken sane and
calm on the morning of June the 13th and who by
nightfall would in all probability have joined the lost
legions on the long roads to the South.

Where was the voice that should have calmed them ? Where was the hand that should have stopped them ? Had Weygand, Pétain, Reynaud, finally failed ? Had the women sensed defeat in the uncertain, wavering, wireless bulletins ? Or had the true news been whispered from town to village, from village to farmhouse, gathering impetus, wildly, falsely embroidered, distorted and re-shaped with each telling ?

The convoy moved slowly down the hill as, one by one, the cars drove in to the hospital, were loaded and left for Sens. At last it was our turn. A delirious man was brought out first ; he was half-conscious, moaning slightly and muttering to himself, his right arm heavily bandaged and in a protective wire cage. He kept plucking with his other hand at the bandages. The *infirmier* tucked the blanket firmly round him, as his chest was bare, then tied his left arm by the wrist to the iron rail which ran along the side of the ambulance. It seemed cruel, but short of an improvised straitjacket, it was the best means to keep him from tearing off his bandages. An injection seemed to quieten him.

He was on the upper rail ; by his side they put a Colonial soldier. He was the darkest shade of black that a man could be. He had been wounded in the legs but as he was covered we could not see the extent of his wounds. He propped himself on one arm and stared at us with enormous eyes, curious and a little frightened, but we reassured him with a smile and his big white teeth flashed at us as he smiled back. He lay down content, knowing that at any rate he was with friendly strangers. The condition of the third man, who lay below, appeared to be not too bad, for he looked quite calm. But it was not always easy to tell from looks ; the fortitude of the men was, almost without exception, extraordinary.

After we had collected our orders and medical reports, Caillemer gave us our parting instructions :

the wounded were to be taken to Sens and if there was time that night we were to return to Provins to fetch another load. If it was too late—and that, we presumed, meant after midnight—we were to make our way to St. Valérien, our new headquarters. We had no maps, only a vague idea of the route, but sensing an even greater confusion on the roads than we had seen during the last two hours or so, and knowing that side roads would be of vital importance to us, we rushed into a garage opposite the hospital gates, determined to find a map. Our search was vain ; we moved out of Provins with a sense of foreboding.

Almost at once we were plunged into the chaos. For miles we seemed to plough through the interminable stream of traffic, crawling along at never more than fifteen kilometres an hour. We were held up for ten, fifteen, twenty minutes at a time. We shouted at the lumbering waggons hauled by teams of horses that pulled out perilously into the centre of the roads ; we cursed the motor-tractors drawing two or three vast carts behind them, that swung out and blocked all movement for miles ; we hooted and banged on our bell at the little cars, which, in an attempt to overtake the slower vehicles, formed a double, triple line of traffic. All in vain, the whole *circulation* was out of hand ; it was every man for himself. Not even the sight and sound of an ambulance in desperate haste penetrated the dulled wits of the refugees, many of whom had come from as far as Holland and Belgium.

We drove all the time on the wrong side of the road, it was the only thing we could do. Thank God, very little traffic came in the opposite direction or there would have been disaster. Occasionally a despatch rider would pass ; very occasionally a military lorry. Sometimes we would overtake parts of a convoy, which, like us, was doing its best to force a passage. If military drivers possibly could help us, they did, for they knew what our load meant. Rarely did we get any help from the civilians ; they were oafish, stupid, uncom-prehending.

The trudging women, the tired children, the mothers with their new-born babies, the toothless, bent grand-fathers, the whole hopeless mass—we felt no sorrow for them any more. Gone was the first shock of pity at the sight of these sad groups ; gone was our impulse to help. We knew that their presence on the roads could only bring about a gigantic breakdown, the dislocation of everything. What was to happen to the supplies for the troops, to the ammunition convoys, to everything necessary to the mobility of a great army ?

Why could they not be diverted on to side roads ? Then we asked ourselves where were the side roads of France ? And we realised that, broadly speaking, they did not exist. The long straight roads of France, how beautiful they have always seemed to us in England with our countless little curling lanes, our odd little roads that lead here, there and everywhere. The roads of France run long and fine, but beyond these, the best are little more than farm tracks. One of the glories of that country was proving one of its disasters.

The man with the badly wounded arm suddenly became conscious ; the effect of the drug had worn off and the pain of his wounds was nearly driving the poor devil out of his wits. His moaning rose to a scream, he tugged at his wrist that was tied to the rail and kept twisting it into the most painful and impossible positions ; he kicked his blanket on to the man below and lay naked, writhing in his agony. At every stop one of us jumped out to re-cover him and ease his bound wrist ; he begged and entreated us to loose it, but we knew it was out of the question. We would drive on, desperately trying to drown the sound of his screams with the clanging of our bell, glancing grimly round when the noise was particularly loud to see if by some awful chance he had worked his wrist loose.

Several times we witnessed a most touching sight. The negro was sitting up, leaning over his comrade, smoothing his forehead and talking to him softly. From time to time he would moisten the man's lips from a water-bottle by his side, restrain the kicking legs and recover the slipping blanket ; an *infirmier* in fact could not have done more. That Martinique soldier deserves a place in Heaven if ever a man did ; for eight ghastly hours, over bumpy roads and through the awful heat, heedless of his own wounds, he watched and cared for his comrade without respite.

At times the peasants would stare dumbly at our ambulance when they heard the awful sounds coming from it ; at other times they would come up to us with shocked faces and tell us that one of the men inside was naked. On those occasions we would grit our teeth and stare ahead, suppressing an almost irresistible desire to lash out at them with words and fists.

Just after Longueville we realised that we had been on the road at least two hours and covered no more than ten kilometres. It was disastrous. In the middle of one particularly long hold-up one of us got out and walked down the road for four kilometres ; it was a solid block of traffic.

An agitated Colonel was trying his best on a narrow bridge to control this overwhelming mass—a vital convoy had to pass somehow. He was hysterical by now and had completely lost control of himself and the whole situation. He was roaring and shouting but to no purpose : everything stood motionless as the Dead Sea. No credit can be taken for the fact that, after a quarter of an hour's hard work we got it moving again. It was due to years of unconscious observation of the English ' Bobby ' at work—to him must go the credit. Moments like Derby Day, first nights in Shaftesbury

Avenue, the Private View at the Royal Academy, came to our mind. We took as our model those calm, blue figures, stolid, unimaginative, determined, heeding no back-answers. How it happened we shall never know and whether a Chief Constable would have approved of the detail of our method is another matter, but the principle was sound and the result proved it.

It also proved another thing : the simple fact that these blocks need not have occurred. If only at that minute, we thought, some competent policemen could have been distributed along these roads, this chaos could have been regulated—not abolished, that would have been impossible, but at least had some measure of order imposed on it.

At Bray-sur-Seine the main stream of traffic appeared to be taking a road to the right which skirted the town. Wanting at all costs to get away from this main road, we drove into the town itself, hoping to find a less congested route. The military police knew nothing. Practically all the civilians we asked paid no heed to our questions but begged for lifts—not to anywhere in particular, but just in order to get away.

In this town, as in so many others, the panic was growing. The sight of the refugees struggling past and the growing rumours, now wildly out of proportion, had unnerved the inhabitants and we knew that within a few hours, unless some firm measures were taken, Bray-sur-Seine would present the same hopeless scene as had the terror-stricken town of Provins.

What had happened to the Government that it was unable to prevent this catastrophe ? Here were sane people allowed, for want of leadership, to become insane. It was still not too late to forbid civilians to use the roads.

The spirit of the civilians was excellent ; if the authorities had come forward to encourage and employ them in preparing the defences of their villages and towns, they would certainly have rallied immediately. They would have fought for their streets and houses as they had done before. Even if they had been deficient in the arms for fighting a modern mechanised army, they could have proved invaluable as *saboteurs*. They could have built and held barricades to delay the German advance ; they could have watched for parachutists ; they could have held up or captured the light mechanised German advance guard, who went ahead to seize strategic points and cut communications ; they could have proved their value as snipers. The French army would then have had time to re-form. But there was no one to explain to them that by leaving the countryside uninhabited they were merely helping the enemy, whose agents could then carry out their sabotage undisturbed.

There was no telling how many enemy agents may have been among the refugees themselves, they were nowhere subjected to control. False alarms and panic ran like lightning down their lines, they always thought that the Germans were only a few kilometres away. So sudden was their arrival, so dramatic their passage, that they quickly destroyed the resistance of those who had not yet caught the panic.

In the stampede, terror prevailed over reason and the staunchest peasant abandoned his home and launched out on the aimless trek southwards ; that was their undoing. Short of food and probably of money too, separated from home, their family and their friends, they quickly lost heart and added to the panic. No one had told them that they would have been far safer in their houses than on the roads, where they could so easily be machine-gunned or bombed. Hundreds were being killed quite unnecessarily.

We stopped at every garage we passed and tried to buy maps, but there was not one to be found. Someone, a little more coherent than the others, gave a vague indication of a route ; hopefully we plunged on to the left.

Some kilometres out of the town we came to a cross-road. The indications on the sign-post were useless— names of villages of which we had never heard ; but we saw a small garage and once again went optimistically in search of a map. The whole place was shut, there was no sign of life inside. We thought for a moment of breaking in and doing a little burglary, but as it was an open spot and there were soldiers about, we decided it would be wiser to make enquiries from them before we resorted to such violent methods. They were in a small group and as we approached we discovered a General talking to them. This was a little awkward. It would hardly be correct to ask our way from anybody so grand ! Before we had time to speak, he spoke to us, and to our surprise asked if we had a map of the region. A General without a map ! It was inconceivable ! We apologised, told him we too were without one and explained our dilemma. Fortunately he was able to help and told us that the road to the right would lead through Sergines to Pont-sur-Yonne and on to Sens. He cursed the authorities who were responsible for posting military police without maps in districts with which they were unfamiliar and, at the same time, raged at the absurd shortage of these essential guides.

From now on we met very few refugees, but passed countless military convoys of every possible descrip-tion : tanks, heavy artillery, petrol supplies and troops. It looked as if the line of resistance was being re-formed on the Seine ; their whole formation and the area they covered suggested organisation rather than the result of casual halts. We were heartened at this thought and it did a lot to dispel the black despair that had enveloped us after the past few hours' experience. The road was awful, at times almost as bad as the little clinker path at Villiers-sur-Marne ; the screaming man behind made us feel as though a knife was being turned in us at every pot-hole and every stone over which we had to pass.

He kept shouting for us to stop. At one point we did. The poor chap forced himself to be lucid for a moment and explained faintly that if only we would give him a few minutes' rest he would do his best to be controlled for the remainder of the journey. But he lapsed back again into his babbling agony almost at once. While we were debating what we should do, it was the negro who suggested we should press on. He was right ; there was nothing to be gained by prolonging the ordeal in which we were now all sharing. The essential thing was to reach the hospital and prompt medical attention. So we struggled on.

In Sens we found an enormous number of refugee cars piled high with luggage and with the almost inevitable mattress tied on the roof. But our main impression when we arrived about 6.30 was of a busy Saturday evening in any big provincial town. The café at the big cross-road was full of people leisurely sipping their *apéritif*, busy housewives laden with their baskets were completing their week-end shopping and in the courtyard of the Hôtel de Paris, opposite the Cathedral, the tables with their chequered cloths and gay umbrellas were already laid for the evening meal.

We discovered a number of our own cars in the press of traffic : Pierre D . . ., Allard and others. They had come from Jouarre : evidently there was a big-scale evacuation of hospitals to Sens. An awful thought crossed our minds : could the hospital take all the wounded ? Or would we be sent on somewhere else ? After nearly five hours of such indescribable misery the thought was unbearable and we quickly dismissed it from our minds. To our horror our worst fears were only too true. At the gates of the vast hospital we were greeted with the call of " Hospital full, no more cases can be taken. All wounded must go on to Auxerre."

Auxerre. . . . Our hearts sank. Sixty kilometres away and the only road to it the Route Nationale Six. It was bound to be full of those damnable refugees. Could it be possible that we had to face this new nightmare ? How could we force a way through these impassable hordes ? And then, what about the dark, moonless night before us ?

An agonising scream from the naked man behind decided us. A doctor must be found. Somebody must help us, the responsibility was too great. Despite the warning shout of the porter at the gates, we drove up to the hospital.

The vast courtyard presented an extraordinary spectacle. Hundreds of ambulances, parked here and there without any attempt at order, were being loaded and unloaded at the greatest possible speed ; nurses, doctors, *infirmiers* and stretcher-bearers were threading their way through the maze of cars in and out of the many doors of the hospital buildings. They looked tired and bewildered by the unmanageable influx of new cases that had suddenly been flung upon them. Many of our own Section were standing about looking equally tired and bewildered. Some were lucky and had been allowed to unload their wounded ; others, who had been waiting some time, had just been told that they were to go on to Auxerre and were pulling themselves together to face the journey.

Having braved the porter and forced an entrance we were determined to get some assistance before we embarked on the second stage of our hazardous journey. We drove round and round the hospital buildings, through small courtyards, down alleys, in an attempt to force ourselves upon somebody. We accosted doctors, nurses, any and every official we could see, until finally we attracted the attention of a young medical officer.

We showed him our naked man, begged him to find an inch of space in one of the wards, or if this was really out of the question, at least to give him some injection to stop the pain and still the awful screaming for a few hours. He promised us help, pointed to a place where we should wait and disappeared. We stood about for some minutes in dismal gloom. Would he forget us ? Would something more pressing appear and take him away, maybe for hours ? But our fears were unfounded, for in a very short time he reappeared with a nurse carrying a hypodermic syringe, phials containing injections and cotton wool.

" Sorry, absolutely no room here," he said as he turned away, " but the nurse will do her best for your man before you leave."

The nurse was an old friend from Villiers-sur-Marne and we were delighted to see each other again. Hastily we exchanged our news. Our stories were the same— evacuation and evacuation again, hopeless disorganisa- tion and lack of supplies. " I know we shan't be here long," she told us wearily. " That's why it's better to take the poor chaps on to some place where there's a chance of them being able to rest for a few days."

She did miracles with our naked man ; calmed him, reassured him, adjusted his left wrist, which by now was twisted into an agonising position, and gave him an injection. She looked at the negro's legs, made him a little more comfortable and said some comforting things to him, for we had told her of his extraordinary kindness to his comrade. After a quick glance at our third man, whom she pronounced to be fit for the further journey, she bade us a hasty goodbye and ran back to her other duties.

Now our immediate problem was petrol. To move out of Sens without a full tank was out of the question, but where to get some was another matter. We drove round the town ; the garages were mostly without

supplies, and those that had any would not give it to
military cars without coupons. We saw Allard and
Herrera, who were enquiring their way to St. Valérien
from a pedestrian in a side street, but they were unable
to help. Finally we found a military policeman who,
by way of a change, was actually able to assist us. He
directed us to the military depot which lay some two
kilometres north of the town.

At the depot we found Miss Juta, Miss Bennet and
other English women drivers with two ambulances.
They had left their wounded in Sens and were just
returning to Provins. We were pleased to see one of
the doctors from Villiers-sur-Marne ; he was now
attached to the hospital at Sens and had accompanied
the girls to the petrol depot. As the girls were going on,
we were able to give him a lift back to the town after
our tank had been filled. He was in a state of great
depression and during the short return journey gave
vent to his feelings. As far as he could judge, the whole
organisation had collapsed. Nobody knew which way
to turn, what to do next. Places like Sens, supposed to
be base hospitals, where all the major operations were
done, were now being used practically as dressing-
stations; the wounded were being sent on to smaller
places, ill-equipped and unprepared in every way for
the vast influx of cases. On the other hand, doctors,
surgeons and nurses were not being sent further south
with the wounded, with the result that they were falling
over each other and had very little to do. He was a
surgeon and had been at Sens for three days without
performing a single operation.

We dropped him at the cross-road by the big café.
" God knows what conditions will be like at Auxerre
when you get there," were his parting words.

As we passed the Hôtel de Paris the courtyard was
already full of people dining, and there was a long queue
eagerly waiting to seize any vacant table. But on the

whole the town seemed calm and more preoccupied with its daily life than with the refugees.

Certainly the road to Joigny was quite full of traffic; mostly refugee vehicles, but there was also a number of convoys. However the road was negotiable and there was no sign of the panic we had met during the earlier part of our journey.

Joigny itself was as calm as Sens, if not calmer. There was no sign of disorder, no undue traffic, no crowds in the streets or on the roads by the river; it was as peaceful as ever. As we crossed the bridge we thought sentimentally of the many times we had travelled this very route on our way to holidays in the south; indeed, but for the fact that we were in uniform driving an ambulance instead of a car, we might have been doing it again. There were even the familiar loafers leaning over the bridge gazing down into the river below and the old men with their fishing rods on its banks. Nothing seemed changed.

The rest of the journey was equally uneventful. The naked man in the back was quiet after the injection, the negro lay clutching his water-bottle and occasionally looking to see if his comrade was all right. The man below was asleep.

It was about 10-30 when we arrived at Auxerre. All light had gone from the sky and we were thankful and relieved to have completed our journey before night had finally fallen.

We started to look for the hospital. We asked our way and found our goal at last, at the end of a narrow street, down one side of which were parked a row of ambulances, waiting their turn to drive in. We took our place and walked on to the hospital gates to see what was happening. It seemed impossible to ask our men to have patience any longer; they had been on the road for eight hours and the naked man was in a desperate condition.

In a little square in front of the gates were some of our own ambulances, empty and without their drivers. The porter at the gate knew nothing and told us to go on into an inner courtyard where was the reception ward. Here was a crowd of ambulances unloading and the work was being done by a few very overworked nurses and some boys, volunteers from the town.

We explained our urgency and they agreed to let us drive in at once. As we arrived the air-raid warning was given and all the lights in the hospital went out. It was quite dark by now and we wrestled with our stretchers as best we could. It was difficult and unpleasant work carrying them up a long flight of unknown stairs in the dark to the wards on the first floor. It needs at least three people to unhook and carry a stretcher if the wounded man is not to be severely shaken in the process. But there was no help available, everyone was much too busy. Aeroplanes roared overhead, the guns blared and the whole place shook as bombs were dropped.

The sight that confronted us upstairs was terrifying. From every corner came the sound of moaning. The floors of the corridor and of all the wards were covered with stretchers, a man on each. We had to pick our way carefully between them and set our burden down in an empty space. There were a few nuns running about with torches supervising the arrivals and one or two doctors in overalls completely distracted and overwhelmed by events. Somewhere in the middle of each ward a candle or two would be burning and this was the only other light. The nuns were doing everything possible to help the sufferers quickly. There was a constant call for beds; the volunteers were doing what they could.

Going down the stairs again one had to be dexterous to avoid the stretcher-parties coming up. We found a young man outside and enlisted his help to carry in our second and third stretchers. We groped our way through and set them down upstairs. Then we had to find someone to attend to the naked man. " Yes, I'll be with you in a minute," was all anyone had time to say as they ran on.

The doors of the operating theatre would open to disgorge the latest case, waves of chloroform would fill the corridor and then the next stretcher would be carried in. Finally, with the aid of our young man, who seemed to know the whole staff, we succeeded in holding the attention of a doctor. We gave him the papers, told him the facts and added a special word of praise for the negro. We urged him to do something quickly.

The negro was content to wait. He asked for a glass of water, which we fetched, and then we had to leave. We said goodbye and thanked him humbly for his magnificent behaviour.

Before leaving we had to find three stretchers in exchange for those on which we had brought our wounded. Tonight our task seemed hopeless. Every available stretcher was being used as a bed, there were no free ones anywhere. It is one of the ambulance driver's responsibilities to see that he always has the correct number of stretchers. We could not go without them, yet we could not leave men lying on the floor. At last we found a kindly nun who procured us what we needed. Whether she took them during a man's absence in the operating theatre or simply made the less seriously wounded get up and sit on chairs, we knew not. At all events we had three stretchers and we were thankful to leave.

The organisation of that hospital had collapsed, if it ever existed. It was clearly not intended to deal with anything like the number of wounded who had suddenly arrived. There was only a very small staff and probably a lack of equipment. Even the stretcher-bearers were volunteers from the town. It was the same in every other hospital for miles around. The advance was so rapid that hardly was a hospital properly staffed and beginning to work than it had to be evacuated. As we left Auxerre hospital, the ambulances at the gate were being sent on to Vichy. We departed feeling that we had abandoned our three men to meet their death.

By now it was 11.30. Our other ambulances were still outside but there was no sign of their drivers. The air raid was just over and, as we looked back, we saw more light in the hospital. We were sagging with hunger and worn out. There seemed very little prospect of finding food in the town at that hour, but we drove to the market square and parked before starting to look. We realised it was too late to think of going back to Provins; we could not possibly reach it before morning, by which time there would be no one left. Then the thought of having to force our way again through the streams of refugees, especially going in the opposite direction, terrified us. We reasoned for a moment and decided to eat and sleep where we were, and go in a few hours to St. Valérien. Even if we only slept for four or five hours, we argued, we could still reach St. Valérien in the early morning, which would be soon enough. What is more, we would have rested and could make the journey by daylight; those were considerations not lightly to be dismissed.

So we locked the ambulance and set out in search of food and a bed. The town was practically dead. We could not even find anyone of whom to ask our way. We tried the Hôtel de l'Epée. Pinned to the front door was a notice, " Full up." We decided to try our luck all the same—perhaps for two soldiers there might be some bread and butter and a couple of arm-chairs. We rang and waited. Then, by some curious chance, the young man who had helped us at the hospital, came walking past. He recognised us at once and offered his assistance again. He knew the *patronne* well, if it was possible she would certainly arrange something for us. At length she appeared, a sad figure in a dressing-gown. Not a crust of bread, not a bathroom, not even an arm-chair free.

"The refugees—it is terrible, messieurs. It has been like this for two days now. The market-hall is full of them, and you will find a canteen. There you might get something to eat and perhaps some straw to lie on."

We apologised for disturbing her and left. The market-hall was out of the question; we could not deprive the refugees of food or a corner in which to lay their head. Our young friend offered to take us home to share his room; he warned us though that he had no food and that even his house was full of refugees. Again we felt obliged to refuse. He had been working since early morning; we urged him to go home and get some sleep while we set off to visit the few other hotels close at hand. But as it was his native town he insisted on accompanying us to see that some hospitality was forthcoming.

We were greeted with the same reply at every door, so we abandoned the search and returned to our ambulance. There at least were two bloodstained stretchers, even if our home would be the Place du Vieux Marché, Auxerre. Suddenly we remembered the bottles of wine which we had hidden. By the light of torches we found the bottles, and the bread; we found some butter too, another relic of Sézanne. Then to our joy we found a large tin containing a ham. We had kept this specially against an emergency.

Our midnight picnic, with ham sandwiches made by torchlight, was complicated but satisfactory, even our young friend remarked on that. Before we had finished we were discovered. Two very young sentries, suspicious of our activities and our foreign language, came to enquire what we were doing. Then two women from the refugees' canteen in the market-hall arrived to offer us some coffee. We satisfied their curiosity as quickly as we could, appeased our hunger and retired to sleep. We were too exhausted to talk.

Friday, 14*th June*
IT WAS JUST dawn when we awoke. Still tired, exhausted and miserable, we pulled ourselves together and got ready for the journey to Sens and our new headquarters at St. Valérien. There was not a soul about; the sentries of a few hours before had disappeared; in the square, the dusty, heavily-laden cars and lorries of the refugees seemed lonely and abandoned. But as we walked about trying to restore the circulation to our cramped limbs, we could see here and there in the cars the still, sleeping figures of their guardians crouched in the most uncomfortable positions. Most of the cars looked already derelict and we wondered bitterly how far they would be able to go, if they could be induced to start, before their final collapse reduced them to becoming new additions to the scrap heaps of old iron already littering the roads.

Our minds were still obsessed by the panic of the day before. We could think of nothing else. No matter how we argued or reasoned to ourselves we could find no solution to the awful new peril that had suddenly and so unexpectedly presented itself. As we drove out of sleeping, peaceful Auxerre at about 4 a.m. we had half persuaded ourselves that perhaps this awful thing, so foreign to the stolid French peasants and bourgeois, was a passing madness that by now had been taken in hand by the authorities, the capable and omnipotent Prefects and Mayors of France and especially by the people themselves.

Our journey to Joigny gave us no cause to doubt our renascent faith; although the broad road was lined at regular intervals with conveyances of every description, they were in orderly lines, and those drivers and occupants who were already awake appeared calm and were preparing in an almost leisurely way to resume their journey.

Near Joigny we were overtaken by Jean P . . .; we stopped and talked for a moment. Like us, he had slept in Auxerre for the few hours before dawn. He told us that others of our Section had been with him and were following, making their way to St. Valérien. He went on ahead but we lost sight of him at Villeneuve-sur-Yonne.

Joigny had been dead, we had not met a single moving car, but in Villeneuve the movement of the day had started again and there was considerable activity going on between the two vast stone gateways that guard the little town. Only a single line of traffic could pass through and the advance of a heavy military convoy was causing a great deal of confusion. Everybody was sleepy and cross, it was still early, but after a lot of unnecessary argument, the civilian traffic was pushed to one side and, with the convoy, we sped along the remaining fifteen kilometres to Sens.

We parked in a little square opposite the Hôtel de Paris. It was 6.30. The town was very much awake for such an early hour. There were quantities of vehicles everywhere, lots of people walking about and already quite a flow of cars driving south.

The sight of a large hotel had made us conscious of our condition; we were dirty, hungry and still tired. We had already learnt that we had to fend for ourselves; it was essential to be washed and revived before returning to the Section. There might be work to do immediately, there might be no provisions at St. Valérien. We arrived at the door simultaneously with a girl delivering a basket of *croissants*. This was heartening; if there was bread we would be able to have some breakfast.

The night porter was old and sleepy, deaf and slow-witted. He must find the *patronne* first; breakfast might be available in half an hour, but meanwhile there was nowhere to wash. The refugees were occupying everything, even the bath rooms. There were no shops, no cafés open in the town yet, and we had to have food. The *patronne* appeared in her dressing-gown; yes, we must wait.

A captain came in; he, too, wanted breakfast. There would be no coffee for half an hour; he went out. The front door opened again and three elderly people came in; two old ladies dressed in black and a man wearing his Legion of Honour. They wanted the same as ourselves, so we sat and waited together, a melancholy, stranded group.

One old lady began to talk. What was happening in the war? Where were the Germans? Where was the French army? She had come from Paris with her sister and her husband. They had been on the road for two days, struggling in the traffic. The situation was intolerable, completely out of hand. The morale of the people had finally broken when they learnt that Paris was not to be defended. Then they had all taken to the roads rather than remain to see the Germans enter Paris. We asked if the order for evacuation had been given, but were told that it had not. Those who wanted to, left; the police did not even attempt to stop them at the gates of Paris. In any case, many of the police themselves had left.

" Oh, messieurs, it is terrible—terrible! How can we have let them get so far? What will the end be now? Where is our great army? " She was nervous, excited and terrified. Then she added: " But we are going to win. We will win, won't we? You do believe we are going to win, don't you? "

We were in no mood to reassure her, we no longer knew ourselves which way victory lay. We had had no news for twenty-four hours, but we had seen what was happening on the roads. If that state of affairs existed all through France, there seemed to be no chance of organising effective resistance. If civilians were allowed to take flight, block the roads and spread their panic, then no wonder the situation was desperate. We were saved from becoming engaged in too dramatic a discussion by the porter, who told us that as one visitor had just left there was a bath room free if we wanted to wash. This seemed almost too good to be true and we hurried after him as quickly as we could.

When we came downstairs a little later, the hotel was in an uproar. The old lady was clamouring for breakfast and so were several other people. The *patronne* was dressed by now and was dealing with them all firmly. There would be no breakfast; there was no coffee and no bread, the hotel was closing immediately and she was leaving. The Germans were practically in Sens. The Mayor had left and now the citizens were going to leave; no planned evacuation had been decreed, *sauve qui peut* was the order of the day. The safe in the office was open and her assistant was busy packing up papers and bundles of francs. Panic had seized them all. We remonstrated with her; after all we had seen the *croissants* delivered, it was not true that she had no bread. She could not deny that we were right; the *croissants* were sent for and she handed them out. We took what we could and left the hotel.

Still in need of coffee, we walked down to the big café which had been so full the night before. Now it was closed, its doors bolted. The tables and chairs had been piled up outside but many of the refugees, in their desire to rest for a few minutes, had seized what they needed and were making a hasty picnic. We decided to try elsewhere. It looked hopeless.

The stream of traffic coming from the direction of Paris had swollen to ugly proportions. The streets were jammed and even military cars were unable to force a passage. The pavements were packed with a frantic tearing crowd. Every available inch of space was occupied by some kind of vehicle which had either stopped in flight or was being loaded ready to leave. The food shops were besieged; everyone was scrambling to purchase as much as possible. Most of the shops were not opening anyhow, and that made the onslaught fiercer on the few that were. One sensed a feeling among the people that they might not see food again for many days. There were no newspapers to calm their fears, no garages to attend to repairs, no petrol to help them on their journey, and no police to control them. Desperate, they seemed unable to decide whether it was more important to fight for the food they needed now or take a risk and escape before the arrival of the Germans.

In the space of one hour, Sens had become a *ville en panique*.

Our way led past the great door of the Cathedral. Some instinct made us go inside; perhaps it was a desire to escape for a few moments from the raging rabble in the streets, perhaps the wish to have one last look while it was still intact. We did not get very far. Every inch of the floor was covered with recumbent bodies, every available chair was occupied. It was impossible to tell whether the crowd round one of the side chapels was watching Mass or taking refuge. We came back into the street; there was no time to waste.

In the side streets, we decided, our chances of success were greater. Here the confusion was slightly less. There were even a few calm housewives armed with string bags attempting to do their daily shopping. They seemed to accept defeat with disdain, going from shop to shop determined to find what they wanted. But most of the shops were already sold out and the owners were standing in their doorways looking on the scene around them with eyes of wonderment. Others were loading their stocks into cars or delivery vans: piles of linen, sheaves of paper, baskets of hardware. The more canny

G

food merchants had refused to sell and were taking their supplies with them. Perhaps they thought that they would be worth more in a day or two. We found a baker and to our surprise he still had some bread. Quickly we bought the two largest loaves and hurried back to the car.

By now it was 8.30. We had fifteen kilometres to drive to St. Valérien—by 9 o'clock we should be there. But first of all we had to get out of Sens. We knew the way, it was sign-posted at the big cross-road only two hundred yards away. But we needed petrol. The depot, we knew, was at least two kilometres out of the town. We had no time to go so far. With any luck we hoped to find one nearer.

We started off and pushed our way through to the cross-road. A military policeman was on duty, trying to clear a passage for a convoy; but the civilians no longer respected military priority. First come first served was their rule now, and they were all equally determined to be first. Everyone was pushing to go in a different direction, the noise of horns, cracking whips and angry swearing was almost deafening. Our bell, hammered on arrogantly and with equal anger, succeeded in making itself heard. We forced a passage and appealed to the policeman for petrol. He was completely distracted and replied that there was none. As we moved down the avenue we looked hopefully for a barrel or pump among the masses of military lorries parked under the trees in the centre. We even dared to stop, to interrogate the driver of a tank. No one knew anything, so we decided to risk it and drive on. We had enough, we knew, for about twenty kilometres.

We ploughed our way towards the bridge over the river Yonne. Aeroplanes were circling overhead but they were French. It took us a long while to get on to the bridge itself. Civilian cars were fighting the military to get there first and the congestion was not

eased by crowds of straggling soldiers on foot, bicyclists and horses. The traffic was mostly going
towards Montargis, so that when after a few kilometres
we turned off to the right we hoped to find the road
fairly clear.

We had not gone far before there was a deafening
series of explosions. Bombs. We stopped. Yes, there
were the 'planes. More explosions and then still more.
We saw columns of smoke and dust rising from the other
side of the river. There was a popping of machine-guns
and then the enemy 'planes made off. We got back into
the car and hurried on, hoping that we had enough
petrol.

The bombing had dislocated the traffic again. By
banging on our bell we were able to thread our way
through a few hundred metres, but eventually we were
halted in the jam. We decided to try the experiment
again of turning policeman. Once more it worked and
after walking two kilometres the way was cleared.

A woman was standing in the gateway of a farm sur-
veying the scene. As we stood beside her watching the
traffic sorting itself, she spoke to us, sympathising with
our efforts to break this lawless abuse of the roads.
" Where is it all going to end ? We must have help from
America." Our answer to this familiar cry was curt and
obvious. " But they cannot ignore Reynaud's ' new
and final appeal ' to Roosevelt," she went on.

To what was she referring ? We had heard nothing.
" He spoke on the wireless last night of the world's debt
to France. It was very moving." Her voice wavered as
she then repeated his solemn phrases: " It is a question
today of the future of France, of the very life of France.
. . . Forces *must* come from the other side of the
Atlantic and crush the evil forces which dominate
Europe."

Now we knew the worst. Reynaud was calling on his
" miracle " to happen.

It was 10 o'clock when we reached St. Valérien, a pleasant little village. It consisted of a very broad and long main street with houses and shops on both sides. As we drove along we looked for familiar faces, nor were we disappointed. There were our friends the nurses; there too was the *Médecin-chef* from the Château des Minimes; then a few hundred yards further on a group of our own ambulances. We parked beside them, thankful to find that we were not alone.

René de S . . . and Sarazinski came up at once, so did Pierre D . . ., Ido M . . . and Jean P . . . They all had stories to tell of their experiences during the last twenty-four hours. But we were too exhausted to stand about gossiping; we needed food.

There was a café not far away and we went to it. It was a peaceful little rural *bistro* which offered us boiled eggs as well as coffee, bread and butter. It seemed so strange suddenly to find a little community living normally so close to the scene of uncontrolled panic from which we had just escaped. We ate a hearty meal and talked. We were all in the same angry mood. Where would it end ?—And when ?—The more the people panicked, the easier the German advance became.

The chief preoccupation of everyone was the mysterious disappearance of Bouveret and Caillemer. Neither of them had yet been seen in St. Valérien, nor had the kitchen-lorry nor Erwtemans, nor Merckx, nor the breakdown lorry. Several others of the Section were missing, too, but they were probably on missions, whereas Bouveret and Caillemer were coming direct from Provins. All we could do was to wait for them.

We finished eating, left the others and walked out into the main street. Here and there were a few large tanks, as effectively concealed as possible; there were some large guns, too, and several lorries. A battalion seemed to be busy packing and preparing to move.

Our ambulances were parked in front of some railings which flanked the entrance gates to the *château*. One could just see the *château* itself at the end of a long avenue of noble plane trees; there were military cars in the grounds. We started to walk up the drive; someone had already invented the story that we were going to install ourselves here.

The first person we saw under the trees was the American Commandant with his dog, standing between two of his ambulances. We exchanged a few words; he was still very worried. Four of his girls were missing, amongst them Miss Juta and our friend, Miss Bennet, and two ambulances. Why did we not go to Vichy and get away from this chaos? The wounded needed peace and quiet; Vichy was a town full of large luxury hotels which could easily be commandeered and which offered sufficient accommodation. Things could not go on as at present. Take yesterday for example; the wounded had been arriving all the morning at Provins and in the afternoon the hospital had had to pack up. Now we had lost half our Section and there were no orders. He was sick of it.

The *château* was a large, very pleasant building. Officers were going in and out and there were several cars at the door. The *châtelaine* came out with her children, got into one car packed to capacity with luggage, and drove off. There were a few tanks hidden under trees and in the stable yard soldiers were loading barrels of petrol and cooking utensils on to lorries. Yes, they were leaving immediately. This had been their headquarters now for two days. Did we not know that the Boche would be here in a few hours? This shook us considerably; obviously, we would not be staying here. But their statement contrasted oddly with the calm of the villagers. We went back to the village to see if it had changed.

The sight of a barber's shop opposite the gates of the

château reminded us that our hair was growing long. We went over to see if it would be possible to have a hair-cut. René de S . . . and Sarazinski were already in the only two chairs; two others were waiting. We staked our claims and decided to clean our ambulance in the interval. It needed it; dust was inches thick everywhere. We sweated away in the gruelling heat, wondering nevertheless whether such cleanliness was still worth while.

Then our turns came at the barber's. It was the most curious hair-cut we had ever had, for half-way through an air-raid started. The barber and his cross-eyed assistant wanted to stop work, but we fixed them with what we hoped was a martial stare and commanded them to finish the job. The possibility of sudden death was nothing to the prospect of our ridiculous appearance with a half-finished hair-cut. The effect was that they went on cutting like demons and would have gone on blindly until not a hair remained on our heads, had we not suddenly realised what was happening and, with two yells of horror, stopped them just in time. All the same we felt quite smart when we came out—a bath and a hair-cut in the same morning, that was luxury.

As we appeared there was an excited yell from the other side of the street. It was Miss Bennet, breathless and bursting with excitement. " Hi, boys! " she tried to look tough, " if you want to know where your commanders are, I can tell you. They have all been taken prisoners by the Germans. Juta and I were captured, too, but we ran away—we had to leave two other girls with their ambulance. There's another of your fellows among the bunch—a Dutchman with black hair; jolly matey with the Germans he's being, too—giving all our names, laughing and joking with them. He's Fifth Column all right. I'm off to report him now."

She was gone before we could ask any questions, there were so many other people to tell.

Bouveret, Caillemer prisoners ? The Section without commanders ? What on earth would happen now ? But who was the Dutchman ? We started to count. It could only be Erwtemans. Yes, ambulance No. 13 was missing. That was not funny, because despite his misplaced humour, we liked Erwtemans, and also because we suddenly realised that we had lost all our luggage! Not only did it mean that we now had practically no clothes but—and this was almost worse —we had lost three bottles of whisky and a bottle of champagne! We decided to seek out Miss Juta and hear a clearer version of the story.

We did not have far to look. Miss Juta was striding down the drive of the *château*. She waved, joined us and started her story. When she had last seen us at Sens, she and Miss Bennet were just starting to return to Provins to fetch a second load of wounded. They had been accompanied by another ambulance of their unit driven by Miss Myers and Miss Darby. Frightened of the heavy traffic and congestion on the road which they had taken in the afternoon, through Bray, they had decided to risk a detour and go back through Nogent-sur-Seine. It was not quite dark when they reached the outskirts of the town and were suddenly stopped by a German sentry who leapt into the middle of the road. They had been taken off to headquarters and there found several members of our Section who had been caught coming in the opposite direction. We questioned Miss Juta carefully, in order to identify the missing men but she had not had time to observe them in detail. Bouveret, Caillemer, Estevez, ' Jack-and-Jim '—these she knew. Then we asked about Erwtemans. She was more reserved: he had talked to the Germans in German, had given the names of his fellow-prisoners and information about the Section with which they were serving. It was most suspicious; perhaps he was a member of the Fifth Column and had led them into a trap. Lenoir ? Merckx ? François ? She did not even know them by sight.

After interrogation in Nogent, they had been told to get back into their ambulances and had been taken off in a column under escort. They had passed through Sézanne, which had now become a German hospital base. From a conversation between the officers, which she had overheard, she gathered that they were being taken to Verdun. Some kilometres beyond Sézanne they had been halted and cleared off the road to make room for a long German mechanised column which was hurrying up to the front. They heard talk of a French counter-offensive already launched. Apparently their guards were more interested in admiring their own destructive engines than in watching the prisoners. Seeing that she was unobserved, she quickly turned her ambulance round and made a dash for safety, thinking the other girls would follow. With her foot hard on the accelerator she had driven right through the German lines, not stopping till they met a French tank and found that they were again in friendly territory.

It was an exciting escape and only Miss Juta's courage and remarkable presence of mind could have carried it off. These two women were evidently not lacking in bravery and could look after themselves in an emergency. Nevertheless, all the women, French and English, apart from nurses, who had found their way to the front were a persistent nuisance. Subconsciously every man felt a responsibility towards them and this was a perpetual irritant. Many of the women obviously resented this and wished to be accepted on equal terms. But instinct and human nature are stronger than reason. No doubt this was why one of Weygand's first acts on assuming the supreme command was to order the withdrawal of women from the front lines.

We decided to consult with the few companions who had arrived; Raymond was missing, there was no other obvious new commander. Everyone seemed to agree that the best thing was to report to the Colonel of the Service de Santé of the 17th Army Corps and put ourselves at his disposal. But we had to elect a new *brigadier* among ourselves. The choice was not clear, and one or two evidently coveted the position. We ourselves hoped for the prompt return of Raymond; we knew that he was not a prisoner as he had been seen in Auxerre. If Raymond did not appear it was a matter of indifference to us who became *brigadier*, so long as he was pleasant and competent; we suggested Allard. The intrigues were too boring for us to take part, so we left our comrades and went for another walk in the village.

We saw a woman carrying a bundle of lettuces. They made our mouths water. For over a fortnight now we had not seen a fresh green vegetable. Avidly we asked where there was a fruit shop and were directed to a market garden a few hundred yards along the road. It was a lovely garden and contained rows of tall, firm Cos lettuces. The owners were pleased to see a customer and cut us quite an armful. Inside the shop we found baskets of delicious fruit—cherries, strawberries and greengages—of which we ate quantities and then bought more. We bought some carrots, too. There was a special price for soldiers; we had a large supply for a few francs. Perhaps they gave us more than necessary just to get rid of it. They had not actually taken the decision to leave, but they were wavering. A car stood ready at the door, neighbours came in and gossiped, the luggage was packed—but they had no news. Should they go ? They appealed to us. Our firm and negative reply was not what they had expected; perhaps they then regretted their generosity, at all events they looked disillusioned.

We found that a lunch had been prepared for us in

one of the cafés of the village. We walked along and took our seats with the others at tables in the courtyard outside the kitchen. The efficient nurses who, with considerable difficulty, had organised the commissariat, were there too.

As we were all assembled it seemed a perfect moment to hold a roll-call and reorganise ourselves. In the interval one clique had dominated the others and we were given to understand that the new *brigadier* was Herrera. He was short, dark, snobbish and Guatemalan. We had watched him trying for a long while to ingratiate himself first with Bouveret, then with Caillemer ; but neither of them had shown any inclination to rely on him and he had remained inconspicuous. All we knew was that he shared an ambulance with Allard. There arose the question of reporting to the Colonel, but as Herrera did not know him by sight, and we had just spent two days under his command, we offered to make the approach when the time came.

In the middle of lunch Miss Bennet and Miss Juta arrived, bringing with them two R.A.F. men, part of the crew of a 'plane which had been brought down. The injured pilot was being looked after by one of the doctors in the *château*. They sat down not far away from us. They knew we were English—after all, we were talking English—just as surely as we knew that they were. But with that seemingly unobserving frigidity, with which only English people can conceal their longing to speak to a fellow-countryman, they sat at table staring curiously at us, not daring to begin without a formal introduction. We never heard their story, they never heard ours, but the *convenances* had been respected.

Lunch over, we set off to look for the Colonel. At the officers' mess in another café we learned that he was making a tour of inspection with the General and would not be back for at least another two hours. We could wait; we had plenty of things to do. Now that we knew our baggage and food were definitely lost we felt that some of it had to be replaced; St. Valérien might be our last chance. Our ham was now a more precious possession than ever; we bought a sheet of cellophane in which to wrap it. We added a few tins to our depleted reserve and bought a few of the more essential pieces of clothing. Then we needed petrol, this was kept in our breakdown lorry, but that had still not appeared. The village pumps were dry; eventually we found a military supply at the far end of the village and were allowed to fill our tank.

Two of the English girls came out of the *château* gates just as we were parking again. "Have you enough petrol? Can you take us to Orleans?" The English airman had to be taken to hospital there and their ambulance refused to start; Miss Juta was having trouble with her engine, too, and the third one was full of baggage and equipment. We agreed to do it if their Commandant consented. He was found and granted his permission, but by the time we returned to the *château* someone had remedied the mechanical defect and our services were no longer needed.

In due course the Colonel reappeared. We found him walking down the street with the General and the *Médecin-chef*. We reported our situation. He decided to assume direct command over our remaining twelve ambulances, and told us to report to Lieut. Bez, his military adjutant.

The General was very friendly and interested, and asked several questions.

"Are you sure no other meeting place was mentioned? Could some of your people be waiting elsewhere?"

We thought hard for a moment, convinced that there could be no question of a mistake. There followed a moment of doubt. The mechanic had said something to us outside the hospital at Provins; what had it been?

" See you at . . . ? " We asked if we might study a
map. There it was: Champigny-sur-Yonne.

" *Mon Général*, the name of Champigny was mentioned. If you wish we can go there at once and see
whom we can find."

He consulted with the Colonel. It was dangerous,
but the risk was necessary. " Yes. Go at once—but
hurry back. We may not be here long."

In the meanwhile Herrera presented himself as the
new *brigadier* and we left them in conversation.

It was about 3.30 when we started down the dusty
lanes towards the Yonne. Champigny was about
twenty kilometres; we still had no map, only the names
of villages written on a slip of paper. We hoped that
we would not get lost. For the first few kilometres the
lane was clear and we pushed along, throwing up great
clouds of dust. Once or twice the lack of sign-posts was
bewildering, but we decided to go straight ahead. The
first obstacle we met was a company of African troops,
led by an officer on horseback. They were marching
more or less in formation and occupied almost the full
width of the lane. We found ourselves on the verge. It
was a pathetic sight; even these noble black troops,
whose resistance to heat and fatigue is so great, were
obviously exhausted. But they tramped and trudged
courageously in retreat, smiling, chatting, staring very
oddly at us.

The road clear, we drove on again. Then we met a
long column of heavy artillery. Guns of every size were
being hauled by caterpillar tractors down that narrow
lane. We were forced again on to the verge. The drivers
stared at us curiously and one of them called out: " You
are going in the wrong direction, my friends ! " We
came back on to the road once more. Now we met in
succession: a column of ambulances, a caravan of
unruly refugees, another negro company, a supply
column and then more refugees who had succeeded in

making the road impassable. The traffic had stopped in two parallel lines and among this jumble of cars, carts, buses and tractors was a group of people swearing, gesticulating, crying, accusing. We hammered at our bell and ordered them to clear a passage. Evidently some impetuous refugee, furious at the delay and over-estimating his capacity as a driver, had pulled out to pass the line ahead of him. In so doing he had forced another car off the road and into the ditch, where it was now embedded. A woman in tears, carrying a baby, appealed to us. What would happen to her now? How could she escape the Germans? We must go and fetch a policeman to arrest the selfish criminal. We promised falsely to do what we could if a passage was cleared immediately; it was, though with reluctance.

We started off again. The road would be clear for a few hundred yards, then we would meet another retreating column, either marching or resting in the shade of a wood. Everyone stared in such amazement as we passed that finally we felt impelled to ask if we were on the right road. Yes, the road was the right one; but what did we want in Champigny? " You had better be quick, the Boche must be almost there by now."

A little further on, the road was blocked again. A company was resting in a ditch on the left; their arms and vehicles had been untidily left about the road. We stopped, waiting for them to clear it. For a moment there was no movement; they were feeding and appeared too exhausted to comprehend or even to move. There was a table with bottles on it. We rang our bell. Then an officer tottered towards us unsteadily. He was short, fat and scarlet in the face. " Be patient, my friends! " He lurched slightly and hiccupped; a half-full glass was in his hand. " You must excuse our being in this condition. . . . We are the front line. . . . We have been in the front line for ten days— always under heavy fire—we have marched from

Soissons . . . now at last a few minutes' rest, the men need it. . . . I have found them some champagne—there's no harm in that." Sweat was streaming down his face and he was mopping his brow; it was a very hot day. We asked if it was safe to go on. " Yes, as long as you don't cross the river, but it's only two kilometres to Chaumont." By the time he had finished talking the road had been cleared and we passed on.

So now we were through the front line. That must mean that we were in No Man's Land. We shuddered a bit, then laughed—we might as well go on. Nevertheless we half expected Germans to appear from behind almost any tree. When we found another group of French soldiers further down the road we were reassured.

There was still a military policeman at the cross-road at Chaumont. Here we had to turn right for Champigny. Despite the efforts of the policeman it took quite a long time. Military and civilians were all fighting to get along the narrow street; we were the only ones trying to go towards the Yonne.

Champigny was even more crowded and chaotic. The villagers were adding to the panic by running in between the vehicles. At the cross-road in the centre was another military policeman, almost distracted with the difficulty of guiding gigantic vehicles round a corner too sharp for them to negotiate without backing. Our approach made his task more difficult. When at last we were allowed to advance we stopped and asked if he had seen any of our ambulances. " Yes, down there on the square." He pointed down a long avenue on the left at the top of which he was standing; the usual endless stream of traffic was pushing up it. At the far end we could see the bridge over the Yonne and the hills beyond. Somewhere over there was the German army.

A hundred yards down on the left-hand side was a large square in front of the Mairie. Crowds of lost soldiers, tired and despondent, were under every tree and on the steps of the public buildings. Here, right on the edge of the road, looking very miserable and conspicuous, just as lost as the others, we saw the breakdown-lorry, one ambulance, the mechanic, his assistant, and Grignard. We had found them!

" Thank God, somebody's come at last! We've been here nearly twenty-four hours, not knowing what to do."

" It was lucky you mentioned Champigny to us yesterday in Provins; just by chance we remembered. If it hadn't been for that you would never have been found. Anyhow we came on a gamble."

" Thank God, we've been fetched, we expected to be taken by the Germans any minute."

" Well, you wouldn't be the only ones. Bouveret, Caillemer and several others were captured last night coming from Provins. If we don't leave at once we will all be taken."

We gave them the route and told them to make as much speed as possible, but we knew that the lorry could not keep pace with us along the narrow lanes. We agreed to wait for them in St. Valérien, then we turned our car round while they started their engines.

A soldier disengaged himself from a little group and came towards us. " *Médecin-chef*," he said wearily, " can you do something for my wound ? I'm frightened it may get poisoned." He held up a roughly bandaged arm. We had been addressed as " *médecin-chef*," it was flattering, but we knew that we were incompetent to deal with anything serious. However, it seemed too absurd, covered with Red Crosses as we were, to refuse even to attempt to help. " Let's have a look at it," we said, with enormous assurance. We trembled as he unwound the bandage. Supposing it were really serious ? Fortunately it was only a gash and not very deep. We cleaned it, covered it with antiseptic ointment, and applied an adhesive bandage. The psychological effect of seeing such a small dressing was prodigious. " Is that little bandage enough ? " he inquired with delight.

" Yes; it will be healed in two or three days." Pressing into his hand the last drops of a bottle of whisky, we added: " That's good for wounds, too."

" Do I rub it in ? "

" No, drink it! " He clutched the bottle and roared with laughter. There never was a more complete recovery.

Then we left. Our return journey was almost as difficult as the outward one, but now at least we were moving in the same direction as the other traffic. Overtaking was complicated but possible; we had to hurry to be certain of finding the unit before it moved.

St. Valérien was calmer than it had been earlier in the day. The main street was empty of military cars and we thought for a moment that perhaps we were lost. We parked our ambulance at the *château* gates, where we had told Grignard and the mechanics to meet us. We looked to see if they were coming, but there was no sign, so we walked down the road to the café. The American Commandant was outside, drinking. We found that the Section had moved a few kilometres beyond the village to the Château de Vertron; the Commandant was just going there himself. We asked him to inform Herrera that we had found two cars in Champigny.

Inside, at the counter, were two drivers of the Tank Corps who spoke to us. They were still optimistic and talked freely. One of them described how he had repaired his tank in the middle of a battle; he enlivened us with the humour and vivacity with which he told his story. They were not downhearted at the long retreat; a stand was going to be made on the Seine. As we were talking, one of them was called away. He returned in a few seconds with a grave expression. " I've been ordered to go and destroy my tank. It's two kilometres down the road. No reason given. It seems a bit hard, she's been a good friend." Then they both went out.

While we were still waiting, a small car driven by an officer drew up. He had brought a wounded man with him and wanted the hospital. We told him that our Section was at the Château de Vertron, where the wounded man could probably be attended to, and offered to take him in our ambulance.

We were just discussing what to do about the breakdown-lorry, which had still not arrived, when we saw it coming down the road. Now everything was all right and we started for Vertron. The *château* was approached down a broad avenue, and we found our Section parked under the trees on both sides. Our arrival was greeted with delight by our comrades.

Up at the *château* the officers and nurses were eating. We found the lieutenant on duty, and he came to examine the wounded man. He arranged to dress the wounds immediately, but that was all. The unit was leaving as soon as the meal was over; St. Valérien was no longer safe. The man must be taken on to Joigny, from where a hospital train was due to leave at midnight.

After our meal, we walked down the drive to report our new departure to Herrera. He was ruffled and unhappy about his new responsibilities; his gratitude for our rescue work was almost excessive. No other of our ambulances had appeared. Now Allard had left for Joigny; he told us to look out for him and bring him back with us.

We returned to the *château* to see if the doctor's work was done. It was after 8 o'clock, and we were anxious to get our drive over in daylight. We found the wounded man ready to leave. The *Médecin-chef* appeared with our final instructions: G.A.C.A. was moving immediately to Château-Renard, where we should rejoin it.

If we failed to find it there, we should apply for information to the *Régulatrice* in Montargis.

It must have been at least half-past eight when we returned to St. Valérien on the first stage of our journey to Joigny. The village was now full of troops, most of them the footsore, weary men we had passed on the road to Champigny. They were standing about looking dejected and half-starved. No provision had been made for them in the village, we knew; food was scarce, it had been difficult enough to organise the feeding of our Section earlier in the day, and now the locust-like passage of many refugees and the fact that the shop-keepers themselves were already beginning to pack, made it quite obvious that the men would have to move on again before nightfall. We wondered how it would be possible to set these unfortunate men in movement; we felt that before many minutes they would drop where they stood.

As we drove down the main street we saw Ido M . . .; some wounded were being put in his car. We had no time to ask his destination; we just waved to each other, passed on and turned down a little side street to the right which led to Courtoin.

Our single passenger was not in a serious condition, he was also fast asleep, which was a consolation.

Dark clouds had gathered, anticipating dusk by at least half an hour ; deprived of a decent start in daylight, we hurried along as quickly as we could, not looking forward to our journey with any degree of confidence. Our task was not simplified by the route which we had been told to take, for it was completely unknown to us. We had been warned by Lieut. Bez to go nowhere near Sens as it was in all probability by now in German hands ; although the names of the villages on our road had been given to us, we wondered what would happen once night had fallen. Courtoin, Vernoy, Piffonds, St. Martin, Cudot, Précy—without a map they might have been a list of words from a dictionary of some obsolete language, for all the sense they conveyed. Mindful of the recent fate of Bouveret and our other companions who had taken a false route, we scrutinised every sign-post with the greatest care.

This part of our journey was tedious and tiring ; we could make no pace ; either we were perpetually stopping to enquire our way or slowing down to avoid some vast lorry which, in the most terrifying way, would loom up at us out of the half-light.

A few kilometres outside St. Valérien almost the worst thing that can happen to any driver in such circumstances happened to us. The self-starter jammed. We had no time to start fiddling about then, and anyhow, it was too dark. Fortunately, at that moment we had stopped on a slope and a gentle push started us easily enough. In any case we were reassured by the sight of the starting-handle at our feet.

When it was quite dark, and that seemed almost at once, we had the most enormous stroke of luck. The insistent ringing of an ambulance bell behind us made us pull in to the side of the road. A *Section de Santé* ambulance overtook us, then stopped, its driver motioning us to do likewise. The assistant driver sprang out, ran back and, in a strong Marseilles accent, asked us the route to Joigny. We were both bound for the same destination ; beyond our list of villages, which he also had, we were unable to help him. After a short consultation we agreed to stick together and follow his lead.

It was indeed lucky ; St. Christopher himself could not have traversed that irksome way more efficiently than the little ' Marius.' He was insistent, indefatigable and cheerful, always conscious of the importance and gravity of his work. He never lost a second when we pulled up to find the way—and we stopped dozens of times—he always ran, his directions were always clear. He was a perfect example of a fine body of men. These *Section de Santé* drivers and their assistants were drawn from the French conscript army; theirs was not a vocational job, but we never noticed a moment's slackness in their work ; they treated the wounded in their charge with the same care and, in some cases, with the same skill as professional *infirmiers*.

We arrived at Joigny along a back turning. There was an Egyptian darkness, no fog could have been more impenetrable ; we could hardly see the car ahead. Blindly we turned down unfamiliar roads, hoping eventually to reach some part of the town which we could recognise. It was strange and awful ; although we could see nothing, we could feel an enormous press of traffic all around. Nothing of these particular moments remains coherent ; we seemed to cross a bridge, pass somehow through a mass of army lorries, mighty tanks and swearing men, on to a road by the side of the river, then up a steep hill winding and curling to the summit on which the hospital was perched. We stopped at the first gate. The miniature St. Christopher darted backward and forward and then on to another gate. We followed. From gate to gate he ran, questioning, shouting, appealing. Cars, ambulances, lorries slipped past us down the hill in the darkness. He came back waving his arms in a final gesture of despair.

" They won't take us. The hospital is being evacuated."

It was exasperating. Where are they going ? Auxerre is out of the question, we know it is full to overflowing. There's supposed to be a hospital train leaving to-night from Joigny. Isn't there somebody who knows ? "

We found an officer and plied him with questions. " A train ? " he laughed mirthlessly. " There'll be no train from here to-night. We'll be lucky if the Boche aren't here before dawn. Get to Auxerre as quickly as you can, you may find something there."

We turned, went back down the hill and plunged once again into the nightmare below. Like so many other places we had been through in the last two days, Joigny overnight had become a madhouse. It was impossible in the blackness to distinguish between military and civilian cars ; the bulk of the traffic appeared to be military. What they were or what they were trying to do was impossible to tell ; it seemed like a gigantic whirlpool moving slowly round and round. The shouting and confusion was appalling ; somebody inadvertently flicked on his side-lights. If the culprit had been discovered he would surely have been lynched, for the cries and threats that greeted this very pardonable lapse were horrifying.

" Lights ! lights ! lights ! " came the roar from a hundred throats. " Bloody selfish swine, have you no thought for others ? The Boche are overhead, that's all that's needed to set them off. Let us get at you— you'll have no lights by the time we've finished."

We pressed on grimly, terrified lest our engine should stop and make us unwillingly add more confusion to this already chaotic scene.

We had lost our friends by now, but by a miracle found our way out of the town.

Whether the broad road swallowed the traffic and made it seem less or whether the majority of it went in another direction, it was difficult to tell ; but once we had crossed the railway bridge the road certainly seemed clearer. Progress was difficult. It was impossible to see the whole breadth of the road, at the same time dangerous to drive well in on our right side because of the cars and carts parked on the verge. We did our best to steer a middle course, but an occasional reckless driver coming towards us made it very uncomfortable going.

Not very far out of Joigny we were hailed by a considerable group of soldiers begging for a lift. They were

infirmiers and stretcher-bearers from the hospital who
had been told to make their way to Auxerre as best
they could. We put as many as possible, with their
baggage, inside the car with the wounded man, but
regretfully had to refuse the dozen or so who perched
themselves on the mudguards, steps and every possible
corner of the car. Apart from the springs—and we
could not have cared less about them in such an emergency—we explained the hazards of the road and
refused to take the responsibility. They got off
grudgingly, thinking us unreasonable ; as we left them
to continue their trudge we felt that perhaps we were
being unnecessarily cautious.

We had not gone more than a few kilometres before
we realised how lucky our decision had been. A
civilian car, driven at break-neck speed, ran headlong
into us. Everybody concerned was in too much of a
hurry to embark on the usual tirade of recriminations,
and as neither of us was seriously damaged, the other
car moved off after a few strange oaths had been
exchanged in the darkness.

Our wounded man was all right, in fact he was still
in a drugged sleep ; the *infirmiers* had transferred themselves to a passing lorry of their own section and after
a Herculean performance of disengaging our bumpers
from the front wheels, we set about starting the engine.

Full of hope, we took out the starting-handle. No
words can describe our horrifying discovery. The smart
new bumpers and tricolour decorated number plate
blocked the passage and defeated our every attempt to
engage the engine.

Nothing would make the bumpers budge another
inch, nothing would move the number plate above
them. Even if we had had the necessary tools it would
have been impossible to do the job in the darkness. We
looked at each other blankly ; no self-starter, no possible
means of cranking the car, an unwieldy ambulance to

push every time the engine stopped. It was a grim thought. Better not to dwell on the prospect of the engine stalling at the next hold-up, nor on the additional fact that our brakes were almost useless. Mercifully, we were facing uphill, we pushed the car backwards, the engine was hot, it jerked, and started almost at once. The thought of the wounded man made us feel as if every bone in our body had been dislocated, but he went on sleeping.

The Germans had started a terrific bombardment of Joigny by now. Although we were quite fifteen kilometres away the din was terrific. Over Auxerre, parachute flares were dropping. The sky and countryside were lit up more brightly than in the brightest sunlight. One felt naked in the dazzling glare. "They'll be bombing Auxerre next," we said, as we drove into the brilliance.

It was long past 2 a.m. when we stopped outside the hospital. The courtyard was full of ambulances into which the wounded were being feverishly loaded. A nurse ran out of the gates into the narrow lane.

" Everybody is being evacuated," she told us. "There's a hospital train due at the station before dawn."

She was going down to the station herself and offered to direct us.

The 'planes were already overhead when we arrived. Soon the bombs began to fall. There was an unbelievable jumble of cars in the station yard and unloading was going on in complete darkness. The waiting-room and platform were cluttered with men on stretchers and already there was very little space left for new arrivals. After a long search we found a doctor who had time to listen to our story. He agreed to take our man. " Goodness knows if the train will arrive before either the station or it are blown sky high. If only the local anti-aircraft guns would stop until we've got this load off," he said despairingly.

We found a place on the platform and left our man.
He was still sleeping.

It was no easy task to manœuvre our way out of the
station yard, the cars had grown thick behind us. On
the floor of a lorry at our side a number of bodies lay
huddled together. " I've just brought them from
Troyes," the driver said. " They were machine-gunned
there two days ago by Italian 'planes ; their wounds
haven't been dressed yet, the town is half destroyed
and the hospital abandoned."

When we had extricated ourselves we decided for a
second night to snatch a few hours' sleep in the town.
This time we chose the Cathedral Square, which had
the advantage of being on an incline. Here we could
safely shut off our engine ; we had a good downhill
run in the morning, at least we would be able to start
without trouble. To make doubly sure we parked on
the highest point, at the Bishop's front door at the far
end from the Cathedral.

As we tumbled on to our stretchers we saw groups of
nurses going backwards and forwards between the side
streets and the Cathedral. Was there a service ?—Were
refugees sleeping there ?—Or wounded ?

We were too tired to go and see for ourselves.

Saturday, 15*th June*

WE WOKE LATER than we had intended. It must have
been about 6. The sun was shining brightly, the clouds
of yesterday had gone and the new day promised to
be hot.

We scrambled up, shaved and washed rapidly at a
water tap in the square, took a gulp of wine, which at
that hour tasted disgusting, and hopefully gave our car
a push down the hill. It moved slowly past the
Cathedral and—started !

Would there be a garage open ? That was our first
thought. Perhaps Auxerre had not yet caught the

panic that was running down the roads of France. We felt that we had a fair chance of finding a mechanic somewhere in the town.

In the light of our awful discovery of the night before, the self-starter had to be repaired. We were told by a passer-by that the Citroën and Renault service stations were on the road to the right by the station. This was excellent ; it was the road which led to the bridge over the river and the direct road through Toucy to Château-Renard.

Our hearts fell when we arrived at the cross-road at the north entrance to Auxerre. As far as we could see, in front of us, to the left and to the right, where our direction lay, there was a sea of traffic. It was worse, far worse, than the conglomeration of vehicles at Provins. It was a confusion beyond control, beyond imagination.

Cars and carts were in a solid block, over-riding the pavements, jammed tightly across the width of the road from house to house. It was like some fabulous, fire-breathing, gargantuan, malevolent monster. The body moved—perhaps at no more than two miles an hour, but it moved. At every little turning, it seemed to throw out tentacles, absorbing into its heaving, jerking mass all the cars that stood tremulously on its fringes. It swept everything before it. The pedestrians ran among the cars, calling for lifts, holding up their worn-out shoes and showing their bleeding feet, in noisy appeal, like oriental beggars exposing their sores. Each time they disappeared from view one thought of the frenzied crowds around the Juggernaut, throwing themselves under the wheels of the angry, unappeased god.

We had no option but to be swept into this awful thing. It filled the only road to either of the places we wanted. We were forced past the Citroën and the Renault garages, which anyhow were closed and boarded up, over the bridge and up the hill. In three hours we covered three kilometres.

Then, from overhead, with the zoom of death cutting
through the deafening sounds below, the German aeroplanes dived and started a devastating attack on
Auxerre. The people on foot ran here and there in
incoherent fright. Frenzied women and children, lost,
weary soldiers on foot, jumped into the back of already
overcrowded lorries. Some drivers of civilian cars
attempted to get out and take shelter, but they were
driven back to their steering wheels by their terror of
the monster of which they were now a part, for it shook
off the bombs like a rhinoceros shaking off an impudent
lizard and moved inexorably on.

We too had our uninvited passengers : first an
infirmier, then an officer from the *Section de Santé*, with a
woman. We asked them where they were going ; the
place they wanted was not on our route, but they told
us we could help them a little towards their destination.
So they stayed, sitting gratefully behind, munching
roughly made sandwiches of ham and lettuce, and bits
of chocolate.

Progress was slow. We moved when the rest of the
traffic moved and stopped when it stopped. For anything trying to travel in the opposite direction it would
have been impossible. Even the ditches were full of
exhausted soldiers who had finally collapsed. Officers
walked among the stragglers encouraging and helping
them. Everyone had made a new friend, someone with
whom to share his misfortune. At one point we passed
a detachment of Annamite troops in their native
costume. They were marching, not in formation, but as
a group, still with their commanders. They looked like
a girls' school of coolies, each with a little bundle on a
stick carried over the shoulder.

Suddenly every head turned towards the sky. " *Les
avions ! Les avions !* " echoed along the road. We heard
the roar of the engines. Luckily we were driving along
a stretch of road which was wooded on both sides ;

there was no difficulty about cover ; we stopped and flung ourselves into the ditch, with the officer and his friend. The *infirmier* disappeared among the trees. We were just in time. There was a series of deafening explosions which shook the whole countryside and left us almost winded. Trees shook, boughs fell, there was a clatter of glass. Some of the traffic was still bold enough to move on ; we knew that the bombs must have fallen on the road hardly a kilometre away. Then we saw the 'planes themselves, wave after wave of them, flying quite low. There were more explosions, this time further off, but still sufficient to frighten us. Evidently Auxerre was still the target. We must have spent about half an hour in that ditch, with bombs dropping all the time, and an occasional aeroplane machine-gunning up and down the road. When it was all over we crawled back to our car. We looked grimly at the windscreen—right in the middle of one pane was a neat hole.

Pillars of smoke and dust had been thrown into the air over Auxerre and, to judge from the red glow, it was in flames. We continued our journey, grateful for another lucky escape ; we were at the most five kilometres outside the town.

Shortly before Toucy the congestion seemed to in-crease and movement ceased altogether. One of us walked ahead to enquire the reason. At the junction of a small and unattractive looking lane, down which the traffic was being diverted, stood a military policeman. He was having some difficulty with the larger vehicles for which the angle of the turning was too sharp. " Nevers this way," he kept repeating.

" What is wrong ? "

" Toucy is in flames, you can't go through."

" How do we get to Château-Renard ? Is there a way round ? " We were still without a map, and ignorant of these country lanes.

" I don't know. You must go down here."

The *infirmier*, the officer and his friend decided to leave us. They preferred Nevers to Château-Renard. When our turn came, we plunged steeply down the little lane. It was quite incapable of holding all the traffic which it now had to carry. Charabancs and lorries were stuck in ditches on both sides, delays were endless. Refugees were camping in almost every field ; when they left there were always enough clothes to dress a regiment lying abandoned on the grass ; they soon tired of their fine raiment.

We followed the lane, guiding ourselves by the clouds of smoke issuing from the town. We wanted to go north-west ; if we could go two-thirds of the way round the town, we expected to meet our main road. The heavy traffic to Nevers turned off at last, but we went on.

We approached Toucy by the road that led out of the town to the south. As we turned on to it from the lane it seemed as if our car trembled for a moment, then braced itself to meet the shock of the frenzied crowds pouring out of the burning town. Down the road they tumbled helter-skelter, charging, battering each other. Horses reared and neighed with terror as the pall of smoke curled and eddied round them.

If it was foolhardy to advance further, it did not occur to us ; too many factors made it vital to reach the only road that led to our Section. So, heedless of the startled looks and warning cries around us, we plunged on—the only car going into Toucy.

By the level crossing on the outskirts of the town, where several roads met, a military policeman was on duty. He stood motionless and powerless, the traffic swirling around. He looked like the centurion of Pompeii. A tense, white-faced woman, bent desperately over the steering-wheel of her car, in the back of which two children were cowering, screamed out to him for some direction. But he shrugged his shoulders and looked straight ahead, while she was hustled on by the cars behind.

An old man and woman stood leaning on the front gate of their little cottage, which nestled under a steep bank opposite the crossing. They watched the passing crowds with calm, wondering eyes. The woman made a movement with her hand as if to brush the all-enveloping smoke from her face, the old man smiled and whispered something to her. Then very slowly the two imperturbable peasants walked up the steep garden path back to the little cottage.

The station, which was an important junction, had been the main objective ; as we went over the level crossing, we could see it was a tangled, smoking ruin. Not much of it was on fire, there was nothing left to burn. Two petrol tanks close by had been hit and were ablaze.

We turned one corner and were in the main street itself. It had been the sort of high street one can find in thousands of small provincial towns all over the world—about a quarter of a mile long with the Town Hall set back a few yards from the road, a grand new garage with the most imposing shops and buildings in the rather wider part at one end, a bridge over a river, then a narrower stretch with smaller houses and shops, petering out as the open country was reached again.

Now it was an extraordinary sight : exciting, fearful, horrifying in the extreme, and yet beautiful. There was no thick blanket of smoke as we had expected, but an enormous, brilliant, blinding brightness along the whole length of the street. On either side, the houses were enveloped in hard vermilion and yellow tongues of flame. They curled slowly up, round and over the houses, leaning lazily out of doors and windows. Although here and there shattered roofs showed where

incendiary bombs had fallen, the scene had no relation
to the hand of man, it was too awe-inspiring, too important in its devastating beauty.

We must be pardoned if, at that first moment, our
thoughts were not of the human suffering around us,
the destruction of precious homes, of the life's work of
countless people, of the proud records of generations of
civic endeavour ; but, faced with such a sight, man
pales into insignificance.

The heat was terrific, almost unbearable. Every
inch of the road was covered with broken glass. As we
drove along, there was a crunching sound under the
tyres and we dared not think of punctures. The faces
of the refugee drivers, peering through their wind-
screens, were strained and set, their shoulders hunched
as if to give them extra force to urge their cars more
quickly through this vast pyre. It was necessary for one
of us to get out and lead our car through the frenzied
onrush. The sight of a man in uniform with a Red
Cross armlet walking in their path checked their mad
progress and gave us a chance to pass. But for this, we
would surely have been battered to pieces.

There was a tantalising moment when we saw a
petrol pump—our tank was practically empty—could
we ?—dare we ? We both had the thought at the same
time, for we laughed at each other, shook our heads
and went on. The garage behind was already in flames,
it was a question of minutes before the tank would
blow up.

Nobody was attempting to beat out the flames, they
were long past control. Here and there, a few dazed
people were standing hopelessly gazing at their burning
homes, some with hastily gathered bundles were
already running out of the town. One young man had
his precious canvases under his arm, an easel slung over
his back. A large dummy packet of Lux with a burning
halo stood solitary in the glassless window of a grocer's

shop. " By Appointment to the late King George V "
it proudly read, and the royal arms of England stood
out defiantly amid the flames. Further on, Monsieur
Larousse, whose birthplace it was, stood on his pedestal
clasping his top-hat.

The bridge was narrow, there was just room for two
cars to pass. " Can you manage ? " we heard a young
voice enquiring calmly and politely. We were surprised—who at this moment had a thought for an
ambulance ? We looked into the passing car. A boy
no more than thirteen was at the wheel. Crowded in
the car around him was his family : mother, grandmother, other women, and countless children. Here
was the head of the family driving his womenfolk to
safety in his soldier father's absence.

Outside the town our road was clear, for we were
going west ; the hordes of refugees were coming south
from Joigny, and Toucy lay directly on their road to
Nevers. For a while we took no advantage of the open
road before us, but drove slowly. We were shattered by
the awful experience through which we had just passed.
There are some sights to which one can never become
hardened, and it was really only after we had left the
town that we realised the full horror of it all.

After about a kilometre, we saw a tall, distinguished
old man, accompanied by an elderly woman, walking
slowly down the road. Thinking he was possibly walking into Toucy, we stopped and warned him that the
town was in flames.

He bowed gravely and thanked us. " I thought I saw
some smoke," he said. " It is extremely kind of you to
tell me ; however, it is not my intention to visit the
town to-day. I am taking my morning walk." We must
have appeared surprised, for he waved his hand—it was
an elegant movement which seemed to embrace the
whole countryside—and explained : " This is my property. You see the *château* there to the right—I am the

châtelain. It is my custom to take a walk each morning."
Then he looked at us hard before he spoke again. It was
clear some disagreeable thought had crossed his mind.
" Tell me, messieurs, is it true the Germans are
near ? "

" Not at all, sir, a wild rumour. They are kilometres
away."

" I thought so. Thank you, messieurs. Good
morning." He bowed, and with his lady, walked on.

At Villiers-St. Benoit we were stopped by a military
policeman. A long military column coming towards us
was being directed down a road on the left, in the
direction of St. Sauveur. The excited villagers, as usual,
were all in the street watching the traffic go through.
A woman in the crowd, seeing an ambulance, rushed up
to us. She said that she was the village nurse, that there
were three infectious cases and some old people who
had to be evacuated. Could we help her ? She had
been waiting for an ambulance from the larger centre
of Charny since the previous afternoon. We explained
that our orders strictly forbade our accepting such
work, but offered to do what we could in Charny.
She gave us the name of the head of the Red Cross
there, and asked us to reiterate her urgent demand.
" The Germans will be here at any minute now, I
must get my patients away."

More and more we found ourselves faced with the
problem of whether or not to disobey orders. The issue
on infectious cases was clear ; we could not possibly run
the risk of carrying them. But what should we do about
the aged and infirm ? Instinctively we wanted to render
any possible service ; but where could we take people ?
We could not take them to our base, nor to a military
hospital, nor could we take the risk of transporting them
to a hospital even twenty kilometres away. Times were
too uncertain. Again and again we explained that sick
people were better left in their beds than taken to a

hospital which might have shut before we arrived. The
question of overcrowding was never even considered.

The panic was spreading from the bottom upwards.
Those whose duty it was to stay behind and attend
to the sick and infirm had cast all sense of duty to
the winds, and were as selfish as the others in their
desire to take to the roads. Those whose position
imposed the responsibility of setting an example, by
remaining calm and at their post, had now caught the
panic from their inferiors. The Mayor of Sens, for
example, had left the town before the citizens. The
police of Auxerre had run away, leaving chaos to
defeat itself. Supposing this spirit of panic was so
infectious that not only the whole hierarchy of func-
tionaries and politicians but indeed the heads of the
Army and other Forces succumbed? We knew what
that meant ; we thought we saw it happening.

So great was the congestion at the cross-road that we
might have been delayed for at least half an hour.
Luckily there was a by-pass which the nurse, in her
anxiety to have her message delivered, was at great
pains to make us take. We dragged up a very steep
cobbled hill in first gear, and turned left beside the
church at the top. From here a lane brought us back on
to the main road one kilometre outside the village. The
line of military lorries and waggons stretched well
beyond this point. We pushed ahead as best we could.

Suddenly a boy sprang out from behind a stationary
car and waved to us to stop. Then his mother appeared.
They seemed very agitated. " Somewhere along the
road in the next few kilometres you will meet a green
lorry, very heavily laden with furniture and luggage.
Would you please be so kind as to tell the driver, M.
Verdurin, my husband, that we have broken down and
are parked beside the road ? I am so frightened that, if
he does not know he must look out for us, he will be
carried along in the stream and then we shall all be

H

separated, lost." We promised to do what we could, but there are always so many green lorries on every road. We watched each approaching lorry, then we looked to see if it was green. At least ten times we must have stopped drivers and asked if they were M. Verdurin.

Further along the road, just outside St. Martin, we were stopped again, this time because the level-crossing gates were shut. There seemed to be quite a number of cars halted on the other side. The keepers of the gates had come out of their little lodge and were talking excitedly to the crowd. Then they came over to our side. " Toucy is in flames ; the Germans have arrived there already and set fire to it. Montargis too is captured. The Boche are closing in on us on all sides. Tanks are rumbling down the road behind you now. They can't be more than five kilometres away. We have just heard it by telephone."

The occupants of two cars, which had drawn up behind us, came forward to hear what was being said. Their terror turned to panic : after all, railway employees must know the truth, it was passed on officially down the line. Our protestations that we had just come from Toucy, that the Germans were not there, and that they were certainly not within fifty kilometres, were of no avail. It was obvious that, in the space of a few minutes, those level-crossing keepers had succeeded in creating among the occupants of some twenty cars a condition of misery and panic based on the slenderest facts. Women were crying, men were bewildered ; they had friends or relations in Joigny, Auxerre, Montargis, Nevers. What should they do ? Should they go and rescue them ? Should they leave them to their fate ? Could they have escaped ? Families were scattered, out of touch, homeless. There had been no news for ten days of fathers and sons in the Army, and they in their turn would have had no news of their families left behind. We seemed to be alone in grasping the fundamental facts : if the families had remained in their homes they would not have been separated ; secondly, they would not have lost touch with their menfolk in the Army ; thirdly, there would have been no rout. Our thoughts were on this subject when the train at last rolled by : it consisted of a chain of goods waggons in which were penned some thousands of refugees going like lost sheep towards Montargis.

We arrived in Charny at last, but were halted before we could enter the main street. Just before the cross-road, at the exit from the town, a strong barricade of concrete and barbed wire had been built across the street. There was just room for one vehicle at a time to pass through, and there was no doubt that the endless column streaming towards us was determined to maintain its priority. We parked under some trees, daringly stopped the engine, locked the ambulance and set out on foot to find the Red Cross.

Everything in Charny was shut, windows and doors shuttered and bolted. The centre of the street was occupied by the long and motley procession of vehicles to which we had now become accustomed. There seemed nothing particularly distinctive about this procession except that it was rather more lumbering and rather less mechanised than usual. In fact, the only cars seemed to be touring cars. We looked again; there were practically no military vehicles. Yet there were a great many soldiers. But now they had joined up with the civilian population; horse-waggons, tractors, pony-carts were being driven by soldiers, while their owners rested. The stragglers, tired of walking, were paying for their transport by taking a share in the work. There seemed to be a great many more bicycles ridden by soldiers; others were riding horses, and we saw an officer sharing his charger with a lady-friend.

We watched in amazement as we picked our way along the pavement. We tried to find a native of the town to direct us to the Red Cross, but every person we stopped seemed to be either a refugee or a soldier. Even the cafés were closed. We walked boldly on, then all of a sudden we saw a dignified old couple sitting at their open window. She was knitting, he smoking his pipe; quite unperturbed by everything that was happening, they were carrying on as usual, exchanging at the most an occasional dry comment. It was like finding two coldly sane human beings in a madhouse. Nor did they allow themselves to be disturbed by our enquiry for the Red Cross. Mechanically the old man replied: " Last house but three on the left-hand side at the end of the village—Mme. Montaigne."

We found the house and knocked at the door. It took some time to get an answer. We knocked again. A strange figure in a dressing-gown appeared at last; it was Mme. Montaigne. She was ill and unable to attend to anything; her mother too was ill upstairs. She had no ambulances available, they had been lent to some friends the day before to leave Charny. Now she had no means of getting away herself with her mother. Could we find them a car ? Commenting, perhaps super-fluously, that Red Cross ambulances were not intended to be private caravans, especially at the moment when they were most needed, we left in disgust.

Our business in Charny was over; it was now 5 o'clock, and we were in a hurry to reach Château-Renard. A few onlookers helped us push the ambulance to get the engine started. The traffic at the barricade was held up while we passed through, then we drove down the main street. It was most unpleasant being the only car travelling in our direction; like intruders, we were made to fight for our rights. At the far end of the town was a second barricade, which we negotiated too by the repeated process of forcibly stopping the refugees. The barricade is an admirable defence work against the enemy, or indeed one's own population, if supported by machine-guns, but when it is allowed to become simply a hindrance it produces fury. It is doubtful whether the barricades of Charny survived our departure by many minutes.

We were glad to be clear of the town again. It was getting late and we wondered seriously whether our Section would still be in Château-Renard. We had really very little petrol left now, but there had been no chance of filling-up in Charny; it was so little, in fact, that we dared not measure it, for fear of learning the worst. We saw ourselves stranded on this awful road. There was nothing to do but hope for the best; we continued to fight against the traffic.

A little way beyond Charny a group of officers were standing in the road outside the gates of a *château*. All traffic had been stopped. Heavy horse-drawn waggons with outriders, part of an artillery column, were being directed into the *château* grounds. It was quite impossible even for us to pass, as they filled the whole road in turning. We stopped. Then we decided to ask for petrol before going any further. The Colonel was courteous but uninterested; his mind was on other things. All the petrol he had he needed, he had given away so much already. Even the ten litres which would have sufficed for our journey to Château-Renard could not be spared. In any case he refused to let us pass till his whole column had arrived; we were made to drive through the gates and park in front of the *château*.

Petrol was now so short that we did not dare keep the engine running. We found ourselves beside a kitchen-lorry hidden under some large trees. The cook was busy plucking a chicken which had just been killed on the road. We asked him about petrol supplies. He agreed to ask one of the lieutenants if he could spare ten litres. But we were again refused. Then the cook had a great idea. One of the heavy lorries full of refugees might be able to give us some. Unhopefully we set off, can in hand, towards the village. At the *château* gates, three or four refugees were now pleading with the Colonel for petrol; he was adamant and brushed them aside, interested only in the arrival of his column. We walked along the road and asked several times for petrol, but the lorry-drivers were as unhelpful as the Colonel. So we were forced to return empty-handed to the *château*. The column was still arriving, there was no chance of getting away. Again we appealed to the cook. He thought for a while, then went off to make some enquiries. He returned smiling. Somewhere at the back of the horse-drawn column was a group of motor-lorries, among them the breakdown-lorry, which carried the petrol supply; we could stop them and ask for what we wanted. We measured what was in the tank: under five litres. Our situation was critical.

We must have waited outside that *château* for at least three-quarters of an hour. Finally the last waggon arrived and we were allowed to drive on. The cook helped us push the ambulance, and we managed to start the engine again. We drove out on to the road feeling frightened. There was still a horde of refugees coming against us, and we knew that we had to watch carefully in order not to miss the possible supply of petrol. We drove as slowly as we could. At last we saw a convoy of lorries coming towards us. We drew up quickly, leaving the engine running, stood in the middle of the road, and signalled to the leader to stop.

" Have you any petrol to give us ? We have been told to stop you."

" Stop the breakdown-lorry: the last car but one."

He drove on hurriedly. We were more hopeful now; as we watched the rest go by it looked as though we had found the right people. More and more lorries passed, driving at intervals of at least fifty yards, then we saw the breakdown-lorry and stopped it. We had two five-litre cans in our hands ready to be filled.

" Ask the permission of the lieutenant in the liaison
car behind," the driver said. We signalled to the little
touring car which brought up the rear of the procession. The door opened, two full tins were handed out,
our own empty tins taken from us, a sign made to the
driver of the breakdown-lorry, and the cars had moved
on. It was all over in a flash—but we had ten litres of
petrol. Now we were certain of reaching Château-
Renard.

We little expected to find the chaos which existed in
Château-Renard, but by now we were accustomed to
anything. We found ourselves at length, about 7
o'clock, in a little *place* in the middle of the town. We
had been on the road almost twelve hours. We parked
firmly beside the statue in the centre; it was impossible
to move any further. Down every street from the
north, west and east, came a convoy; they were all
converging in the *place* and fighting their way down the
only other street which led south to Châtillon. There
was no sign of any member of our Section. We questioned the two military policemen who were attempting
to control the convoys, but they had only arrived in the
town a few minutes earlier, sent ahead by the convoys
in question. We had learnt by now not to despair; we
decided to walk round and round the town until we
found either an ambulance or some information concerning the latest move. We obviously could not go on
to Montargis, the convoys were coming from there.

In the milling mass of men and machines it seemed
unlikely that we would ever discover our Section, but,
undaunted, we started the search. The pavements were
full of straggling soldiers, bustling, terrified civilians,
and a great many children; the roadway was as much
occupied by stationary vehicles as by those trying to
pass through the town. Only half the people seemed to
be making for a fixed destination, the others were lost,
like ourselves. Here and there in corners, exhausted

soldiers had collapsed, elsewhere in doorways and on the floors of shops, the lightly wounded, who could go no further, were lying. One distracted soldier, seeing our Red Cross armlet, came and begged us to attend to his sick comrade. We promised to send him a doctor if we saw one. We scanned every face that passed, every car, hoping to recognise something we knew. But it was all desperately unfamiliar, unknown.

At the south end of the town, where the road to Châtillon crosses the river, we came upon a traffic orderly. He was expecting us; we could hardly believe him. The Section had left an hour previously and had gone to Dammarie-en-Puisaye, some fifty kilometres south. He gave us a slip of paper with the route written on it. It was obviously in Herrera's hand-writing; we were saved.

Now two problems presented themselves: firstly how to get hold of enough petrol, secondly how to get hold of a map. A mere list of villages would be no help at night. Nor would our ten litres, of which we had used almost five, suffice for fifty kilometres. There seemed no end to our difficulties. The orderly was quite unable to help us; everyone in the town was looking for petrol, and there was none left. We walked back towards our ambulance.

We passed a garage; the glass panes in the door had been broken and there were some soldiers inside des-perately trying to find petrol in the few drums which were lying about. With one leap we too were inside. The search for petrol was futile, we did not even try; maps mattered just as much to us. Pillage or not, we ransacked the drawers and shelves of that garage until we found what we wanted. We came out again with three excellent Taride maps. Even if we did not have enough petrol, we at least knew how to get to Dam-marie.

We returned to our ambulance, filled one of our

water-bottles at the pump in the *place* and entrusted the
other to a small boy who knew where wine could still be
bought. There remained the problem of petrol. We
asked several more people, but they merely laughed.
Everyone wanted petrol.

As we waited for the boy to return, wondering what
on earth we should do, we saw a large bus full of civil
police forcing its way down the road. It stopped for a
second in the *place*, one of the men jumped out, waved
goodbye to his companions, then it swung off on its
journey. The policeman gave a hurried look at the
names of the streets converging on the *place*, consulted a
map, then immediately assumed control of the traffic.
Some authority had taken the whole of the Versailles
police off their usual duties and distributed them over
the countryside. That they probably had no idea of the
district was not so important, they knew where the
main roads led, that was enough; but their knowledge
of handling traffic was their greatest asset. We could see
how, almost at once, the policeman brought some sort
of order to the chaos in the *place*.

Then an officer came over to us. We saw from his
tabs that he was a doctor. His plight was as bad as
ours; he was on the Medical staff of the 17th Army
Corps, and had orders to go to Bonny-sur-Loire, only a
few kilometres beyond Dammarie. He had a car, but
no petrol. Could we give him some? It was our turn to
laugh. We told him about the ill soldier, and proposed
that if he could get some petrol, we should all travel
in our ambulance. He agreed, and went off to attend
to the sick man.

In time he returned with two soldiers, one sick, one
wounded. We were to take them both to Dammarie.
We regretfully pointed out that our petrol supply was
not sufficient to take us so far, but that it would at
least carry us twenty kilometres. He decided to take the
risk, abandoning his own car, and we left.

The horde on the road to Châtillon was still as frightening as ever. If we had to continue our struggle on these roads, the journey, we knew, might take seven or eight hours. We consulted our maps and found a perfectly adequate side road through St. Maurice, Aillant and Bléneau. Perhaps in one of the villages we would find some petrol. The officer agreed, and we turned off the main road. Now there was only an occasional waggon full of refugees; the road was calm.

But once again we were lucky. As we came into St. Maurice we saw an army petrol lorry parked on the edge of the road. Here at last was our chance. The doctor wrote out an order for forty litres, our tank was gladly filled.

One of the soldiers standing by the lorry looked desperately miserable and while our tank was being filled we spoke to him. The story he told us was one of the saddest we had heard. That morning the lorry had been stationed in a little village and by chance the soldier had met one of his oldest friends; they came from the same town and had known each other from childhood. When the time came they had done their military service together, but shortly after the outbreak of this war the friend had been discharged as medically unfit and they had lost sight of each other. Now there was this chance meeting. They were over-joyed to see each other and had talked for a while. The friend was in flight with his wife and child. They were about to celebrate the chance meeting before going on their ways when there was an air-raid. The civilians ran to take cover, a few bombs dropped, but it was soon over. The soldier went to look for his friend; he found him, with his wife and child—all three dead.

We thanked the soldiers and continued with our minds at rest. The side road was our salvation; we met practically no traffic. Every village we passed through was full of troops, preparing, as we thought and hoped, to defend the Loire. But between them and the enemy was this uncontrolled, panic-struck horde of refugees and other military elements, unable to move back, unable to move forward to the attack. It was too late now for a great counter-attack.

We arrived in Dammarie a little after 10 o'clock. The little village centred round a big cross-road. On one side was the inn and a few houses were grouped round about. When we stopped to enquire where our Section was to be found, the first person we saw was our Colonel standing with Lieut. Bez and Herrera. We reported, presented the lieutenant whom we had brought and asked what we should do with the two wounded men. After a conversation with the lieutenant and Bez, the Colonel decided that the men should stay the night in Dammarie and that we should take them on to Cosne in the morning. They were directed to a building where they could sleep and told to report again at the cross-road at 6 a.m.

Very deferentially we presented our case to the Colonel and asked if it would be possible to send some other ambulance in our place. We explained the condition of our car and the inadvisability of carrying wounded until the brakes and self-starter had been mended. He immediately agreed and said that other arrangements would be made. Herrera was delighted to see us and took us to a nearby house, our quarters for the night. On the way he told us that apart from himself, Ackerman and the breakdown-lorry—who had come direct from Château-Renard—we were the only members of the Section who had arrived. The others were rescuing people from St. Valérien, which had been destroyed. He was extremely worried and wondered if we should ever see the others again. We had an impression that he was not finding his new duties as *brigadier* too pleasant.

Our quarters turned out to be the house of the local

notaire. The family had fled, evidently in great haste, the remains of a hurried meal were still on the table in the kitchen. It was a depressing sight and at first we felt uncomfortable, intruding on the privacy of our unknown and unknowing host, but we were tired after our journey and, when Herrera informed us that there was a real bed to sleep in, we quickly overcame our hesitation.

Ackerman was mouching miserably round the house. He was one of the Section we knew and liked least. He was thin, dark, and had a slight limp, he was noisy and generally an unattractive person. He had been accepted as a volunteer because of his knowledge of cars and was an unofficial assistant to the mechanic.

They told us that food was to be found in the inn where the Section kitchen had been established. Beyond trying our excellent bed we ran up the road without further delay to find our meal. We ate with a Commandant of the Air Force—a liaison officer—and his chauffeur. The Commandant told us that he had set out early that morning to visit seven bases, but owing to the awful confusion on the roads Dammarie was the first he had reached; now he found that the Air Force had moved and we had taken possession. He was calm but at his wits' end to know what to do next. He was reticent about the general situation and seemed to think that the hoped-for aeroplanes from America would reach France soon; beyond that he said very little. He was most scathing about French politicians in general. " I would be very happy to discuss archaeology with Monsieur Herriot," he said, " that is a subject he understands. But politics, never! "

When we got back to the *notaire's* house after our meal, we were surprised to find that Herrera and Ackerman had not yet gone to bed. They were sitting round the dinner-table, talking hard. Ackerman's eyes were bright with excitement. The moment we walked

into the room he jumped up, beckoned to us mysteriously and disappeared through a door into a sort of
still-room that lay beyond. We followed and found him
pointing greedily to a large cupboard, the doors of
which were wide open disclosing rows of preserve jars
and about a dozen bottles. Some of the jars were filled
with cherries, not very good, for we tried them at once;
the bottles contained a home-brewed *pruneau*, a good
strong liqueur; needless to say we tried that too and it
was excellent.

Rather shamefacedly Herrera suggested that we
might take them when we left; we quite agreed. We
had lost our kitchen with all the supplies. We had been
told that no food should be left for the advancing
enemy. The *notaire* and his wife would surely be happy
to think that their own hungry and needy soldiers,
rather than the Germans, had taken their preserves and
liqueurs. It would be a useful act of sabotage to empty
the *notaire's* store-cupboard.

The argument convinced Ackerman of a great deal
more, for an immensely crafty look came into his
shifty eyes. "And the empty jars, we need them too.
The food must be stored carefully now that it has to go
in the breakdown-lorry." This was reasonable enough.
Petrol, oil and food were not good travelling companions. We all agreed that the jars should be taken.

But Ackerman had no intention of stopping there.
"Perhaps there are other things we should take," he
said as he limped up and down the room flinging open
cupboards and pulling out drawers. "The cellar?
What about the cellar? There may be wine there."

By the light of our torches we descended the narrow
stairs. We gathered the few bottles of wine which we
found and hurried back. By now we were feeling a little
guilty. But Ackerman searched the cellar more
thoroughly and followed with a jar of preserved eggs
and a pot of butter.

Then we heard him clumping upstairs; he called us excitedly. We found him kneeling in front of a cupboard on the first floor landing. " Look, jam! Several pots! " There was a row of pots neatly labelled: strawberry, gooseberry, damson. We tasted some, it was delicious. The *notaire's* wife certainly knew how to make jam. We fetched it downstairs and started to pack our spoils in various boxes.

Every corner upstairs was picked over, Ackerman looking everywhere. It was indecent, outrageous, we had to stop him. It was one thing to sleep in the *notaire's* beds, to take his food, but quite a different matter to ransack his private affairs. " We will take what we need, nothing more," we told him. " We will not tolerate looting." He glared at us malevolently and hated us from that moment.

In silence we finished packing the food and drink. In silence we went to bed.

Sunday, 16th June

WE STRETCHED OURSELVES luxuriously as we awoke. It seemed hardly possible to believe that we had spent the night in a real bed. Nothing will ever be as comfortable as the *notaire's* feather mattress seemed that night. Before us was the enchanting prospect of washing and shaving in lots of hot water. The gas-stove worked, we had noticed the night before; we could boil as many kettles of water as we liked.

Curious noises from the kitchen, which was next to our room, broke our peaceful reveries and made us rise abruptly to discover the cause of the disturbance. We were only just in time to prevent a major catastrophe. Ackerman, who had been brooding all night on our curious attitude, had obviously decided on a master stroke. If he was not to be allowed to pilfer he would have to confine himself to one big *geste*—a *geste* on a big scale! He intended to present us with a new kitchen installation, so he was removing the gas-stove—it was a Butagaz—cylinder and all! We had a short but extremely heated argument, the stove was replaced at once, and within ten minutes two big kettles were already on the boil.

A few of our ambulances had turned up from Cosne during the night and various members of our Section now appeared at the *notaire's* house. As the order had been given to stand by for an immediate move the unit's kitchen had ceased to function, so we soon found ourselves preparing a rough sort of breakfast for our exhausted comrades. The *notaire* had taken his coffee and it was amusing to see our cups of tea being rapidly gulped with every sign of enjoyment.

We had another short passage with Ackerman when we refused his offer to stow our spoils in his car, preferring to leave them in the more certain charge of the mechanic's assistant, the acting cook. We suspected our shifty friend of removing the bottles for his own consumption, but we thought it was better to say nothing then.

It was about 10 o'clock when we left. We were moving to Les Naudins, on the other side of the Loire, some twenty-five kilometres away. We followed the leaders down to Bonny, along a peaceful country lane, but as soon as we emerged on to the main road beside the river, we found ourselves wedged in the familiar mass of traffic. The alternative route from Paris to the South was as impassable as the other. Luckily, we needed to cover only two kilometres of it to reach the bridge. Parked beside the road were several mechanised columns, lorries and heavy artillery.

During one of our halts we noticed a most incongruous scene. A group of drivers, dirty and unshaven, but in tremendous spirits, was gathered round a lorry. They were drinking, not as we might have expected, the habitual mug of *pinard*, but a bottle of the finest champagne—Moët and Chandon '29. They must have noticed our surprised and envious looks, for they offered us some, then, in the grandest manner possible, suggested we might like a case! We were astounded, but the explanation of their generosity was simple; they had spent the night at a large *château* whose cellar they had been told to empty. Quickly we opened the door of our ambulance, and the case was transferred. Fifty bottles of champagne was a handsome present.

Once across the Loire the roads were clear, the main stream of traffic was following the river. We reached Les Naudins by 11 o'clock. Here we were met by Lieut. Bez, who shepherded us along a side road and down a narrow grass track where we were well hidden by trees. Quietly, with a few brief directions, he explained how we should manœuvre our cars in the event of an attack on the village, in what order we were to park and leave. It was refreshing: we were not used to being given clear, comprehensible instructions without a display of shouting and counter-orders. We all took a great liking to Bez from this moment. Here at last was a lieutenant who commanded our respect.

For the moment there were no further orders; we had to wait for our other ambulances. We walked up the village street to see who had already arrived. The American Commandant was there, having successfully billeted his girls in a cottage. Two more were now lost, those who had gone to Orleans. We congratulated ourselves on another lucky escape.

The nurses had arrived, too; they were sleeping on the floor of the church. The *Médecin-chef* was dealing with a woman in tears; she had run out of petrol and was pleading to be helped in her flight. We could ill afford it by now, as our own stock was almost exhausted and there seemed little possibility of replenishing it, but generously she was given ten litres. An orderly was sent to see what could be commandeered in the village.

The great event of the morning was the return of three more ambulances from Cosne: Pierre D . . ., Jean P . . . and van A . . .. For the first time, we heard now the story of the end of St. Valérien. Nothing was left of the village, tons of bombs must have rained down on it. The streets were strewn with dead bodies, thrown about by the force of the explosions. Even the *château* had suffered considerably in the raid, which had occurred within a few hours of our departure. Almost the only people left alive had been a few madmen who had escaped from the workhouse and were wandering freely among the debris. Our friends had worked for hours, rendering what assistance they could, then they had taken the wounded to Cosne. There seemed no justification whatever for the raid; certainly the village had been used as a base by the Tank Corps, but they, of course, had left before us. One of the many German reconnaissance 'planes must have observed this.

Van B . . . was particularly bitter about the destruction; apparently, on the previous day, he had offered to pay half-price for a bottle of Pernod in one of the cafés, but the proprietor had refused to sell. Now the café was in ruins, the proprietor dead, and the Pernod wasted.

This seemingly heartless attitude was due to the pace at which things moved. Provins, Sens, Joigny, Auxerre, St. Valérien: each had been calm and normal when we arrived, yet, within twenty-four hours of our passage, each had been either abandoned or destroyed. There was no time to think in terms of individuals.

Lunch was quite a festive meal. By the road at the end of the grass track where we were parked was a little cottage inhabited by the village carpenter; in his workshop we built a table out of trestles and planks, and seated ourselves as comfortably as possible round it. The meal was brought to us by a soldier driver we had not seen before. He was talkative and said that he and his father owned a hat shop in Toulouse. The carpenter's wife brought a few chairs from the cottage, one of the cooks had provided a good meal, and we added some bottles of champagne. Even Lieutenant Bez came along to see that we had been properly fed. For a while our existence seemed to have recovered something of its lost stability. In addition, we were allowed to enjoy the luxury of a good sleep in the afternoon; we were certainly in need of it. We slept soundly, except for the occasional disturbance of heavy bombing raids in the distance, until about 6.30 p.m. Herrera called us to a glass of *apéritif*. It was horribly sickly and sweet, and tasted faintly of tar, but it was a present from Lieut. Bez, who was drinking with us.

In the meantime, others of our Section had returned: René de S . . ., Sarazinski, Horiot, and a Norwegian ambulance. Cosne had been almost destroyed. The bridge over the Loire had been bombed, killing several hundred people, mostly refugees, and plunging many more into the river. Several bombs had been dropped on the town itself, even one on the hospital. The medical staff and nurses had all escaped immediately, leaving the wounded as they lay; after the attack, the hospital resembled a mortuary more than a hospital, and Raymond, with one nurse, had decided to remain to do anything possible. Our other drivers had had to fight their way back along the Loire to Bonny to find a bridge still intact.

We were more numerous, therefore, at the evening meal, and Herrera organised a roll-call. There were several unexplained absentees: Allard and Ido M . . ., who had not been seen since St. Valérien, Mazella, 'Mustapha,' E . . ., and three other Norwegian drivers who had not been seen since Jouarre. We were now reduced to twelve ambulances and a breakdown-lorry. There were several problems to settle. Since we had no kitchen of our own, we had to rely on the cooks

of other Sections: which should it be ? In addition, the
Section no longer possessed any cash; that had disappeared with Bouveret and Caillemer. Would the 17th
Army Corps provide ? We were out of touch with our
own headquarters, which we imagined were now in
Bordeaux. Should they be informed of our plight, and
if so, how ?

Meanwhile, it was important not to lose Raymond,
he must return. We all sincerely hoped that he would.
He was the *brigadier* we wanted. Everyone respected and
liked him, he was always good-humoured and bright,
efficient, painstaking and imperturbable. It was typical
of him always to do his fair share of the work, to help
as much as possible. He exaggerated, perhaps, but he
was an actor; his theatrical background encouraged a
certain display, yet he was not an exhibitionist. We
knew that something in his character throve on a
situation such as there must be at Cosne; he would be
in his element, and undoubtedly proving his efficiency.
It was not the glory but the drama which he sought.
There was general doubt whether he would ever reappear, and that doubt fostered disappointment, the
desire to do something.

We were all in a nervous, taut condition. Dinner
ended in a scene. How it was caused we did not have
time to grasp, but suddenly the planks were overturned
and Horiot was on his feet, purple in the face with
frenzy, shouting: " *Lâche! Lâche!* " at Jean P . . . .
Luckily they were seated on opposite sides of the table,
or there would have been a violent struggle. Both had
risen to their feet and were pulling off their jackets ready
to fight, shouting one louder than the other. Each was
restrained from the use of force by his immediate
neighbours, but the bawling continued on a rising
crescendo. Suddenly there was a deafening bang on
what remained of the table. The carpenter's mallet was
brought firmly down, and a voice even louder than the

combined voices of the two combatants yelled: " I hate
people who shout! " The shock was so sudden
and unexpected that both disputants were paralysed.
When they recovered, the fight was over and both
warmly thanked and congratulated the peace-maker.

By the end of dinner, fears for Raymond's safety had
so increased that it was decided to send someone to
rescue him while there was still time. We all accepted
Herrera's curious proposal to draw lots to settle who
should go. The impossibility of reaching Cosne in the
absence of the bridge seemed to have occurred to no
one, nor indeed was any concern felt at the possibility
of losing a second ambulance. The lot fell to van
A . . ., who, though he was quite happy to make any
possible effort to fetch Raymond, was equally sceptical
of his chances, especially at night. He left directly.

With René de S . . . and two other drivers we
repaired to the *bistro* for a cup of coffee—a great rarity
—before retiring for the night to our customary
stretchers. As we walked up the road there was a great
deal of excited whispering and giggling; they confided
that there was a brothel in the village, but when we
found that the place was full of soldiers and heard that
the attractions were a negress and a lady of very uncertain age, we all decided to investigate no further.

Monday, 17th June
WE WERE WOKEN at dawn. The hospital at Ouzouer-
sous-Trézée, some twenty miles away on the other side
of the Loire, had to be evacuated. We set out at
4.30. In addition to our own ambulances almost
every car of the unit was in the convoy; there was
evidently a big job to be done. It was a straight drive
and there was not much traffic on the road, but on the
grass verges, in the ditches, fields and woods beyond,
there were soldiers and civilians in hundreds, most of
them still asleep.

Beside the road were many abandoned cars and carts; some had just broken down and been left to their fate by the distracted owners, others had crashed and were an unsightly tangle of body and wheels, others still were completely burnt out. Once or twice we saw a deserted horse lying in the ditch on its side kicking feebly in its last struggles.

We reached Châtillon-sur-Loire in about an hour. Our convoy stopped in the long road that led to the bridge; there was a hold-up. We waited in our cars while Bez walked to the bridge to find out the cause of the delay. After about fifteen minutes he returned looking grim and gave the order to return to Les Naudins. " All the bridges over the Loire, from Orleans to La Charité, have just been blown up," he told us. " It's lucky we did not arrive ten minutes earlier, we should have been cut off."

It was another lucky escape; once across, with the bridges gone, we would have been completely isolated.

On the way back we were stopped by a woman who begged the lieutenant to take a dying man to the nearest hospital. Bez agreed to do so and the man was put into an ambulance. Out of gratitude the woman gave each of us a cup of milk and that, with the promise of bread and hot coffee at Les Naudins, cheered everybody up considerably. Whether as a result of this, or from some other cause, the remainder of the journey was made at break-neck speed. As we watched the car in front of us bounding along we could not help feeling sorry for the dying man. On our arrival at Les Naudins we jokingly remonstrated with the driver, but he was unrepentant. We looked inside the ambulance expecting to find a corpse, but the old man appeared quite unaffected by his shaking.

Les Naudins was without bread, but Bez was determined that we should all have breakfast after our early fruitless mission, so we moved two kilometres down the road to Aubigny, where we parked in the garden of the workhouse. Again, we were unlucky, there was no bread here either. We hung about the dismal garden wondering what the next move would be.

A certain number of patients—all civilians—had to be taken from the workhouse of Aubigny to Bourges. There was a call for ambulances. We volunteered for the work; our shattered windscreen was already weakening, and we were anxious to have it replaced at once. Bourges was a large town and seemed to offer an excellent opportunity. The lieutenant agreed, and told us to find a second ambulance. René de S . . ., who was at hand, joined us.

A series of large huts had been erected in a field behind the workhouse to serve as additional hospital accommodation; they had been filled partly with tubercular patients, partly with victims of air attacks on refugees. These were the people whom we had to take to Bourges.

While we lined up at the door, a small touring car, weighed down with an excess of luggage, was pushed into position beside us. Then someone began systematically to unload it; suit-cases, hat boxes, cushions, candlesticks, saucepans, blankets—a variety of junk was soon lying on the grass. Amused, we walked across to look more closely. Then we saw that one side of the car was riddled with bullet holes, about twenty of them. The machine-gunner who was responsible had certainly performed his filthy task thoroughly. But the engine still worked and the car would do its duty. It was to accompany us to Bourges with other patients. The lieutenant, sceptical, sent an orderly to fetch a chain for towing.

The owner was brought out on a stretcher; it was a woman, talking volubly. She had been wounded in the leg. At the sight of her car and of her belongings on the grass, she sat upright on her stretcher, nearly upsetting everything, and clamoured to be set down. She had to be certain that nothing had been stolen, and started enumerating the contents of her car. The lieutenant politely asked her to lie down and remain silent, as everything was being done correctly and under his supervision. The doors of our ambulance were opened to admit her. But first of all she had to be persuaded to lie down, which she seemed to have no intention of doing, being far too interested in watching her belongings and chattering, protesting ceaselessly. She lay down under pressure, but finding herself suspended on one of the upper rails, she sat upright again and protested that she would be sick, that she could not breathe, that she would faint if she were not allowed below. Everyone's patience was rather short, and so was time; she was left where she was, and the doors of the ambulance closed. Now that she was in position she sat upright again, and her voice continued to pour through the open window.

Meanwhile, the luggage had been sorted and replaced, and a useless pile of bedding and cardboard boxes left on the grass. A nurse appeared carrying a handbag, a suit-case and the woman's shoes, the equivalents of the soldiers' bundles. The door was opened while they were put on her stretcher; once more there was a flood of protest and abuse. This time she claimed to be well enough to get up and attend to the packing of the car herself. Failing that, she wished to take all her luggage in the ambulance, lest the car break down or get lost.

" Madame, if you cannot be quiet I shall have no hesitation in removing you from the ambulance and leaving you beside the road! " The lieutenant could contain himself no longer. His words had their effect— but only for a few minutes.

Some very old men with drawn, pallid faces hobbled out of the hospital and took their places in de S . . .'s car; two more women, advanced cases of tuberculosis, were brought out on stretchers and put in ours. They, too, had their complaints to make. We commented that the first grumblers we had met were civilians, and none of them in very great pain. Two or three people got into the little car, but the lieutenant insisted that one of us should drive it. Lastly, a very sour-faced old man, in an ancient yachting cap, appeared and sat with bent back on the front seat of our ambulance. The doors were shut, final instructions given, and we started. The woman was still protesting.

It was about 10 o'clock when we left Aubigny. Bourges was fifty kilometres along a dead straight road, so we expected to reach it by lunch-time. We knew beforehand that a decree had just been issued ordering the refugees to remain where they were and to clear off the roads. So we started with hope. Indeed, our hope seemed to be not altogether unjustified. There were no more waggons visible, nor any of the tractors with their string of trailers. So far as we could see, the traffic was almost exclusively military with the exception of a few private touring cars. But the more closely one looked the more one realised that civilians and military were now inextricably mixed in their flight. Lorries carrying soldiers had increased their complement with groups of civilians, women and children, while civilian cars often contained an officer. At the side of the road, the same lines of straggling soldiers on foot were trudging south, more dusty and footsore than two days earlier. Again and again they begged for a lift. We saw again the groups of Annamite troops whom we had last seen outside Toucy. Line of Paris buses stood empty, artillery columns idle.

The women coughed, spluttered, grumbled and moaned. The old man in the yachting cap coughed, too, as he sucked a grape-fruit. He stared at the sights on the road, and carried on a monologue. Only a week before, the whole group of tubercular patients had been moved from Bourges to Aubigny to make room for wounded soldiers, now they had to go back again. He hated the hospital at Bourges, he was allowed no freedom, and the food was bad. Still, it was better than at Aubigny, where, for the last two or three days, the nuns in charge had given them almost nothing to eat. ' You'll see, they won't admit us at Bourges, they were so glad to get rid of us they'll turn us away." On and on he mumbled, telling his life story in the end. It appeared that in the last war he had been attached to a company of the Royal Engineers at Calais; he spoke English quite well, and had acted as interpreter. His mood seemed to improve during the drive, and he told a few anecdotes, but he was a gloomy companion.

Arrived at Bourges, we drove straight into the courtyard of the Hôtel-Dieu and reported to the Reception Officer. At first he declined to receive any civilian, as the hospital was full, like every hospital in the town; he told us to go on to Châteauroux. But by now orders were orders, and we had strict instructions from the Colonel to go no further than the town stated on our order. As we had this in writing, no argument was possible; the Reception Officer agreed to find room.

Outside in the courtyard several ambulances were being unloaded, and nuns dressed in white were going about their business. The Mother-Superior, recognising our patients as we brought out the stretchers, came over and spoke to them. She did not hide her surprise at seeing them again so soon, but went to look for beds. The little car was parked under the trees and locked to await its owner's recovery; the keys were given to her and she was still protesting as she was carried into the hospital. A solemn little procession of two nuns carrying a stretcher, on which lay the very battered and blood-soaked corpse of an old man, crossed the courtyard and disappeared into the mortuary. Then the stretcher-bearers, who complained of overwork, returned and our other patients were carried upstairs.

We were thankful to be rid of our tiresome load, and glad to leave what seemed a gloomy and unpleasant hospital. But it is only fair to the staff to say that, during the few preceding chaotic days, only the unexpected had happened. It was not incompetence but unpreparedness which defeated them when the test came. There were not enough dressing-stations or clearing hospitals, because they had to retreat almost before they could be opened. A better distribution of the wounded among the hospitals that did exist was prevented by uncertainty and transport difficulties. In the first place, there were practically no trains: lines had been cut, stations and hospital trains destroyed by German bombs. In the second place, ambulances, like everything else, were lost in the rabble on the roads, and when eventually they returned to their base, they often found the base gone.

Every officer on the road, every lorry driver, every hospital staff was crying out for ambulances; they all had wounded men to be fetched or carried. Many of our own drivers we knew, had stayed in places where there was work to be done, accepting orders from any commander. So long as the Army existed, as such, in formation, there is no doubt that the G.A.C.A. of the 17th Army Corps had to remain in formation, too. But for almost a week now it had not operated, and the staff of doctors and nurses were retreating in idleness. Of this they were acutely conscious, and it made them angry, because they were proud of their profession. There was plenty of work to be done, each hospital we went to provided the evidence. Doctors and nurses were not allowed to expose themselves to the dangers of capture or injury from bombardment; their skill, their power to save the lives of future thousands, had to be preserved intact, even at the cost of abandoning present hundreds. To condemn this attitude on humanitarian grounds is easy, but in this war the Red Cross is treated by the Germans as a military objective, and no doubt its personnel is no longer immune.

As we reached the hospital gateway, a lorry started to drive in. Piled up inside it was a horrifying mass of mangled, bleeding humanity. These were the latest civilian victims of a German bomb and machine-gun; some were dead, disfigured beyond recognition, others still struggling with life.

It was just before midday when we left; there was still time to reach the Citroën garage before it closed for lunch. Even at this stage we still expected to find the conventions of peace-time respected among the towns-folk. We found the garage and it was closing as we had expected, not for lunch, but because the owner was leaving. We asked for a pane of safety-glass; it was unobtainable—there was none in the town.

We drove on towards the station, which was a few hundred yards beyond. Outside, on the square, were hordes of enraged and despondent human beings, civilians and soldiers. The train services of France, north of Bordeaux, had been suspended, there was no longer any possibility of flight. The civilians seemed to mind most and were enraged, the soldiers, exhausted beyond words by ceaseless walking, were resigned and set out anew. The depot which they should have found at Bourges had already left, now they had to go on to Châteauroux and Poitiers. At intervals of a few yards, people leapt on to the running-board and begged for a lift, soldiers, seeing two Red Cross armlets, would rush up and ask for their regiments, their depots.

The hotels and cafés round the station were all closed. We drove back into the town and stopped opposite the first large hotel we saw: Hôtel de France.

We had been told to eat our midday meal in Bourges.
The door was locked, but the hall was full of people.
We knocked and rang until it was opened. The *patron*
appeared, utterly distraught; there was no question of
any food, the hotel was packed with refugees and in any
case would be abandoned in another hour. Did not
we know that the Germans would be there after lunch ?
They had already crossed the Loire at La Charité and
Nevers. We assured him that it was untrue, but he was
determined to stick to his story and spread the panic.

A little further up the street was a large restaurant
where meals were being served. Every seat appeared to
be already occupied, but we decided to walk to the
back and see for ourselves. As we did so, a voice
spluttered out of an exhausted loud-speaker fixed on
the wall: " *Ici Radio-Journal de France. . . .*" A complete hush fell throughout the room; waitresses stopped
where they stood, dishes in hand, conversation ceased,
eating ended.

The voice went on: " The Cabinet met three times
yesterday and in the evening the following special
communiqué was issued: ' In the present circumstances
the Council of Ministers, on the proposal of M. Paul
Reynaud, has deemed that the Government of France
should be entrusted to a high personality, enjoying the
unanimous respect of the nation. . . . M. Reynaud has
accordingly placed his resignation in the hands of the
President of the Republic. M. Lebrun has called on
Maréchal Pétain to assume the reins of Government.' "
There was a gasp of mingled surprise, horror and satisfaction, but before the assembled company could
recover the voice had announced the Maréchal himself
addressing the nation.

We listened to the cold, quivering tones of a tired old
man: " Frenchmen! On the appeal of the President of
the Republic, I have to-day assumed the direction of
the Government of France. I am, in heart and thoughts,

with our admirable Army. . . . My heart goes out, too, to the poor refugees who have had to endure so much. . . . I give myself to France to help her in her hour of misfortune. . . . It is with a heavy heart that I say we must cease the fight. . . . Further destruction of our precious country must be avoided. . . . I have this night applied to our opponent to know the conditions on which he is prepared to agree to a cessation of hostilities."

Then a band played the *Marseillaise*.

The crowd in the restaurant was dumbfounded. Critical as the situation was, no one had expected this blow. They did not know whether to rise to their feet while the National Anthem was played, or remain seated. As the last note sounded, the moment had come for a gesture. But what should it be ? Each person in the room seemed to be asking himself the same question, as they all hesitated between relief and revolution. Then one man, quicker than the rest, raised the cry of: " *Vive la France!* " At first only a few voices took up the refrain. Then suddenly, with a shout, the whole room echoed the phrase; afterwards there was silence again while the news bulletin was read.

The news bulletin was short; it announced the composition of the new Cabinet, that the Government had moved to Bordeaux on Saturday, that oil tanks at Venice had been bombed, that the Germans had taken Auxerre and Avallon, and advanced on Dijon. Then there was silence again.

The crowd started to eat, then to talk. What had the Maréchal said ? Did it mean that a state of Armistice already existed ? Were the English also sueing for peace ? Were hostilities to cease against Italy, too ? These were the questions on everybody's lips. We had all heard the same speech, yet no one had rightly understood. It was a masterpiece of ambiguous phraseology. Like others we collated our version of what had been said.   Some maintained that hostilities had already ceased, others that no Armistice had even been asked for, while still others professed no interest whatever.

Nothing could have been more calculated to destroy a Frenchman's pride and sense of responsibility, to sow doubt and disunity.   Only forty-eight hours earlier, Reynaud had maintained that the capture of the whole of France mattered but little; there was always the Empire, and the Government was preparing to retire to Africa and to carry on the war from there. This thought had consoled all of us as we moved south. It was unthinkable that France could have been defeated so quickly.

Only those in the Army knew the awful truth; they alone knew that the great and justly famous French Army had not been beaten in open combat. For several days now there had been nothing but sporadic encounters in the East and in the West;   most of the soldiers on the road had never even seen the Germans. The Army of France had been defeated by panic among the civilian population which it was fighting to defend. It was the civilians who had met the enemy face to face and, in their fright, taken to the road, sweeping back with them the troops who were advancing to protect them.   This was the tragedy which Pétain and the Commanders-in-Chief decided to end, but no true Frenchman believed that such a dastardly solution had been forced on them.

We found a table at last and ate a hurried meal. Food was scarce; the refugees had large appetites, so the waitresses told us.   Then we walked up the main street to buy some cellophane tape to secure our windscreen.   By now the populace was showing its reactions. Almost every shop was shut, the streets were crowded, and in every doorway stood groups of people disputing.

" I say it is not possible; it was certainly the voice of

an old man, but it was never Pétain. This is some German propaganda trick to ruin us. Now that they have so many of our wireless stations how are we to distinguish between the true and the false ? Remember they did the same sort of thing in Poland and in Holland, now they are doing it to us. It is not true, I tell you. No Frenchman would sue for peace from Hitler."

There were as many different opinions as there were people, but the majority refused to believe that an Armistice would be signed. We ourselves inclined to the belief that it might be a time-wasting ruse to enable the Army to re-form; but the objection to this seemed to be the inadmissibility of troop movements during an Armistice. If there were an Armistice, and if France admitted her defeat, we reasoned, then our own position would be most anomalous. We comforted ourselves with the thought that we would not be alone; the situation would be equally unpleasant for our Dutch, Belgian and Norwegian comrades.

A solitary, mournful, young soldier, in a steel helmet and carrying a rifle, accosted us. " Are you from England ? " We said that we were. " Well, so am I." He stretched out his hand, and we shook it. " I am Czech. I have lived in London—in Harrow, rather— for twenty years, my family are still over there. I don't know what to do now, I'm lost. I want to get back to England, find my family, and join the army. Can you help me ? "

Regretfully, we had to reply that we could not. He seemed terribly downhearted. He had been fighting with the Czech Legion, had lost them, and had had no food for two days; he had no money, no regiment, no outlook. For the last few days he, like many others, had been living as a refugee on the hospitality of the owners of cottages or farmhouses along the road. When we asked him what had happened to the Czech Legion, he shrugged his shoulders, made a gesture of despair,

and said: " Routed." Then he tapped the butt of his
rifle and pointed to a date: 1915. " You can't expect
soldiers to defend themselves against aeroplanes and
modern machines with rifles dated 1915. It's not a
question of their efficiency—but one just doesn't have
confidence in a rifle which is twenty-five years old."
We advised him to direct his steps towards Bordeaux,
wished him luck, and parted.

It was 3 o'clock when we left Bourges. In the space
of two hours the aspect of the town had completely
changed. There were more people on the streets, more
shops closed, more soldiers, more movement. The
townsfolk were leaving, but there was no sign of the
Germans. We were quite happily going fifty kilometres
to the north.

To avoid the crowds and congestion on the main
road, we decided to go by a series of cross-country
lanes through Allogny, Neuvy and Presly. The distance was not much greater and we hoped to reach
Aubigny more speedily. For a while everything went
well, and there was very little traffic, but in Allogny we
encountered again the familiar stream. Aubigny, too,
was in a hubbub. Convoys were pouring into the
market square and leaving by every possible road.

Back at the workhouse we found only the American
Commandant and his girls. The unit had left for
Allogny earlier in the day and we were expected to
rejoin it there. We all left together and arrived about
6.30.

We parked in the centre of Allogny while we went in
search of our Section. Traffic was still pouring through
and the little square was a bivouac. As we walked down
the road, we were stopped by a despatch rider. His
eyes were inflamed and red from the dust; he could
hardly see. He took off his goggles and tears streamed
down his cheeks, washing their way through the cover-
ing of dust. Luckily we had a bottle of Optrex and

some boracic powder in our ambulance; we had been
suffering ourselves from the same complaint. He
followed us back to the ambulance, thankful to find
someone who could relieve his pain; but he was not
alone. From somewhere on the street he collected at
least ten other members of his unit, all similarly
afflicted. The air was thick with dust, a result of the
phenomenally dry, early summer and the abnormal
traffic on the roads. Thousands of soldiers were suffering with their eyes.

While we were administering the eye-bath, a detachment of the Tank Corps came clattering through and
stopped. The drivers got out and added themselves to
the group. They, too, were suffering from swollen eyes
and had not seen a medical unit for several days.

We talked while we treated them, anxious to hear
their opinion of the Armistice. The despatch riders
knew nothing of it; they were horrified to learn what
we had heard in Bourges. The tank drivers knew
already, but were completely at a loss to understand,
and were furious. They were proud of their tanks, they
had served them well and there was plenty of fight still
left in them. They had taken part in the battle around
Laon, so they knew the excellence of French tanks.
" All we want," said their leader, " is to turn round now
and go for the Boche. Our tanks are in perfect condition
and we trust them to smash any force of Germans.
Sooner than surrender, we will blow them up." If that
is typical of the Army's reaction, we thought, the
Armistice proposal will be short-lived.

We found our Section parked down a grass track, so
we fetched our ambulance and joined them. Van
A . . . had returned, but he had not brought Raymond;
he had been unable to cross the Loire. Food seemed
to be the chief thought of everyone; there was practically none and for what there was one had to fight.
Ackerman and Herrera fed the Section on the spoils

I

of Dammarie.   A mixed meal was produced: eggs,
strawberry jam, bread and wine.

Everyone was talking about the Armistice, but we
were the only ones who had heard Pétain's speech.
No one knew anything more, no one understood. There
was no news from headquarters and no information
that hostilities had ceased. It was a great mystery. We
decided to wait till the following day to consult Bez
about our own position; perhaps by then, we thought,
things will have clarified and we shall know more. But
it looked as though the war in France was over. Still,
we did not believe it.

As we were going to bed we heard the sound of
shooting. We enquired what it could be. " Oh, the
sentries don't bother to make people turn out lights,
they just shoot them out now," was the casual reply.

Although it was completely dark we hesitated after
this to even use our torch. So we put up our stretchers
and undressed in the dark.

CHAOS

WE AWOKE TO the sound of a heated argument. It was Horiot clamouring for bread. Breakfast this morning was as deficient as the evening meal of the previous day, even coffee was not available. As *brigadier* Herrera was hardly proving a success, he had completely neglected the commissariat. We cut Horiot a slice of the stale loaf which we still had left, he then went up to the village to buy some fresh. We knew now the value of our little stove and the small quantities of supplies which we had assembled. Our only concern was how long the foodless state would continue; on the one hand our supplies were limited and on the other we, like the others, could not afford to continue much longer buying it for ourselves. For we were running short of money, with no certainty of getting any more.

Horiot soon returned from the village; the bakers' shops were closed, their stock exhausted and no possibility of a fresh baking. There was almost a riot. Even washing was difficult this morning; the only source of water was a well about half a mile away. At this point the demijohns of Vittel proved useful, both for washing and making tea. We boiled innumerable kettles.

About ten o'clock Bez gave the order to leave. We filed out of the grass track back on to the main road. But to-day the Colonel had a surprise for us; we were to serve as transport lorries for the *infirmiers* and stretcher-bearers. A party of eight were detailed to our ambulance, the doors closed on them and the caravan set forth.

We did not get far. In the centre of Allogny two main roads cross; military and civilian traffic was trying to proceed along both. The heaviest vehicles, guns, Paris

255

buses, charabancs blocked the passage of their rivals
in their determined effort to pass first. As a result no
traffic was moving in either direction. At length some
officers, more irate than the others, took charge and
established the precedence of the north-south stream,
until the patience of the defeated ones was exhausted
and the old situation returned. Ours was the worst
predicament; we were facing west and trying to turn
south, but at the end of half an hour our turn came
and we joined the torrent rushing south.

To-day we had no route, we had been told to follow
the cars in front. Even Bez did not seem to know our
final destination. It felt as if we were just on the run,
escaping south as fast as we could, to save our skins
and our material. There was no attempt at work; we
did not even go through Bourges, only fifteen kilometres away. Panic had given way to chaos; there
was no pretence of organisation or plan. We suddenly
realised that we were part of the greatest rout in
history and from that moment our attitude changed.

A little " *Système D* " had always been necessary, but
in future it had to be applied whole-heartedly; nothing
came to him who waited. One had to fight for self-
preservation, for food, for drink; one had to accept as a
fact the collapse of the country one loved and admired,
then try to protect oneself while trying to study dis-
passionately what one saw and heard, to feel and to
mark one's every experience as something unique and
valuable. There was no hiding the fact that we were
pleased to think of ourselves as possibly the only
Englishmen to whom this unique experience was being
granted. But our nationality had its complications.
There had been no mention of England's attitude to the
Armistice, but we knew that the Allies had contracted
not to make a separate peace. At the same time we
knew that England must continue the war. What would
be our position supposing England went on fighting ?

For hours we debated as we sat hemmed in by traffic. We had no news of the latest developments, nor any prospect of hearing news; the unit was without a wireless set and newspapers were printed so far in the south now that we never saw any. All the news we had gleaned in the last few days had been by chance.

Why was there this silence about England ? What was there to hide? We weighed up our own situation carefully. If the Armistice was a feint—as many people thought it was—there seemed no cause for worry. But if it were genuine—and against our own feelings we began to believe that it might be—then obviously we had to choose between the probable alternatives of re- turn to England or a concentration camp. In the way of this choice stood duty. We had enlisted in the French Army, it was impossible to go back on that. But we had a Red Cross armlet; that should give us some immun- ity, even if our experiences hardly confirmed the belief. In any case we had only our military papers in our pockets; if we were going to stay in France we would have to obtain at least some money, if not other papers. The Government was in Bordeaux, so the British Em- bassy must have moved there, the banks would all be there and also the headquarters of the S.S.A.F. Clearly a visit to Bordeaux was indicated; but when ? We were still a long way away, the English girls were still with us, neither the Colonel nor Bez showed any concern, obviously we could wait until we knew more.

It was a long, dreary morning; the hours dragged by while we struggled along at little more than crawling pace. The hundred and one things that go to make convoy driving complete hell came back to us with a rush and we realised with surprise that it was less than a week since we had lost our officers and half our Section. It was impossible to believe that so much had happened in that short space of time; we had covered so much ground, we had suffered so many awful experiences—and all in five days.

Military convoys of every description, refugees, soldiers on foot—all the now only too familiar sights—were everywhere along the roads; sometimes the road would be comparatively clear, other times seemingly impassable, but Bez with skill and firmness managed to clear a way and after stops and delays we always moved on.

The ' Grandmother of Snow-White,' ever desperately conscious that his car was labelled Number I, strove to manoeuvre himself into a leading position, but as there were so many missing numbers in the remnants of our Section and as we were mixed up with the other cars and ambulances of the 17th Army Corps, of which we were now a part, he achieved nothing beyond making himself a perfect nuisance to all the drivers.

At times it was not too easy to keep together or to prevent extraneous lorries and cars from joining the line of our convoy, but during our countless halts in villages and hamlets, these intruders were ruthlessly eliminated. During these pauses in our journey we noticed the village folk standing at their front doors, in little crowds in the street or gazing out of their windows, watching with dumb apprehension the vast armies flowing past their homes. We could see the worrying thoughts that passed through their puzzled minds as they discussed and argued the reason of our passage; each and every one was thinking only of flight.

We crossed the Yèvre at Mehun, then the Cher at St. Thorette. In every place we passed the bread shops were besieged by large crowds, sometimes in an orderly queue, mostly in a sullen, despondent mob. The temper of these people was quick and, at times, ugly. Once, when passing some oncoming traffic in a narrow street, we were unavoidably obliged to pull well into the kerb by a baker's shop. The outer edge of the waiting crowd instinctively drew away from us; then, as we stopped for a few seconds, turned round angrily and in a fit of sudden rage pushed with their hands on the side of our ambulance in an attempt to turn us over.

In another village, where we were held up for about fifteen minutes, some women offered to post letters for us, while others ran down the long line of the convoy offering cups of tea to the drivers.

It was nearly midday when we were halted at the forked roads on the outskirts of Charost. Scant rations of bully-beef, sardines and bread were handed out to the nurses, officers and drivers, but no orders had been given about our small band of volunteers. We were overlooked in the general scramble for food. Miserably we trailed down to the village to see what we could find in the shops. There was not a scrap of food to be bought anywhere, but we got a bottle of wine and after bravely pushing our way through the clamouring crowd outside a baker's shop, we were given the allotted ration of bread—about half a small loaf—because we were in uniform.

On the way back to our car we passed the Town Hall; it was surrounded by crowds of refugees. We caught sight of a sinister notice posted on the door, it ordered the civil population to surrender their fire-arms immediately. This, in itself, was a serious admission on the part of the authorities; by it they recognised the fact that already they had lost control of the stampeding hordes. Did they think that by taking away all fire-arms they could prevent more serious trouble—perhaps a revolution? Was it premature demobilisation? It was pathetic. We wished that somebody in authority had been present when those angry hands had pushed against the side of our ambulance. It was too late to marshal them now—the rot had set in—chaos reigned.

There were some inviting-looking lettuces in a neatly tended garden by the road where we were parked. We found the owner in her house and asked if we might buy some. " Please take what you want," was her reply. " As you see I have a great many. As for payment, please do not mention that, it is a great pleasure to be able to give to my soldiers." We thanked her gratefully, cut a dozen, one of which we kept. The rest we took to the breakdown lorry where our hungry Section was grouped. Herrera had bought food for them and they were not eating too badly. As we had bread and the remains of our ham, and they little enough, we returned and ate in our car.

A little later we caught sight of a soldier tramping over the garden and pulling out lettuces by the handful. We remembered the kindness and generosity of the owner and rage overcame us. We certainly frightened the rapacious soldier away for we rolled out a surprising series of round English oaths. Although he did not understand the finer shades of their meaning he certainly saw what we were driving at and beat a hasty retreat.

We were proud of our splendid vocabulary and re-marked how fortunate it was that none of the soldiers round had understood and been corrupted by our out-burst. But a soldier, short, dark and with spectacles, leaning on the back of the lorry parked in front of us, evidently had understood, for he roared with laughter and spoke to us in excellent English.

" I can understand all right, though I dare say I'm the only one here who can. After all, it really needs an expert in English to understand all you were saying " ; then he looked at us hard. "I know both of you," he said, " give me a minute and I'll remember your names." He thought hard. " Got it! You're Mr. Cooper; you're Mr. Freeman; now do you remember me ? "

We racked our brains. Yes, his face was familiar, very familiar, where had we met before ? It was no good, we had to confess that we could not remember.

" I'm Bertin from the Ritz Bar."

Bertin! It was fantastic; little Bertin, we had known him for years. But here in uniform, with us in the same service, it was too ridiculous, too absurd! We were delighted to see him, and talked of Frank, all our friends, old times, old scandals, a thousand things from the now so far-off past.

Bertin told us that he was one of the two cooks of the unit and that the lorry in front of us was his kitchen. We then discovered that the other cook was the *maître d'hôtel* we had first encountered while washing in the orchard near Rebais. " If ever you're hungry, just come to me," said Bertin. " I'll always find something for you." This chance meeting was indeed luck, none of us need go hungry again; permission or no, we knew Bertin would help us out. It was very much in keeping with his generous character, for he is a true man of Toulouse.

After about an hour we set off again. Then about 4 o'clock we stopped half-way between Issoudun and Châteauroux. In the interval we had passed through a nasty aerial bombardment and had been machine-gunned, but nobody had been hit and we had continued moving. It was quite a treat to pause and rest on this boiling summer's afternoon.

We were informed that in all probability there was going to be a long wait. The Colonel and Bez had decided that with so many enemy 'planes overhead it would be unwise to proceed further until later in the day. Everybody did what was necessary to their cars; all tanks were filled with petrol; we again tried to patch up our windscreen, which was rapidly falling to pieces. Then we all strolled up and down the long hill on which we had stopped, or lay down in the deep ditch by the side of the road and slept.

At the back of our column a small crowd gathered round a little artillery cart, which was halted beside the road. Sitting on the box, holding the reins, wearing a steel helmet, which was much too large, was the blackest negro imaginable. He seemed completely defeated, uncomprehending, and sat mournfully resting his head on his hands, which were covered in a spotless pair of white cotton gloves. No sight could have been more unexpected. Sweat stood out on the shiny skin of his face which was decorated with elaborate tribal scars, his eyes were bloodshot; he was a solitary but noble example of his regiment, returning home with his faithful horse.

One of the doctors offered him food and drink, but he could not be persuaded to do more than shake his head. Speech came hard to him; he may have understood, he certainly spoke at the most ten words of French. A tin of bully-beef was sent for, also a tin of sardines, then wine; an elaborate dumb-show started, the doctor coaxing, even demonstrating how to eat. But the negro merely stared in silence and shook his head. Then someone lifted up the blanket which covered the rear part of the cart. That brought the negro off his box. Under the blanket were various partitions, the largest one of which was full of hay; this discovery satisfied part of the audience's curiosity—at least the horse was being looked after and fed. But what of the driver? They began to pry; if he could refuse tins of food so generously offered he must either be weakwitted or have a secret reserve. Someone suggested that bully-beef was not part of a negro's diet.

They treated him like a child in their determination that he should be fed and looked after; their solicitude was kindly meant. When at last they discovered a collection of half-chewed crusts, bits of meat and fruit, their relief at finding that he did eat was obvious. The negro by now was dejectedly standing beside his cart watching, in shame and amazement, for what they might do next. Then someone found a piece of baggage with a name and regimental address; they pointed to the name and then at the negro, but he still only shook his head, rattling his steel helmet.

On top of the baggage was a water-bottle; apparently he was human enough to drink. Someone shook it to see if it was full. But then a large bullet-hole was discovered in one side; obviously it was useless. Fingers were pointed, questions asked, the negro smiled enigmatically. "*Copain . . . tué . . . Soissons.*" Then he reached out, recovered the water-bottle and clasped it like a precious doll. He laid it back carefully in the cart, with the crusts around it and covered the whole tenderly with the blanket. The audience was amazed, but the negro looked at them and smiled. Then he moved to the other side of the cart, uncovered another partition, pulled out bread, jam and tins of meat, to which he pointed proudly, spread some jam on a piece of bread and began to eat.

Slowly he ate half the slice of bread, then moved back to the other side of the cart, lifted the blanket and added the remaining half to the collection surrounding the water-bottle. Was he not hungry? Why save it for later when he was being offered more? What was wrong? It passed their comprehension. But one member of that audience had understood. "*Fétiche*," he murmured. The negro turned round, a broad smile of delight lit up his face and his steel helmet shook vigorously in assent. "*Copain . . . tué . . . Soissons*," he repeated. There were still those who did not understand and to whom the meaning of "*fétiche*" and the feeding of the water-bottle had to be explained. Then they asked him where he was going; but of course he did not know, he had probably never seen a map. He waved his white-gloved hand in a lordly gesture, which can only have meant that he followed the streams of traffic. Then unperturbed, uninterested, he set about gathering armfuls of grass, with which he filled up the partition at the back. He did not forget to feed his horse, any more than his dead comrade, his only companions in his loneliness. There was obviously nothing to do about it, so the crowd dispersed. A few minutes later, when he was rested, the negro resumed his solitary, dignified but mournful progress.

We found that our comrades were in a state of mutiny about the food situation. They were saying that it was our *brigadier's* duty to rectify it. Herrera innocently joined the discontented group. He appeared rather vague about his responsibility. Perhaps the heat of the day and the realisation that all of us were rather too much of a handful to manage made him bad-tempered; at all events he became rather truculent and, for some unknown reason, directed his attack chiefly against us. We did not hesitate to defend ourselves and pointed out to him the existence of two kitchen lorries, two excellent and willing cooks, and an adequate supply of food, all of which, with a little organisation, would be put at our disposal.

There was much discussion about our protracted halt; no one knew where we were going. Why were we still retreating ? And for how much longer ? Someone pointed out that we might be on our way to Toulouse, and that seemed quite a reasonable suggestion. So long as we were on the move there was obviously no Armistice; perhaps, after all, it was only a time-wasting ruse. Perhaps even negotiations had broken down; France obviously could not accept unreasonable terms.

What could France accept ? What would be the German demands ? They talked vaguely of ceding Alsace-Lorraine and Artois; but by general consent that was deemed unreasonably generous. France, a Sovereign Power, could not light-heartedly forgo her sovereignty. They expected the Germans not to be too exacting. We expressed doubts.

About 8 o'clock the convoy set off again, passed

through Châteauroux, calm and beautiful in the setting
sun, and on to Argenton-sur-Creuse. It was then dark.
We stopped for a short while by the roadside while Bez
made enquiries about the route. At last we were told
our destination, it was Malicornay, a little village some
twenty kilometres off our present road and in the heart
of the country. It seemed hours before we reached it.
Countless little turnings, puzzling cross-roads and a
moonless night made our progress slower than ever.
The last stages of our journey seemed endless, but at
last, well after midnight, we arrived. With a shock we
realised that it had taken fourteen hours to cover a
hundred and twenty kilometres!

We were parked on what appeared to be the village
green. Through the darkness we were conscious of a
lot of trees and a stream or pond beyond. It was a
romantic scene; perhaps it was this that prompted us
to throw a party before we all slept. Most of our comrades, with ' James of Old England ' and some other of
our new friends, gathered round Pierre D . . .'s car and
drank the rest of the champagne. It was a pleasant
conclusion to the day and the ruffled tempers of the
journey were soon calmed. Even Horiot, who had one
quick outburst, was soon smoothed down and everybody retired to sleep the best of friends.

Wednesday, 19*th June*
WHEN OUR BIVOUAC came to life in the morning—
rather later than usual—the sun was already shining
brightly through the trees. We had our first view of our
surroundings. We were parked in a compact mass
under a clump of tall trees; in front of us was a large
slimy pond on which several ducks were swimming,
behind a group of five or six farmhouses. In the yard
of one of these was a pump round which many people
were washing and shaving. We took our turn in the
crowd, then made our usual cup of tea.

Even so early in the day there was a lazy, disconsolate atmosphere of improvised domesticity. We had
intruded on the peace of the village, but it refused to
respond; we were subdued. There was no bustle, no
roar, no tumult; we were off the map.

Herrera came across to our ambulance and said
almost casually: "Freeman and Cooper, you will be
kitchen orderlies and responsible for the feeding of the
Section." He was out to draw the dragon's teeth; but
we were prepared. The first move obviously was to find
Bertin; he was already busy with the commissariat and
offered to consult the Adjutant on our problem. Between us we soon fixed matters and it was agreed that
we should draw our food from his kitchen. Nothing
could have suited us better; we went down to the village
to gather supplies.

The road through the village was full of people,
members of our unit, standing about in groups talking.
There was no sign of agitation, no intimation of departure. The *Médecin-chef* was talking to the Colonel,
as usual a map trembling in his hand. The nurses, too,
had appeared and were in conversation with some of
the officers. They greeted us and we spoke for a few
minutes. They, too, were complaining of the lack of
food and had decided on a protest to the *Médecin-chef*;
their tempers had not been improved by spending the
night on the floor of the church, which was not surprising since the officers and the English girls had been
comfortably billeted.

Bertin set about his work methodically, visiting the
few shops, calling at the farmhouses. But there was not
much food available and it soon became apparent that
he would have to go to Argenton to find his supplies;
so he left. One farmhouse had plenty of fresh eggs and
they proved a valuable addition to the menu, especially
as the good woman was prepared to boil them for us.
She also had a newspaper, published in Châteauroux,

which had just been delivered. We seized it avidly and
read.

Hitler and Mussolini, it stated, had met yesterday in
Munich to discuss the French proposal for an Armistice.
That was all that we were allowed to know, though
under prominent headlines came the extract from M.
Baudouin's speech: " France will only accept honour-
able conditions of peace." Still no mention of the
English attitude nor of whether England was taking
part in the negotiations.

Dropping our concern over the provision of food, we
hurried back with the newspaper to show to our friends.
Here at last was some definite information.

Everyone was idly waiting about in ignorance, though
the more energetic ones had found things to clean.
With René de S . . ., Pierre D . . ., Sarazinski and the
nurses, who had come up to visit our encampment, we
were soon engaged in a vigorous discussion. What was
meant by " honourable conditions " ?

We ourselves were rather pessimistic, but the
majority of the French were encouraged by the news.
The Germans, after all, had not defeated the French
Army in battle, nor had they overrun the whole of
France. There was always the Empire to which the
Government could retire, as Reynaud had indicated; if
therefore the Government was prepared to stop the
war now—and it was significant but unremarked that
Pétain's reason was substantially the same as that of
Leopold of Belgium, namely to avoid further destruction—then it was clear that the Germans must be
prepared to respect French autonomy. There was no
cause for undue alarm. Of one thing they were all
certain, that if the German demands were too exor-
bitant the negotiations would collapse and the war
continue. The cession of Paris, for example, could
never be tolerated. (We only learnt to-day for certain
that Paris was occupied, though we had assumed it for

almost a week.) There seemed no reason for us continuing the discussion as we were caught between
prejudice and ignorance. Perhaps we were being too
wise before the event, but it seemed essential to
envisage the worst.

We retired to continue our discussion together; we
could not think of anything else. There still seemed no
purpose served by leaving the Section; we could not
light-heartedly escape from our engagement, duty was
still duty. At the same time we needed guidance; what
was happening to other English people in France?
What was it possible for us to do? Obviously nothing
without money and papers. Bordeaux was our only
hope, but that was still over 250 kilometres away.
There were many reasons for going there in time; we
had consulted in the meanwhile with some of the others
and discovered that René de S . . . had friends and a
family bank there, that van A . . .'s family were there
and possibly van B . . .'s, too. The Dutchmen realised
that their situation would be as hopeless as ours in the
event of French capitulation and had no intention of
giving up the fight. We resolved to act together, but in
the middle of such chaos it was difficult to decide to
seek permission to quit the Section which offered a
certain protection.

Bertin returned with enough food for the day, which
he had found with difficulty, and much to everybody's
surprise again provided a decent meal. For the moment
our popularity was enormous. The lack of bread was
the only complaint, but again there was none in the
village.

There appeared no likelihood of our moving during
the afternoon; the officers were vague, evasive when
questioned, but they thought we would remain in
Malicornay till nightfall. The ambulance had not been
washed for days and it was filthy; we had no clean
clothes either. We had time to attend to both; the sun

was hot enough to dry our clothes before evening. We had hardly begun before the whole place quivered. One explosion followed another, and we knew that it could only be Châteauroux which was being destroyed. Evidently hostilities had not ceased; was this a good sign or a bad one ?

The nurses visited us at work, they were despondent and disconsolate. A few of the young surgeons, unable to tolerate longer their enforced inactivity, had taken a car and rushed to Châteauroux. They, at any rate, were determined to do their duty, but the nurses had not been allowed to accompany them. Their only topic of conversation was the futility of our present existence; they thought the unit was probably retiring gradually to Toulouse and advised us to make for Bordeaux when we thought fit. But there seemed to be no hurry, even though everything was so uncertain. Even the immediate future was uncertain; no one knew whether we would remain in Malicornay or move.

The evening meal was another success. Bertin had risen to the occasion well. He had clearly deserved a drink and we asked him to meet us later at the *bistro*. As we walked down the road we passed a doorway in which several people were gathered. It was just 7.30, the hour of the wireless news. We stopped. Hitler had replied to Pétain: let France appoint her plenipotentiaries and Germany would name the time and place of meeting. It was understood that this had been done and that the meeting would take place soon.

Hostilities were still in progress in the Vosges; the Germans had taken Lyons, had crossed the Loire, were advancing on the Cher and in the west were approaching Nantes. The French chaos, which to us seemed deliberately fostered by the reticence of the Government, was obviously the greatest help to their advance.

But we saw it in another light now. The French had lost their power of improvising resistance, of taking risks. They wanted to rescue their property, to preserve the buildings which were dear to them, to preserve the beauty of France; this beauty did not lose its meaning by virtue of the German occupation, they were now too conscious of defeat to realise that it would have been better destroyed by themselves than by the retreating Germans whom they would ultimately have to drive out in order that the beauty might live again.

We sat on a bench outside the *bistro* in the evening sunlight and were joined by 'James of Old England,' the English girls and some members of our Section. The woman who served us was a gay refugee from Paris; the *chic* of the capital was unmistakable. She spoke English quite well and exerted herself particularly to serve us, saying how nice it was to see English people, and how much she liked and admired them.

The surgeons returned from Châteauroux while we were still drinking and some of them talked with us. The bombing it appeared had been severe, numerous people had been killed and the hospital itself hit. They had worked hard, operating and rendering what assistance they could under chaotic conditions. Bourges too, they told us, had been heavily bombed. The nurses added themselves to the group. Again they had nowhere to sleep except in the church. We were rather shocked and agreed with René de S . . . who proposed that they should accompany us to our duck-pond, where he felt certain of being able to offer them an ambulance.

We all left the *bistro*. As we walked up the road a group of soldiers were amusing themselves with the village idiot. He, at the same time, was greatly amused by them. He was quite young and slightly deformed, but harmless in his antics. Most of his display consisted in pulling wry faces, adopting strange attitudes and roaring with laughter. He was good-humoured and well pleased with his audience who, to judge from their expressions, might have been watching a chimpanzees' tea-party. We stopped for a minute, but it was an ill-timed decision. With two or three leaps and bounds the idiot was in front of us. He pointed a finger, started to speak, roared with laughter, then in another bound—encouraged by ' James of Old England '—had flung his arms round Miss Juta's waist and was heard to exclaim " *Ma belle!* " Miss Juta rose to the occasion splendidly.

Van B . . . agreed, as he was alone, to give up his ambulance for the night to three of the nurses, so stretchers were prepared and they went to bed. There remained a fourth for whom to find accommodation. In his absence we appropriated Pierre D . . .'s ambulance. D . . .'s shock on finding his unexpected visitor was considerable, but we had prepared a stretcher for him in our ambulance. So, for the second time, we slept in Malicornay.

Thursday, 20th June

AT 1 A.M. we were woken by Herrera, who opened the door of the ambulance, thrust in a slip of paper and explained that we were leaving at once for Le Gros d'Ognon, some fifty kilometres south. We dressed hurriedly in the dark, again the group of *infirmiers* got in behind and then we left.

We came back on to the main road, turned left, arrived at Argenton, then turned left again towards Limoges, through the countryside made famous by Georges Sand. At this early hour the roads were more or less clear, and we moved rapidly. But driving had its new dangers; our light ambulance, constructed to carry four people in the back, now carried eight, and a great deal of baggage. It swayed from side to side of the road unsteadily, the springs creaking and groaning; at sharp corners it seemed likely to upset, and the weight was too much for the brakes both going uphill and

downhill. Some protest had to be made at the first halt
to restrain the impetuous leader of the convoy.

At one point the road had been bombed and a gaping
crater filled most of its width. There was also evidence
of bombing at Le Gros d'Ognon, where we arrived at
8 o'clock.

It was a hamlet which had grown up round an important cross-road; there was hardly a human being
to be seen, and every house was tightly shuttered. We
turned up a minor road at the end of the village and
parked on both sides under lines of elms. Naturally
there was only one thought in every mind: why had we
come here? and how long would we stay? We had come
to accept these moves now as part of our daily routine;
they were no longer dictated by plan or considerations
of strategy, we had become part of the chaos. When the
German advance came too close, our imagination told
us, we retired; it mattered little where we went, but the
general direction was southerly.

To-day Bez had as little information as yesterday, but
there seemed to be no hurry. Slowly we washed, then
lay down in the sun to rest awhile and collect our
thoughts before beginning our duties. Bertin had to be
found, the feeding organised; he had things well in hand
already, but wine was needed. We went down to the
village to see what could be found.

Le Gros d'Ognon had been bombed three times in
the last few days; there was a petrol dump as well as
an important cross-road. No great damage had been
done, as the objectives had not been hit and the bombs
had exploded in the fields. Everything was dead,
deserted—one *bistro* had remained open, but it had
nothing to sell except perhaps a glass of *grenadine*. There
was no coffee, no tinned food, no wine; everything had
been consumed by the soldiers and the refugees who
had arrived before us. It was our misfortune to be in the
rear of the retreat.

The only thing of value which we did find in the village was a newspaper. This gave a list of the French plenipotentiaries, and stated that they were meeting the Germans this day, but there was no mention of the place. To our dismay we found at the head of the list the name of General Huntziger, the star among the younger French generals, and the author of an heroic Order of the Day calling on his troops to defend to the last the sacred soil of France. Obviously, the end was now at hand. Besides this, was the mysterious statement that the Government denied all responsibility for the speech of General de Gaulle over the wireless from London, that his mission was terminated and that he was recalled instantly to France. For some strange reason the paragraph was completed by an editorial comment and we learnt what de Gaulle had said: " France is not alone. . . . She has a vast Empire behind her. . . . The flame of French resistance must not and will not go out. . . . Every Frenchman who still bears arms has the absolute duty to continue resistance. . . ."

We knew the name of de Gaulle, the expert on mechanised warfare, in which only Hitler and Reynaud had believed; we had read of his sensational successes at Laon and Abbeville, and his subsequent appointment as Under-Secretary of State for War in Reynaud's Cabinet. It looked, therefore, as though French resistance was being given a responsible lead.

Reynaud and Daladier had disappeared as silently as Gamelin, we did not know why, we did not know where. The newspapers made no attempt to help one to understand, their only aim seemed to be to increase the chaos by keeping us all in ignorance. The more we thought of the vast French Empire and of Reynaud's famous speech announcing that he was prepared to carry on the war from Africa, the less we understood what we were reading. But the net did seem to be closing in.

We turned the page, then a minor paragraph caught our eye: " ENGLAND'S PROPOSAL TO FRANCE." Underneath was the text of an official *communiqué* announcing that on Sunday the English Government had proposed a total union of the two Empires, French and English, with far-reaching plans for political, economic and financial union and a system of double nationality. The newspaper made no comment, we were unable to find out whether the proposal was under consideration, nor whether it had been accepted or rejected. Clearly this was immensely important; but why had it not been published until to-day ? Why was it now tucked away on the back page ? Why was there no indication of whether it had been accepted or not; Was this a weapon which was being used to bargain with Hitler ?

Our own position was still no clearer, except that we now presumed that England was not taking part in the Armistice negotiations. It seemed therefore more than ever essential to lay our plans carefully to avoid being caught. We could not end up as prisoners of the French. The time for departure had not yet arrived: we had to resign ourselves to waiting, and waiting in ignorance and doubt.

By now there was a regular flow of cars, buses and mechanised forces through the village, and at the sides of the road the same dismal procession of dusty, footsore, unkempt stragglers, now almost incapable of the least physical exertion. They had thrown away everything to lighten their load—gas mask, rifle, greatcoat and, in many cases, even the steel helmet. One and all must have been practically starving; there was no organisation to feed them, and, except for those who still had enough *sous* to purchase something, what food they got must have been charitable gifts. In any case, as we ourselves were experiencing, food was practically unobtainable.

Some of the officers were so angered by what they

saw that, with members of our Section, they organised a small group to stop every car and force the owner to take as many extra passengers as possible from among the stragglers. Their action was quite unofficial, but the results were interesting and most satisfactory.

First of all about a hundred weary soldiers were collected and hidden in a field by the side of the road. They were to be produced one by one, so as not to frighten drivers in advance with the sight of a great body of men. To deal with really stubborn or offensive drivers, two armed soldiers were hidden in a ditch at the side of the road and warned never to appear until given the signal; then they were to advance slowly, holding their rifles in a menacing way and looking as fierce as possible. They were, in fact, harmless, for there was no ammunition in their rifles.

One-third of the drivers gladly agreed to give the soldiers a lift; the second third were not so pleasant, even if their cars were almost empty, and several times there were angry scenes. The remainder were down-right rude and flatly refused to co-operate. Most of these, however, quickly changed their minds when the signal was given and the two men advanced from the ditch.

One driver even threatened to shoot and produced a revolver, but Horiot rose to the occasion magnificently. He just said, " Wait a minute," advanced slowly towards the man, opened the car door, took the revolver gently from his hand and then threw him into the ditch. Another man sitting beside him, seeing the fate of his friend, immediately produced his revolver. Horiot was not at all put out by this. " Half a second," he said, walking round the car. " I'll come and attend to you." Whether our hysterical laughter or Horiot's calm hypnotised the second man, we never knew, but he sat there motionless until Horiot opened the door and meted out to him the same treatment.

The greatest triumph of all, for which Horiot was again largely responsible, was the stopping of a charabanc full of Paris policemen, who were travelling in considerable comfort with their bicycles on the roof. In the space of a few minutes they were replaced by soldiers in their luxury coach, and left to continue their flight by their own efforts. The little detachment of bicyclists presented a sorry sight as they started off on their new vehicles, cursing and vituperating. It was deplorable to see how those in flight were completely devoid of both ethical and moral sense.

Bertin provided a lunch which was much appreciated. Food played a great *rôle* in our daily existence, but this did not seem curious to us at the time. When we were hard at work we needed it to keep up our strength; when we had nothing to do we needed it as a distraction, in the same way as one's day consists of intervals between meals on a long railway journey or on board ship. Perhaps, too, it became even more interesting as it became more difficult to get. At all events everybody looked forward to their meals, and there were always complaints if the standard was not maintained.

The nurses came to see us after lunch and we talked about the end of the war. Where would the plenipotentiaries meet ? What terms would the Germans demand ? What terms could the French accept ? Rather brutally, we told them the conclusions we had reached. The meeting would, surely, be at Compiègne or Versailles; the Germans would keep at least the whole of that part of France which they had already captured, plus the whole coast to the Spanish frontier; the Italians would probably claim Corsica, Tunis, Savoy and the Riviera. A few people collected round us while we talked, anxious to hear the latest developments. We were laughed to scorn as undue pessimists. The suggestion that the Germans would be allowed to possess over the half of France was treated as outrageous, not to say treasonable. France, after all, was a great nation, she could not be overrun so easily, could not bow down before German high-handedness.

Only the nurses were realistic enough to grasp that the French, least of all, could hope for leniency from the Germans, with the examples of Poland, Holland, Belgium and the other countries before them. Then we showed them the mysterious paragraph on the back page of the newspaper. They all agreed that it was a great and generous offer, even if fantastic; the pity was that it had been made so late, and then withheld from the French *people* for so long. It was impracticable now. The papers gave practically no information, no hint of what was expected; the authorities were exploiting our ignorance for their own ends.

Out of the general vagueness, a heated argument grew. Then the second sister, a distinguished woman, the daughter of a general, who was the most calm and the most rational figure in the group, turned to us and said: " I believe you are right. We cannot expect generosity. I am even inclined to concede that, under the circumstances, it might be better for France to become no more than a colony of England, rather than allow it to pass under German domination." Such was the verdict of an intelligent woman who was definitely anglophil.

The discussion continued for a long while and it was curious and distressing to hear. When the French themselves were faced with the situation which had confronted so many other peoples, at whose capitulation they had mocked, they tended to behave in the same arrogant, incredulous way. But at the same time, most of them agreed that, rather than accept the capitulation of France as the end of the war, they would each do all in their power to get to England or any other part of the world where the fight was being continued.

Then we all went to sleep.

Our rest was broken by a breathless Miss Bennet proclaiming: "We're off!" The American Commandant had made up his mind that the Armistice was imminent and that he would hurry to Bordeaux with his girls. We went over to interview him. He was feverishly at work packing and unpacking apparatus from one ambulance to another, helped by the girls and the two doctors. They were all obviously panicky.

"What's happening?" we asked.

The reply was surly: "I can't take any risks with these girls, the Armistice may be signed to-night; we are leaving for Bordeaux, and if you have any sense you'll follow us." The Commandant was too frightened and too hurried to say more.

The shock was rather sudden, even if we had been thinking of going to Bordeaux ourselves; but it was still 200 kilometres away and, so far as we knew, there was no particular urgency. We decided to consult with Herrera.

Herrera counselled delay, but passed us on to Bez. We sought him out and confronted him with the question: how near was the Armistice, should we or should we not go with the Commandant to Bordeaux? For the first time we were really worried. England seemed determined to continue the struggle, from which we concluded that there was every chance of our being taken prisoners.

Bez thought for a time, then passed us on to the Colonel. The Colonel was sympathetic but reassuring. Naturally, if the American Commandant felt that he must get to Bordeaux with his girls, that was his affair; he was independent, and women, amid the rout, were only a responsibility. In the circumstances, he for one was glad to see the last of them. But after all the Armistice was not yet signed, and the situation would not be clear till then. There was no need whatever

for us to go to Bordeaux to-day. We explained that
we needed advice on our position after the cessation of
hostilities, that Bordeaux was only 200 kilometres away,
and that if necessary we could be back with the unit
by the following afternoon. We did not tell him that
secretly it was our intention to obtain a passport
and some money before the Armistice; we could not
return to England before, at any rate, our military
obligations towards the French had been acquitted.

The Colonel promised to consult the General, who
no doubt would be arriving in the near future; at
present, G.H.Q. had been lost. We begged for a
speedy reply. The Colonel's attitude would have been
reassuring if we had been able to convince ourselves
that it was based on fact; unfortunately we were inclined to feel that it only concealed genuine ignorance
and *insouciance*.

The result of our interviews was unsatisfactory, but
naturally we had no option but to accept the Colonel's
decision. We had no doubt that, in the event of trouble,
Bez would prove our rescuer; he obviously understood
our predicament and felt that our request was sensible.
We must admit that we hesitated whether to take the
law into our own hands and desert for a day. We
returned to consult with the nurses and our friends.
René de S . . . started hurriedly to write a letter to his
family. Van A . . . was prepared to leave, but not
anxious. The sister suggested waiting, but advised
preparedness. She had lost her confidence in the
Colonel, as well as in the *Médecin-chef*, whom she
described as " a broken, trembling reed." Weighing one
thing against another, we were held by our obligations
to the Army and remained; the panic of the Commandant was none of our affair. Nevertheless, we had
a slight feeling of responsibility towards the English
girls. We gave them the best help we could in the form
of a letter to an English official of the Embassy staff

in Bordeaux. We took the opportunity also to ask for advice about what we ourselves should do. But our minds were so confused that the difficulties of getting a reply never occurred to us. Supposing that we might, however, reach Bordeaux one day, we did ask Miss Bennet to leave a note for us at an hotel in the town with her news and any instructions for ourselves.

With an immensely superior feeling of calm, and hardly a qualm, we waved farewell to the Commandant and his gallant, but rather bewildered, troupe. Then, acting on the sister's advice, we asked Bez if, as a precaution, we might fill our tank with petrol, and also keep a reserve supply. He agreed at once and we were lucky enough to obtain a drum of fifty litres, which we covered with a blanket and hid inside the ambulance. Now we had no fears; if we wanted to leave, we could travel a long way.

Then we were at peace again. We sat down on the step at the back of our car and calmly tried to work out the hysterical and chaotic incidents of the past hour. Before many minutes, the nurses and most of our Section had gathered round us in a large semi-circle. They looked at us curiously, it was a most embarrassing experience. Then a flood of questions burst over us.

What are you going to do ?—What did Bez advise ? —What did the Colonel say ?—Are you going to stay with us ?

Some of them seemed to have an idea that we possessed a secret knowledge of events and asked us the most extraordinary questions. Pierre D . . . and Jean P . . . became extremely dramatic and pointed out that their situation was equally, if not more, dangerous. Van A . . . and van B . . . agreed that things would not be too pleasant for them if there was an Armistice and they were handed over to the Germans. Sarazinski capped it by solemnly spitting over all of us as he hissed one phrase: " What about me, I'm a

Jew ? " They all shouted at once; even those who did not really care one way or the other about " the foreigners " put on suitable faces and added their remarks to the general babble. But whatever side issues arose the conversation always turned back to us and to our immediate problem. Finally, there was almost a general chorus of, " Well, what *are* you going to do ? " And then a pause.

It was very awkward; we were going to stay, but we knew our audience expected something more dramatic. The only truthful answer we could have made at that moment was: " We're going to wait and see "; but we knew that would not sound very convincing. So we solemnly looked at the time and said with great surprise, " Why, it's 4.30, naturally we're going to make tea." There was a silence, then Sarazinski burst into peals of laughter and shouted: " *Les vrais vaches anglaises*, what else would you expect them to do ? We'll all have tea."

" I have a tin of milk I'll contribute," said Pierre D . . .

" For those who don't like milk, I'll add brandy," said ' Snow-White's Grandmother.'

" An interesting exhibition of phlegm," said Jean P . . .

Cups, glasses, mugs were produced; they all sat down and soon a regular orgy of tea-drinking was in progress. We were nasty-minded enough to think that there was some ulterior motive in ' Grandma's ' generosity, but said nothing. Only René de S . . . had really understood, for when nobody was looking he solemnly winked at us.

Hardly had we begun to drink our brew when the Commandant and his girls drove shamefacedly back up the lane. We all laughed. " You haven't got far. Have you lost your courage ? "

" We can't find G.H.Q. to get an *ordre de mission*; we

don't want to have any difficulties, so we have come
back to get one from the Colonel here."

This time they decided to leave one ambulance and
a doctor behind. It must have been 5 o'clock when
they finally left. No one seemed to lament their departure. They had done no work for days, as they
themselves had complained, they were a responsibility
and had always been given the best billets. The two
people who were most pleased were undoubtedly their
doctors. After the little group had finally left, one of
them drove down the lane smiling, free at last.

The evening passed quietly, though we half-expected
to hear any minute that the Armistice had been signed.
Ackerman had prepared a surprise. During the afternoon he had collected a variety of vegetables and some
bits of meat; then he had made a fire and cooked us an
excellent stew for dinner, in addition to what Bertin
had provided.

' Snow-White ' was fussing and fidgeting all the
evening. Later, he came and asked if we would give
him our demijohn of Vittel water: he explained that it
was not the water he wanted but the bottle. Sarazinski,
it seemed, had already filled his with petrol, which he
kept in his ambulance, and ' Snow-White ' wanted to
do the same. We temporised, pointing out the value of
the water and the fact that it was not ours to dispose of,
but told him he could have it some time. For the
moment he went away; but not for good. He returned
three or four times to try again; he seemed in a great
hurry. Finally, when we retired to sleep, we put it outside on the grass. He could take it or not, as he wished.

Friday, 21*st June*

THE MORNING BEGAN with a great surprise. Ido M . . .
had returned! We were all delighted and longed to
ask him a thousand questions. Where had he been

since St. Valérien ? What had he seen, what had he done ? And, more remarkable still, how had he found us ? We had to restrain our curiosity, for the poor chap was dead beat and fast asleep. We peered into his ambulance to make quite sure he was there, noticing with surprise that there was a strange figure by his side, then left him to sleep until midday.

We had been woken by ' Snow-White's Grandmother '; the demijohn of Vittel had disappeared but he had still been nosing round our car since early dawn. Once he saw we were really up and awake, he whispered to us his plan to visit his family. The demijohn was already full of stolen petrol, now he only needed to look at our map and he would leave immediately. We asked if he had been given permission. " No, no," he replied, " that's not necessary. Once I've seen that my wife is all right—she's not far from Bordeaux—I shall come straight back." We were astounded at his impertinence, but decided it was none of our business and that, anyhow, if that was the way he felt, the Section was best rid of him. We were certain he would never return. We watched with disgust as he turned his car and sped down the road. His action made us all the more determined to stick to our duty until the last possible moment.

As yesterday, there was no sign of a move. The Colonel and Bez strolled up and down the lane, talking hard but giving no indication of any decision. Everybody questioned us, they were immensely curious. What were we going to do ? What were our plans ? The nurses seemed surprised to find us still there. " You'll have to make up your own minds," one of them confided. " Even if the situation is dangerous for you— and it might well be—you'll get no decision from the Colonel." Then, rather timidly, she added: " Please don't think that any of us would believe it wrong of you to leave. We understand very well about duty, but at a moment like this, with such hopeless chaos everywhere, one has to make up one's own mind. Desertion is an ugly word, but circumstances change everything. We are entirely with you, whatever happens." These women certainly knew the meaning of duty, better than any of the soldiers around them, and we felt consoled that in the event of our having to make a desperate decision we had their moral backing.

Ido M . . . was full of the most hair-raising stories. Perhaps it seemed mean to question the complete veracity of some of the more ghastly details, but we realised that most of them must have been true—he certainly had been through an awful week. His audience was too busy asking questions for us to get a clear picture of his adventures. We gathered that he had unloaded a hospital train of a hundred and thirty wounded—who had been deserted except by one faithful *infirmier*—and transported them to a hospital. He had more or less kept track of our movements, but at every place where he might have caught us up there was always urgent work to be done and so he had stayed. Bez and Herrera took a very bad view of his conduct and from their point of view they were right. " If everybody just went off and worked as they fancied, what would happen to the Section ? There must be some organisation," they argued. " Heroes are all very well, but undisciplined heroism is a perfect nuisance to commanding officers." Ido M . . . was disconcerted, he little expected this reception; perhaps they were unnecessarily harsh. He sat on the step of his car looking despondent and miserable. However, he cheered up considerably when we suggested making vodka with the large supply of neat alcohol which he had " won " somewhere on his journey. He was vague about his travelling companion—beyond the fact that he had picked him up on the road some days before, lost and tired. Nobody seemed inclined to turn him away, and

K

as he was very pleasant he was accepted without further question as a new acquisition to the Section.

Sitting about debating our precarious future was becoming an awful bore; everybody else seemed to be more interested in it than we were. It was a relief to be able to do something; so we set about turning the back of our ambulance into a private still and soon proudly presented Ido M . . . with two large bottles of illicitly-made vodka. He was delighted and gave us one; although still lukewarm we all drank a glass. It certainly was not the best vodka, but oddly enough it was not too bad, especially at that moment. Flushed with pride at our achievement it tasted like nectar!

In the early afternoon Bez came down the road calling for us. There was great excitement; what did it mean ? Had the Colonel decided we should go to Bordeaux ? Bez informed us that there were two injured soldiers to be taken to the hospital in Limoges and we were to leave immediately.

It was very curious. Why had he picked on us ? Our car was not first in the line, nor were we in any way the obvious people to send. Was this an official way of giving us a chance to escape ? We debated all these thoughts as we hurriedly prepared our ambulance. René de S . . . came up to us. " Are you going to make a get-away ? " he whispered. " Maybe," we replied. " We'll see what the news is in Limoges."

"Just in case you don't return, I'll give you a letter to my bank in Bordeaux," he said, and hurried away to write it.

The two injured soldiers were brought along to our ambulance and put inside. They had been riding a motor-bicycle, one driving, one on the pillion, and through fatigue and exhaustion the driver had crashed into a car. They were both seriously hurt and were lucky to find doctors and ambulances on the spot.

As we expected, the traffic along the forty kilometres

to Limoges was prodigious. But our progress was not slow, for everyone was tearing along at frantic speed. There were some lorries carrying enormous pontoon boats; we wondered what on earth they could be doing in this part of the world and where they were going, but as always there was no rhyme or reason for anything that was to be found on the roads.

About half-way we were stopped by some villagers, who asked if we had room for a soldier who had collapsed on the road. We went to investigate and found a straggler in great pain. Quickly we got out a stretcher and loaded him into the ambulance.

A crowd gathered, morbidly inspecting our other two men; annoyed by their curiosity we drove them away.

Outside Limoges we found that the main stream of traffic was being diverted round the outskirts of the town. The authorities had wisely decided to force the refugees on further south. We were allowed through the barrier, but not without a thorough examination of our *ordre de mission*; evidently too many of the military had become part of the refugee traffic and were using their uniform as a passport.

The main streets of Limoges were full of people and traffic, but not unduly so, not unlike Sens on the eve of its débâcle there was the unhurried atmosphere of a calm and prosperous town. We reported at the big Hôtel-Dieu, where the two soldiers from Le Gros d'Ognon were accepted, but the stray had to be taken to the Musée des Arts Décoratifs which was being used as a relief hospital.

The two men were unloaded and as we waited for the empty stretchers to be returned we spoke to two doctors. We had all been looking at some aeroplanes overhead, wondering if they were French or German, when one of the officers turned and said, " Do you suppose the 'planes from America will ever arrive ? "

"They won't be in time now," said the other bitterly.

"And England—you are English, aren't you?— what has happened to the English troops?"

We explained that we probably knew less than he, but that we understood a second expeditionary force had been sent and was already fighting on the Seine.

"Too late, always too late," he muttered in reply. Then, quickly, as if to cover his bluntness, he added: "Forgive me if I appear to be outspoken, but when things are so desperate one is apt to make foolish statements."

Our third soldier was accepted in the Musée and disappeared inside. Before moving off we examined the windscreen; there was no question about it now for, despite the strips of sticky paper with which we had covered it, it was rapidly disintegrating. Something had to be done at once; perhaps there would be glass in Limoges, our first stop would have to be at a garage. A small crowd of interested spectators helped us with our examination, but they quickly dispersed when we moved to the back of the car, and no small wonder. The inside was in an appalling condition; it was a horrible mess of blood, vomit and God knows what else. We gazed at it in despair; more than ever we needed a garage. A thorough cleaning and disinfecting was imperative, none of our rough road-side methods would be of any use in its present state.

As we went to shut the doors we noticed that the stray had left his rifle behind. We took it out, intending to hand it over to the porter at the gates of the Musée. A *Médecin-chef* was coming out; he looked suspiciously at the rifle. "What are you doing with that?" he asked.

"It belongs to a soldier we have just brought here," we replied.

"Take it away at once!" he almost shouted.

"We have strict instructions not to carry any arms," we explained.

" I don't care in the very least what your instructions are! " He was really shouting now. " In no circumstances are arms permitted in the hospital. Take it away."

" But what shall we do with it, Sir ? We can't just throw it away." We longed to dispose of the beastly thing.

" Take it to the armoury at the Cavalry Barracks." He strode away.

By now we felt as if we had unlawfully come into possession of a vast magazine and drove off quickly in search of the barracks. After twisting round endless side streets on the outskirts of the town which, to our surprise, we found very empty, we eventually found the barracks. The street in front was crowded with soldiers and lorries, evidently it was a depot to which stragglers reported. We could see at once that there was by no means a lack of organisation and discipline. It was a very heartening sight and not at all what we had expected. We handed over the rifle and went off in search of a garage.

To our relief the big Citroën service station was open. There was a notice outside announcing that it was serving as a refugee centre and the two floors of the vast garage were crammed with cars and sleeping figures. After a certain amount of argument our conversation with the manager proved satisfactory. He could do nothing about the windscreen, he told us that there was not one inch of safety glass to be bought in Limoges—on the other hand he would have the interior cleaned for us, the car greased and the brakes attended to; all this was again imperative. The man who had to do the cleaning was short-tempered and jibbed a little when he saw the condition of the inside. But we pointed out that it was not for our personal comfort that the work needed doing, but for the wounded who had to travel inside.

" If you don't like doing it, lend us the hose," we said.

He quickly overcame his not unnatural qualms. " Of course I'll do it," he replied. " For the wounded I'm prepared to do anything. Forgive me being a bit short with you, but we've been working so hard here it's difficult to know what one is saying."

Then to make sure the job would be done as quickly as possible, we invented a story about having to do some work at the hospital and said we should need the car in an hour. To give colour to our story, we took out a small bag with a professional air, meaning to suggest that it contained medical instruments; then we strode firmly away.

But the bag contained no Aesculapian secret, nothing more than a sponge, soap and scrubbing brush! We had an hour to spare and once again the possibility of a bath! Escape, food—all the things that had filled our minds for days—disappeared into thin air. A hot bath was the only thing we could think of. We wasted many precious minutes enquiring at hotels, only to be greeted with the same reply. " The bathroom is not available—not even for ten minutes—refugees are sleeping in it."

As we hurried from place to place in our fruitless search we were questioned anxiously by refugees who stood in helpless groups in the hotel lobbies. One woman, who had overheard us speaking English, spoke to us in our own language. " Can you please advise me, gentlemen," she said despairingly. " My husband is English and in London. I am French born but naturally I am now English." She waved her passport and went on, " I am here with my sister and her family, they want me to stay in France, but I think I should try to get back to England. We have a car and petrol and I can get to the coast, where I understand there are still boats leaving for England."

Her sister stood by her side arguing wildly. "It's foolish for her to go. She is quite safe with us. Please, messieurs, advise her to stay."

It was a difficult situation but there were no two answers to the question. "If you are English, madam," we replied, "you must try to get back. If you stay, the situation may prove very difficult for you, embarrassing for the English authorities and dangerous for your family here."

She was immensely relieved. "Thank you. I knew it, my duty is with my husband and with his country. I shall leave at once."

With the little bag lying between us we sat in a tiny café and wondered what we should do. Time was getting short.

We unfolded the newspaper we had just bought. The headlines were larger than ever—"THE PLENIPO-TENTIARIES MEET." In the centre of the page was a photograph of the meeting inside a railway carriage. Where had it been? In the Forest of Compiègne. Hitler had been unable to resist the temptation; it was the old railway carriage of Marshal Foch, dragged from the Invalides. There were no details of the terms proposed, no intimation of what would follow. The editorial was almost optimistic; to us the irony was excessive, it was clear that the people of France were being betrayed.

The rest of the front page was filled with the text of Pétain's latest speech: "French people! I have asked the enemy to put an end to hostilities. . . . I took this decision with the stout heart of a soldier because the military situation imposed it. General Weygand had re-grouped our forces and his name alone presaged victory. The line yielded however. . . . From 13th June the request for an armistice was inevitable. The blow surprised you, and I am going to give you the reasons for it. . . . In June, 1918, we had eighty-five

English Divisions with us. . . . In June, 1940, we had ten English Divisions. . . . Not so strong as twenty-two years ago we had also fewer friends, fewer children, too few arms, too few allies. There is the cause of your defeat. . . . Since victory the spirit of pleasure has prevailed over the spirit of sacrifice. . . . As head of the Government I shall remain with you in the dark days. Stand by me. The fight still goes on. It is for France, the soil of her sons.''

We gasped as we finished reading; it was a terrible admission, a terrible indictment. We dissected it statement by statement. It was anti-English; clearly the Government were trying to excuse themselves by putting the blame on their Allies. If the figures quoted were true—and naturally after the Dunkirk episode English support was temporarily reduced—we felt that he might succeed in his campaign. We were afraid of violent resentment and anti-English feeling—we had not seen the slightest evidence of it yet—we only half believed it would come, but we were on the watch for it from this moment. It was the speech of a frightened, senile and devout old man, pathetic in its naïveté and lack of self-confidence. This was not the utterance of a great leader of a great nation, but the cant of a man uncertain of himself explaining France's downfall in terms of her past sins.

The rest of the news was incidental. Many of the French colonies had telegraphed their solidarity to the Government. In the Vosges fighting was still in progress. Brest had been captured; Bordeaux had been bombed. The Admiral in command at Toulon had announced his intention of resisting the enemy to the end. Obviously hostilities had still not ceased; obviously there were still a great many Frenchmen who had no intention that they should cease. Would there be a revolution ? We played with the thought again. Revolutions are made in Paris, we reflected; it was too

late for that now. What of the Army ? They still had
plenty of firearms and material. The populace ? We
decided that an army of French women armed with
knives were still equal to any mechanised army of
Germans. But the people, soldiers as well as civilians,
were too dazed to revolt; moreover, they no longer
had their property to protect, the Germans had
already taken possession. The dangers of an immediate revolution were past, we decided, there was no
organisation.

Our time was getting short. In desperation we asked
the waitress. " A bath ? Why yes, there's the *Bains
Chinois*." We were amazed ! A Chinese bath, what on
earth could that be ? We thought of Japan and the
stories of ladies who scrubbed the clients, and enquired
more closely. Was it a—well—we did not quite know
how to put it—a place of entertainment, in addition ?
The waitress seemed impatient at our stupidity. " It's
the *Bains Chinois*," she repeated, and turned her back
on such provincial ignorance.

We pulled ourselves together; what on earth were we
quibbling about ? A bath had been discovered, be it
Zulu, double Dutch or Polynesian, what did it matter,
there was certainly no harm in trying it. Perhaps it
would prove to be no more than a form of Turkish or
Russian bath with a great deal of vapour, we argued; if
there *were* additional attractions thrown in we could
avoid or cope with them as the occasion demanded,
although we agreed that we felt little like either
" brutal " or " licentious soldiery " at that moment.

With the little bag swinging by our sides we marched
down the road looking for the Place Gambetta. We
asked our way at a chemist's shop. Rather timidly we
enquired if the baths were all right. The chemist was
surprised. " Perfectly all right," was his reply, and we
went on our search feeling we had made fools of
ourselves.

By the time we reached the *Bains Chinois* our imagination had run away with us; we expected to find almost anything. We eyed with suspicion the lady who took our five francs at the door, expected the most fascinating and curious proposals from another who gave us towels and wondered what devilish scenes the rather weary old man, who led us down a passage past a series of doors, was preparing for us. But alas, our excitement was all for nothing; we discovered that a Chinese bath was identical with its European counterpart—just a tub with running hot and cold water. The taps were our only consolation—they were magnificent brass swans, but they held no wonderful secrets, they merely turned the water on and off.

Back at the garage we found the car ready and waiting for us. We thanked the manager and his assistant and departed. One thing we were definite about, we would not leave Limoges without a bottle of disinfectant. There was none left in the Section's stores; we could not always count upon the lucky chance of an open garage, and it was out of the question to leave the car unwashed. Disinfectant had to be found; it was late, well after 7 o'clock, and the few shops that were still open had none. It looked as if we would have to give up our search.

At one point we were hailed by Herrera, Horiot and Sarazinski. They seemed surprised to see us and asked where we were going. We explained that our mission was completed and that we were looking for disinfectant before returning to Le Gros d'Ognon. They had been buying provisions and looking for Sarazinski's brother, who was somewhere in the town, now they were going to eat—would we join them? We said we would look for them when our search was over. In a final attempt we went back to the Hôtel-Dieu, where after a long hunt we found a nun in an operating theatre who presented us with a bottle from her store.

Herrera's ambulance was parked in a square, but there was no sign of our comrades. By now it was getting dark and we decided it was foolish to hang about waiting for them. We had a short conversation with a passer-by from whom we enquired the quickest way out of the town. He explained and then went on to tell us that there had been an air-raid by the Italians the night before, but added, with the utmost contempt, " They only dropped three little aerial torpedoes which didn't even go off! "

Although it was dark the traffic on the road back was still thick and moving quickly. Progress was a dangerous business. A little way outside Limoges one car of our Section loomed up out of the darkness and rushed past us. More followed; it looked as though the Section was on the move. We ran into the middle of the road and shouted, but none of them stopped; we flicked our lights on and off, but there was only a cry of " Lights, lights! " The cars sped on their way.

What had happened ? Had the Colonel made a decision in our absence ? Perhaps the mission to Limoges *had* been given to us as a pretext to cover our escape and, not expecting us to return, the unit had moved off. But there was Herrera and the other two in Limoges, and then whoever had called out " Lights! " had recognised us and spoken in English. If there had been a general move either Herrera would have been informed before or somebody would have stopped to tell us. In any case, messages would have been left at Le Gros d'Ognon; we decided to continue.

As we drove on we suddenly realised that we had entirely forgotten about Bordeaux and our papers. It was really too absurd. For three days now we had argued and plotted, and then when a sudden chance had occurred to make a get-away, we had been too absorbed in our work and a bottle of disinfectant to remember it. If we had disappeared for a day, even two, with the excuse of having been sent on to some other town and delayed by traffic on the road, nobody would have even questioned the veracity of our story. At all events, we were quite happy to be driving back to Le Gros d'Ognon and to let things work out for themselves.

About twenty kilometres from home we overtook an enormous convoy of empty Paris buses. We were curious and wanted to know where they were going and whom they were to carry—civilians or soldiers. After the busy scene in the Limoges barracks we thought that perhaps an attempt was being made to gather together the straggling army. A long motorised unit approaching from the opposite direction caused a great confusion and prevented us from stopping and finding out.

As we turned up the lane it was a great relief to see that the main bulk of our unit was still there; evidently the cars that had passed us were on some mission. Everybody was asleep, there was no chance of finding out if a move had been announced or contemplated during the night or in the morning. We prowled round the silent cars; van A . . . was still there, ' the Grand-mother of Snow-White ' had not returned, nor was there any sign of our other lost comrades. As we climbed into the back of our now almost unbearably disinfected car, we wondered whether anybody would be surprised to see us in the morning.

Saturday, *22nd June*

WHEN WE AWOKE there was a series of surprises. ' Snow-White ' had returned and was strutting down the lane with a golden retriever. Secondly, under a tree close to our ambulance were two large armoured radio cars. Then word came that we were leaving in an hour.

We were astonished to see ' Snow-White ' at all, but the presence of the dog was even stranger. He confessed that he had spent the day with his wife, had brought

back his favourite dog, also a gun and a good supply of
cartridges.

His escapade, which had passed unnoticed, was impertinent enough, but to return with a shot-gun was
outrageous. Remembering the episode of the rifle at
Limoges, we begged him to get rid of it at the first
opportunity. He was quite well aware that if he kept it
the enemy would have the right to shoot us all out of
hand.

Amid such hopeless chaos capture never seemed very
remote. But he was undaunted; he was proud of the
gun, but whether he intended to hunt Germans or
rabbits we were not told.

We watched to see what would happen. It seemed
impossible that so flagrant a violation of discipline
could pass without comment, without correction. But
Herrera said nothing and ' Snow-White ' cunningly
concealed his gun and cartridges. Obviously discipline
was a word of yesterday.

The radio cars had arrived during the night. We
walked over to talk to the crews to see what news they
might have. They told us that they were a liaison between headquarters and the front line; that the Germans were advancing rapidly and that the situation
was hopeless. Messages were still coming through from
the front, here and there fighting was being bravely
carried on by isolated units, but on the whole the
Germans were sweeping through a deserted countryside. We asked whether they listened to news bulletins.
" We always listen to London," they said, " it's the only
station which tells us anything—even then it's little
enough. If you are still here when the next bulletin
comes we will turn it on for you." They tuned in to
show that they were serious, but it was 10 a.m. and
London was broadcasting its morning service.

" Have you heard anything this morning ? "

" We listened to the news in French from London at

8 o'clock. The Armistice must be near. The French
Commission has reported to the Government and has
left for Rome. *Les salauds!* Our troops are still fighting
and winning on the Italian frontier; we can't give up
anything to the Italians. Our only hope is General de
Gaulle in London, but how is anyone to get there?
Most of the troops don't even know about his revolt."

The whistle blew for our departure. We thanked
them and returned to our ambulance.

Bez was walking swiftly down the lane. He caught
sight of us and stopped dead in his tracks. He smiled
broadly, said " Good morning," looked as though he
had more to say, but changed his mind and walked
straight on. There was no question but that he *was*
immensely surprised to see us. Now we knew that they
had not expected us to return.

Herrera gave us a route; we were going to St.
Yrieix, ninety kilometres to the south. It was on the
direct route to Toulouse; this was another indication
that the unit might be going home. We began by losing
our way in Limoges and continued to do so throughout
the journey. At 1 o'clock we reached the level crossing
at the entrance to St. Yrieix, but nobody seemed to
know where the hospital was. We turned and started on
a tour of the countryside; we careered along lanes and
through villages; everyone's temper getting shorter as
their appetite increased. About 2.30 we found ourselves back at the level crossing and to our disgust discovered the hospital only two hundred yards away on
the left.

It was a large gloomy-looking building labelled
" *Hôpital Complémentaire*," and the carpenters were
still fixing this sign over the gateway. We drove into
the large courtyard and there we found the ambulances
which had passed us the previous evening.

We started out gloomily for the town to find food;
it began to rain. Many of the shop windows were full

of the local pottery set out to catch the eyes of tourists, but now it seemed quite out of place. Alternating with pottery shops were *pâtisseries* full of the other local speciality, the *madeleine*. Then we saw the Hôtel des Voyageurs; this was the obvious place to eat.

We sat ourselves down at a table in a long low dining-room which might have been an 18th-century Assembly Room in any English provincial town. Diffidently we asked what we would be allowed to eat; to our surprise there appeared to be a considerable choice. Probably through habit the old serving woman offered us every-thing of which she could think. As it was already after 3 o'clock our appetite and our hopes both ran high. We began tentatively by suggesting a beef-steak.

" But would you prefer a *tournedos*, of course with *sauce béarnaise* ? Potatoes ? I suggest *pommes lyonnaises*. Then a salad, and perhaps *petits pois* ? Naturally *hors d'œuvre* to begin with; then a *potage*. I'll bring you the wine list."

We ordered it all, our eyes falling out of our heads, mouths agape. A few minutes later the *patronne* herself came in.

" I can manage to give you a sardine, some beef and a salad. I'm afraid you've been misled," she added apologetically.

We were disappointed but realised that we were lucky to get anything. " You seem to have plenty of food here all the same," we said. She explained that the hordes of refugees had not taken the road through St. Yrieix, and that although up till now supplies had been adequate, they were already impossible to obtain.

We ate heartily in an attempt to control our rising irritability. We felt it was petty to be irritable at this moment, but it was the result of increasing incoherence. Everyone was drifting and we realised that it might well go on thus for weeks. No one knew why we were in St. Yrieix, for apparently neither nurses, doctors nor ambulances were wanted at the hospital, nor had we been expected. We felt a sense of injustice. ' Snow-White ' had taken French leave without being censured; Ido M . . . had disobeyed all orders with no serious reprimand; everyone seemed to be doing as they liked; whilst we, by asking, had only been regarded as a nuisance. Here we were, perhaps prisoners of the French or Germans at any minute, with nothing but French military papers to prove our identity. We had not even the immunity of members of the International Red Cross—we were simply French soldiers.

The decision was taken. We walked back to the hospital in the rain determined to find Bez or the Colonel and again seek permission to leave. The courtyard of the hospital was almost deserted; there was no sign of anyone we wanted to find. Even Herrera, it appeared, had returned to Limoges with Sarazinski, who wanted to see his brother once more; an odd trip for our *brigadier* to make. We found van A . . . and told him of our decision; he welcomed it and announced his intention of following us with van B . . . We told him to ask permission.

The nurses were miserably sheltering from the rain in their uncomfortable charabanc, knitting, sleeping or reading. We could not go without consulting them. The sister was the first to speak.

" Well, what are you going to do ? "

" We have decided to ask for twenty-four hours' leave to go to Bordeaux. We must go while the Embassy is still there; besides we need a new wind-screen. Then, too, we must find our headquarters and communicate our whereabouts. Time is short, we must go now; we are looking for the Colonel to ask permission—if he still won't give it we shall have to *filer à l'anglaise*."

" I'm glad to hear it. I think you are quite right. But you can do something for us, too. We must get a letter to the Red Cross; our situation here is intolerable.

If you want any help with the Colonel please use this
as an additional reason for leaving; we will support
you. I will write the letter straight away; please let us
know as soon as anything is decided."

We left her to write the letter and went to see about
petrol for ourselves and van A . . . Our tank was
half-empty but we did not want to break into our
reserve so soon. We looked for the mechanic—the
breakdown-lorry was locked. Van A . . ., however,
had another idea. He knew of a drum hidden in
Grignard's ambulance and proposed that we should
both fill up from this; Grignard, after all, was staying
with the Section so it would not matter. Now we were
ready for the journey.

Pierre D . . ., Ido M . . . and René de S . . . returned
from the village where they had been feasting on
madeleines. M . . . was rather drunk and inclined to be
liberal with a bottle of Grand Marnier. We wondered
whether to tell them of our decision, but for the moment
there seemed no point. We could not take the whole of
the Section with us, that would merely reduce our
own chances of getting through. When de S . . . was
alone we decided to whisper to him our plan; he was
the member of our Section for whom we felt the most
sympathy and respect, the only person we would be
sorry to leave at this moment. He encouraged our
departure; it was the best course for us to take. We
offered to do anything for him during our twenty-four
hours in Bordeaux; he started to write letters of introduction, in case we met with difficulties, and a letter to
his family.

At last, about 6 o'clock, we saw the Colonel and
Bez walking together across the courtyard. It was the
opportunity for which we had been waiting. With van
A . . . we went to meet them.

" *Mon Colonel*, our request of Thursday afternoon is
still unanswered. We feel that it is essential for us to go

to Bordeaux and consult our Embassy. If we stay, without papers, we may only be an embarrassment to you. Will you grant us twenty-four hours' leave ? We can be back with the unit at the latest on Monday."

" I am sorry, messieurs, it is not in my power to grant your request; the General will probably be visiting us to-morrow and then we can ask him."

" *Mon Colonel*, it is a matter of great urgency. . . ." Bez, a representative of the Army and not a member of the medical profession, understood our renewed request and pressed our case; then the sister, seeing our difficulties, added her voice to the rest and handed us the letter.

The Colonel thought for a moment, then a smile passed across his face. " All right, messieurs, if you wish to go I will shut my eyes. But you go on your own responsibility. I cannot give you an *ordre de mission*. You may take one ambulance and don't leave before to-morrow morning. In any case come and see me again in the morning before you leave; I too have a letter for you to take to Bordeaux."

Our faces fell; to-morrow morning might be already too late. However, the permission was granted; there was no point in insisting further.

" Thank you, *Mon Colonel*. Since we cannot have an *ordre de mission*, may we at least have a requisition order for a wind-screen ? "

Again the Colonel thought for a moment, then told Bez to write out the order. This presented no difficulties. Then the Colonel went on his way, followed by Bez.

" I'm not going to wait till to-morrow morning; I'm going now." Van A . . . was the first to utter the thought that had occurred to us all. The sister winked and said, " He's right. You have got the Colonel's permission; he may change his mind before to-morrow morning."

" But his letter ? "

" *Merde à la petite amie du Colonel!* "

That settled it. We would leave at once and drive as far as possible by daylight; we could then be in Bordeaux by 7 o'clock in the morning. We shook the nurses warmly by the hand and thanked them for their kindness.

" Good-bye," we whispered to each in turn, lest anybody should discover our project.

The evening meal was being served in the village and everyone had gone to eat. The *Médecin-chef* of the hospital came out and asked us to move some cars which had been untidily parked. While we were attending to this and extricating our own ambulance, we saw van A . . . and van B . . . slip out of the gates in their car. Thinking they had left for Bordeaux we bundled into our ambulance as quickly as we could and slipped out after them.

ESCAPE

Saturday, 22nd June—Wednesday, 26th June

WE DROVE DOWN the main street of St. Yrieix with the guilty, elated feeling of truants; it was a feeling we could not control. We had been given permission to leave—permission of a kind—yet it was difficult to believe that it had substance. Some members of the Section were strolling along, we waved casually to them, they waved back and seemed not at all surprised to see us. Perhaps they thought that we were on some mission.

At the top of the town the road forked. We asked some townspeople for the Bordeaux road; mutely they pointed to the right, uninterested, perhaps they had been asked that question too often in the past few days. But with the consciences of truants we were surprised that they were not suspicious, surprised that we were not asked for papers—an *ordre de mission*.

In great haste we hurried out of the town, and as the countryside unfolded and revealed itself before us we realised that at last our days of questioning were over. Our Section was behind us, our future lay in our own hands, our own decisions were the only decisions that mattered now. But our hearts were not light during our last stage on the road to Bordeaux.

It was not raining when we started, but quite soon a cloud went over the sun, and in a few drops pattering, there fell from out of the sky the first heavy rain of the summer.

We had to stop. We did not want to; we wanted to drive on and on until there were many kilometres between us and St. Yrieix. But our wind-screen finally dissolved and rain and glass poured in upon us. It ran down the dashboard and started to get inside the

instruments. Something had to be done, so we covered the hole with an old towel.

We had driven " all out," but there was no sign of van A . . . If he had been ahead we ought to have caught sight of him already. Had he changed his mind or taken a different road ? We were a little surprised that he had not waited for us. However, there was no turning back now.

We drove on through miles and miles of beautiful countryside, which appeared almost deserted. For a change there was not even any traffic on the road. For over forty miles the only vehicle we passed was a cart driven by a solitary man. Even the inhabitants of the little villages were not to be seen. It was a curious sensation.

We calculated that Bordeaux could not be reached much before midnight. By then it would be too late to find a place to sleep and in any case this was probably impossible. So we decided to spend our last few francs on a bed and a bath in Périgueux; we wanted to appear presentable in Bordeaux. But this was not to be. A few kilometres before the town we were stopped by an officer at the gates of the military hospital.

" What are you doing ? Where are you going ? " he demanded.

" To Bordeaux by the direct route, *en mission*," we replied.

" You are not to stop in Périgueux; take the outside road and pass through the town as quickly as you can."

" Has there been a bombardment, Sir ? " We sensed something going wrong already.

" No, nothing like that; merely that there are a hundred thousand refugees in the town. There's not a bed, nor food and you can't drive through the streets."

Although our hopes were dashed we were secretly resolved to stop and see for ourselves, so we said, " Thank you," and drove on.

As we drew near to the town we realised that the officer had been right. There was not an inch of room on the pavements or on the streets. The pedestrians, for the most part refugees, looked like a vast, depressed crowd of holiday-makers. They were promenading slowly, gazing with melancholy disinterestedness at the shop windows and the beautiful old houses. We forced our way through and parked in the big square. Here, fixed to the trees, were instructions to Dutch and Belgian refugees. Then as we looked more closely at the faces of the passers-by and listened to their voices we realised that after all these weeks we had at last caught up with the original wave which had swamped the roads of France.

The first hotel at which we enquired had no food left. In the second the *patron* told us that in time he could find a table. He added that there was no hope of finding a bed in Périgueux itself nor in any of the towns or villages on our road. Every town had been occupied by refugees and now that, since two days, their flight had been halted, they were forced to remain where they were.

Then he looked at us enquiringly: " I suppose you have got your papers to get into the Gironde ? "

That was a bit startling, but we looked very casual and said, " Naturally. Is there any difficulty ? "

" Difficulty! Why yes, the *département* is closed, and it is impossible to get into Bordeaux. It has been so for three or four days now. No civilians are allowed on the road; there are half a million refugees there already, and food is short."

We went into the dining-room feeling thoroughly gloomy. How were we going to get into a closed *département* and a forbidden city with only a requisition order for a wind-screen ? Without a moment's hesitation, before even the food had been ordered, we called for writing-paper. Within ten minutes, after two or three

attempts, we had forged for ourselves what we hoped
was a convincing *ordre de mission*. It was a composite
document based on others which we had been given,
but under the circumstances, and to make it completely effective, we added: "*Par route directe.*" It was
signed with a passable imitation of Bez's handwriting.
It ran as follows:

Ordre de Mission Militaire

S.S.B.M.

No. Voiture 30403

Chauffeurs: Freeman et Cooper
    Pour aller à Bordeaux et retour par route
    directe réquisitionner une glace Sécurit
    Citroën, et porter une lettre à la S.S.B.M.
      le 22 juin 1940
      l'Officer Ct. la S.S.A. 17

367e. Cie. Auto de C.A.   P. Bez.

Towards the end of our frugal meal we noticed a
solitary young soldier at the next table. He had been
writing for a long while and intermittently staring at
us. As we rose to go he leapt to his feet, saluted and
introduced himself.

"Aspirant de C . . . of the Foreign Legion."

Mysteriously and in a state of great agitation he
asked: "Are you going to Bordeaux ? "

We said that we were. "Then may I speak to you for
a few moments ? I have something I want to ask you."

Thinking he had something urgent to say and
realising that it did not matter whether we left the
town immediately or half an hour later, we went with
him to the café next door.

He first enquired our nationality, and when he learnt
that we were English asked if we were on our way home.
We told him that there was no question of our going
home unless hostilities ceased in France and England
went on fighting alone.

"France is no longer fighting," he replied bitterly.

" The war is over here, we are beaten. But I do not intend to give up, nor do thousands of others."

As he went on talking it became clear that he was desperate. In his determination to get to England he had run away from his regiment. He begged us to take him to Bordeaux, if necessary to hide him inside our ambulance. Again and again he repeated that the Army was not responsible for the collapse, and apologised for the French for " having let the English down."

It was a great shock, evidently the spirit of the tank drivers at Allogny still prevailed. We had not realised till this moment that French soldiers were really thinking of escaping to England.

We debated for a moment what to do, while he kept on imploring. But we realised that our own chances of getting to Bordeaux were slender enough and selfishly we had to refuse him. The excuses we gave must have sounded plausible, for he took them in good part.

As we left the café a large crowd was gathered round the loud-speaker waiting for the news bulletin. We hurried past, fearful of what we might hear. If the Armistice had been signed there was no point in learning of it in Périgueux—better to go on in ignorance to Bordeaux.

The *patron* ran after us and spoke in English: " Good-bye, messieurs, good luck. If you should get back to England tell them not to think too badly of us. This is a terrible moment for a Frenchman who is proud of his country and his honour."

It was practically dark when we drove out of the town. The streets were almost empty, the cafés closed, there was not a light to be seen. It contrasted so oddly with the crowds of less than two hours before that we wondered whether a curfew had been imposed.

There was little traffic on the road, but we were alarmed and startled when, for the first time for weeks, we met cars with their headlights blazing impudently through the darkness. When we saw the first car we thought that perhaps the driver had gone mad; then when others followed and we realised that all cars had their lights on we wondered if this was a sign that the Armistice had already been declared. Finally, with a shock, we realised that we were so far south as to be outside the war zone.

After about thirty kilometres we saw an ambulance parked facing us on the grass verge on our side of the road. As we passed we recognised it as one of our own cars and drew up immediately. We were hailed by van A . . . and van B . . . In the explanations that followed we discovered that when they had driven out of the gates of the hospital at St. Yrieix they had gone to the kitchen, thinking that we were following. When they missed us they hurried after us as quickly as possible and must have passed through Périgueux while we were in the hotel. We parked beside them and arranged to start together on the last stage of our journey early next morning.

*   *   *

It was still raining when we awoke and our first job was to write another false permit for our companions. They then led the way and when, after some kilometres, we reached the boundary of the Gironde and saw an armed guard barring our way we spent a few anxious moments. Van A . . . produced his false permit, which was carefully examined; it worked like a charm and they were allowed through immediately, ours was not even demanded.

We stopped about 8 o'clock for a few minutes at a café in Libourne. We sat miserably drinking coffee; this was all we could get, the *patron* told us that there was no bread in the town. Little groups of people were talking excitedly. Suddenly, in a far corner, we saw an enormous soldier with a very familiar face, in the middle of the largest group: it was Raimu. This time he had a strange audience; strained, worried faces were listening to what he was saying. We could not hear what was said, but we feared that the worst had happened. We ran out to find a newspaper.

There, splashed across the front page, was: " ARMISTICE SIGNED." Beyond the fact that it had been signed at 6 o'clock on the previous evening there was no further information, no hint of the terms which had been accepted.

It seemed ironical that the Armistice should have been signed just at the moment when the Colonel was telling us not to worry. Now there was not a moment to be lost; perhaps we were already too late. We bundled into our cars and drove towards Bordeaux at breakneck speed.

A few miles out of Libourne we were stopped by an officer of the Air Force, who was in charge of some lorries parked beside the road. He asked if we could attend to one of his men who had been wounded by shrapnel. With some misgiving we unwound the *pansement individuel*, which the man had tied on himself. Fortunately the wound was not serious, but it needed cleaning. We had no antiseptic and were regretting the large store of pure alcohol which Ido M . . . had " won," when we suddenly remembered that we had turned a quantity of this into vodka. We found the bottle and solemnly proceeded to wash the wound; some salve and a clean bandage completed the operation. The man seemed greatly relieved; he had been terrified that the wound was septic. His friends who had gathered round him to watch the performance were also immensely relieved and behaved like a family after a successful *accouchement*.

The officer was very grateful and asked if there was anything he could do for us. Thinking that, after all, Bordeaux might not be the end of our journey, and knowing the lack of supplies, we asked if he could spare us some petrol. This was not quite the reply he had anticipated, for he told us confidentially that he was escaping with material and a ground staff to Toulouse and needed all the petrol he had. However, we had helped him and he would be happy to help us; so both our tanks were filled with about forty litres of aviation spirit.

As we drove off we shouted back to our patient: "You can say you are the first soldier of this war who has had his wounds washed in vodka."

We were stopped again by armed sentries guarding the big suspension bridge over the Garonne leading into Bordeaux. Again van A . . . produced his false permit; again it worked, and by 9.30 a.m. we were in the city itself.

We found our way to the little square where van A . . .'s father's office should have been. We waited anxiously below with van B . . . while he went upstairs. Would the family still be in Bordeaux? Or would they too have fled? It would mean a great deal to the three of us to find a friendly house at such a moment.

We seemed to wait endlessly. When van A . . . reappeared he was beside himself with excitement. "They may still be here," he said, "they were seen yesterday. Anyhow, I've got the address of their flat."

In high spirits we started off again through the crowded streets of Bordeaux. Along the Rue Ste. Croix, up the Cours Victor-Hugo, down the fashionable Rue Ste. Cathérine to the Place de la Comédie, then across the Place des Quinconces to the little street in which the family now lived.

Bordeaux looked unhappy, resentful but intact. Cars and tramcars were running busily along the *quais* and through the main streets, people swarmed everywhere; the café terraces were overflowing, so were the pavements, the streets were full of litter. Everywhere cheap meals were advertised and many places had become

Centres d'accueil for refugees. Number-plates of every nationality could be seen on cars. The Tour St. Michel stood on its mound protecting the mummies in the crypt.

It was a Sunday morning and there were crowds outside every church, especially outside the Cathedral. The Place de la Comédie, the sad and dignified centre of the town where so many beautiful streets meet, was besieged by a rabble. Crowds thronged the portico of the theatre, the temporary Chambre des Députés. Was the Chamber in session, perhaps actually ratifying the Armistice ? We had to hurry on now.

The Place des Quinconces, the large square open to the river, was packed with cars of every size and shape. It was half prepared for a fair; there were several half-built, abandoned pavilions now battered and bruised through neglect or misuse. Everything was wet, resentful of its spoilt beauty.

We stopped at last, about 10 o'clock, outside a house in a little street and van A . . . ran upstairs to see if his family were still there.

There was really no time to waste now. With the Armistice signed there were many things we had to discover. Were we already enemy alien members of an Army which had signed a truce ? We did not even know the terms of the truce. What ought we to do ? What could we do ? No regulations would provide for two such anomalous beings as ourselves. The hotel where Miss Bennet had agreed to leave, if possible, news for us, was on the other side of the square. Telling van B . . . that we would be back in a few minutes, we hurried across.

The lobby of the hotel was crowded with people of many nationalities. Piles of luggage were everywhere. Everyone was preparing to depart, but with no clear destination. Those who were lucky enough still to possess both a car and petrol were loading up, but little did many of them know that it was almost impossible to leave the town by any road because of many un-scheduled formalities. A train full of English people had left for St. Jean-de-Luz earlier in the morning, now there was no further means of escape.

Those English people who, for one reason and another, had missed the train, were clamouring for help and information. Dutch, Czechs, Poles and Belgians, caught like rats in a trap, were equally frantic. No one felt safe; even the Government had moved to Vichy.

What were these English people still doing in Bordeaux ? For that matter what were they doing in France at all ? We heard horrifying stories of escapes from Paris ; but ought any of these adventures to have been necessary ? Even at the time we had left for the front all the English in Paris must have known that the wives of many officials had already been sent home. It must also have been known that since the middle of May the Embassy staff was prepared to leave the capital at any minute. Admittedly, for political reasons, the facts were not published and no official order was issued to the English compelling them to go home. Nevertheless, emergency travel facilities from Le Havre and St. Malo had been advertised and, despite the lack of an authoritative statement, common-sense should have told them that by remaining they could only be an embarrassment to themselves, to their own country and to France. There were exceptions. Naturally, business men representing important allied interests were bound to remain till the end. But Bordeaux at this moment was full of people who had no right to be still in France, and of panicky expatriates railing against the country of their choice. The majority of them had been either too lazy or too stupid to leave before.

They were behaving unpleasantly ; it was an

unfortunate scene. Any discomfort they were suffering
was entirely their own fault and they were imperilling
those who had been obliged to stay. This situation was
not helped by the absence of all authorities.

The British Embassy was closed ; the Ambassador
and his staff had left three days previously. The British
Consulate, too, was closed. At this moment, the
strangest and most terrifying in the history of the
Anglo-French Entente, England had no diplomatic
representative in the provisional capital of France.
The authorities had seen fit to depart first, abandoning
to their fate hundreds of English subjects.

The Dutch, the Poles, the Belgians—all had representatives to take care of their nationals. Only the
English had left.

Provisionally, some assistance was being given by
the American Consulate, but it was limited. A notice
informed English subjects that so long as the sovereign
authority of the French Government was still recognised, the American Embassy was unable to afford
them protection. It was thought that an English
Consul—the only one remaining in the whole of
France—might still be in St. Jean-de-Luz, where there
were said to be boats. But there was no longer any
means of getting there, the last train had left.

That we had arrived so late in Bordeaux was our
own responsibility and as such we accepted the con-
sequences. We did not want to join this band of howling refugees. We must and could look after ourselves.

It was not until this moment that the thought of
escaping to England entered our heads. If we had
arrived too late to find a boat . . . *tant pis !* Whatever
happened to us from now on we could not, in fairness
to our friends, ask them for help.

What then ?

There was something almost funny about the calm
with which we traced out every possibility. To stay

could only mean to be taken prisoner, or at the best to be interned by the French. We thought of hiding in a hayloft till the end of the war. But whose hayloft? It would have to be a friendly one. We went through the list of our friends with whom we might seek refuge. Should we drive straight on to Toulouse? Aix-en-Provence? Puy-de-Dôme? But what use would it be? Our reason told us that we could not embarrass even our most intimate French friends with our presence at this minute. Nor did we know the whereabouts of any of our English friends.

Escape seemed the only solution. But where to? How were we to get to England? There were no boats bound for England in Bordeaux harbour we had been told. Perhaps via St. Jean-de-Luz? After all, we had enough petrol and a Consul was supposed to be there. On the other hand we might already be too late to catch a boat. Added to this was the difficulty of having no papers; the authorities might stop us leaving Bordeaux. Perhaps it was worth risking all the same, perhaps some French authority could be induced to give us the requisite permits. The Red Cross? we had a letter to deliver to the Présidente.

Why not return to our Section? For that our papers were in order and without question there would be a great deal of work to do. There was the question of our nationality. We were not yet " Germans " like our Dutch, Belgian and Norwegian comrades. With the best will in the world neither Bez nor our commanding officers could protect us. We could only prove an embarrassment to them, too.

If the worst happened we could always start back to St. Yrieix and take another road once we had got outside Bordeaux. We had enough petrol to cover at least four hundred kilometres. If everything failed we always had our legs. The Pyrenees? Spain? Portugal? With no papers and no visas we could hardly hope to be allowed through. The paths across the Pyrenees, we reckoned, must be too well worn by now. Our only hope would be to pose as ambulant onion sellers. Mentally, we went through the whole trudge. It was wildly exciting in thought, but almost certainly cheerless in fact. We only had two one pound notes and ten French francs in our pockets. What a lot of onions we would have to sell !

St. Jean-de-Luz was our best hope. We must try and get to St. Jean-de-Luz. If that failed there were always the Pyrenees as a last resort.

With these thoughts in our mind, we went back to the van A . . . 's about an hour later.

We found van B . . . waiting for us. He called out excitedly, " They're here. Isn't it wonderful ! Come along ! "

We went up the stairs and found van A . . . 's parents waiting at the door to welcome us.

To judge from the reception they gave us, we might have been old friends of the family. It was an extraordinary display of kindness and hospitality. They never for a moment discussed or referred to their own troubles, which must have been grave. Their only thought was of the future of their son and of his three friends. They offered us money and every possible assistance. Theirs was true generosity.

We all discussed the situation and what should be done. But the more we talked the more we realised that, beyond an attempt to reach St. Jean-de-Luz or some other port, there was nothing to be done. Mr. van A . . . told us that there had been an English destroyer in the harbour the day before, but that he thought it had sailed. There were no longer any boats leaving Bordeaux. The Germans were dropping mines at the mouth of the river every night and their troops were already at Royan guarding the northern bank. To escape from Bordeaux by water certainly seemed

L

out of the question. Our final decision was to deliver the letter to the Red Cross, ask what we should do and, failing a satisfactory answer, to drive in our two ambulances straight to St. Jean-de-Luz.

Mme. van A . . . broke in on our deliberations. "Whatever you decide to do, you can't do it without food. I'm going to take you all off to lunch. One has to get to the restaurants before 12 o'clock nowadays or there is no food left." It was a surprise suddenly to find that we did not have to think about food for ourselves.

We had to go out to lunch so we thought that we might as well walk round by the river to see if, by chance, the English ship was still there. As we walked across the Place we looked half-heartedly towards the river. It seemed more than improbable that an English ship would still be there; we heard nothing about it at the hotel nor at the American Consulate.

"No," said Mr. van A . . . "I see no sign of it; it must have sailed."

We went slowly across the Place, then, over a row of Customs sheds on the bank, we saw a tiny flag flapping limply in the rain. We looked again; there was no doubt about it. It was the White Ensign.

Our hearts rose as we approached. English soldiers with fixed bayonets were on guard. A destroyer was still at anchor.

We walked straight up to the first sentry : "Have you a Consul on board? We're English and need advice."

He was too surprised to answer "Yes" or "No." He simply turned his head and called in a broad Lancashire accent to some of the sailors on deck : "Send for the interpreter, will you?"

In time a young army lieutenant appeared. We explained our case to him, he examined our papers, looked puzzled and disappeared back into the ship to find the Captain.

He reappeared almost immediately with a senior naval officer. We explained our case again ; he looked more and more perplexed and not unnaturally, for our story must have appeared very strange. After all, it was difficult to explain in a few sentences why two Englishmen were in the French Army. However, the lieutenant stated that our papers seemed genuine ; the photographs on them corresponded with our faces, our fluent English broke down more suspicions and, as we continued with our guileless story, their surprise finally changed to unrestrained amusement. It was not surprising, for the more we told them the more ridiculous it all sounded.

" You do seem in a bit of a mess," the naval officer said, " but it's a bit awkward, for there's absolutely no room on board."

A really grotesque and naïve scene of English politeness followed. " Oh, we don't want to bother you," we replied, " we merely came to see if you had a Consul aboard who could tell us what to do. We can quite well drive on to St. Jean-de-Luz and look for a boat, we have petrol and an ambulance."

We really were behaving in a very odd way. Having decided that we must at all costs now try and get to England, here we were almost declining a potential offer of transport.

The officer was still more amused. " I don't think that would be a very good idea," he said. " I think we had better go and talk to the Captain of this ship."

He went back on board, leaving us to follow with the lieutenant. We hastily explained to the van A . . .'s what was happening and arranged to meet them in a short while at the restaurant. " See if you can arrange anything for the two boys," the father said.

Then we followed the lieutenant aboard H.M.S. ———. We met the Captain on the deck. Briefly, the first officer told him the facts. He thought for a moment and then told us that somewhere he would find room for us ; he was sailing almost immediately. " You're the last two I can possibly take. I have got almost four hundred people on a ship built for half that number."

We immediately started to explain that we were quite prepared to drive on to St. Jean-de-Luz rather than embarrass him. He seemed to think that was out of the question, that the possibility of finding a boat was highly improbable and that anyhow it was far too dangerous for two Englishmen to be wandering about France in uniform.

Then, as if the matter was completely settled, he dropped formality and became a host. He took us below to his cabin and dazed us even more with a large " pink gin."

It was awful to abuse this generous hospitality, but it was our duty to press the case of our two Dutch friends. We could not possibly desert them now. We used every possible argument to get them taken aboard too, or at least accommodated on some other ship. We pointed out that they would be two additional soldiers for the Allies and that both were well known to the Dutch authorities in London. But our arguments were of no avail.

The Captain was extremely sympathetic, but inevitably had to refuse. It was not purely due to lack of room, it was due to a variety of reasons and we believed that he felt as badly about making the decision as we did at hearing it. " You're jolly lucky to find us here, but I'm afraid I can only take English subjects. I can't set a dangerous precedent. All you can do is to advise them to take the risk and go to St. Jean-de-Luz."

While we were talking the Naval Control official came in. He was a civilian and we understood that he was an English business man in Bordeaux who had taken on these additional duties since the war. " The

Admiral has opened up the Consulate, he's clearing things up, I'm going back to fetch him soon."

We were getting more confused every minute. The first naval officer to whom we had spoken was a commander, the Captain a lieutenant-commander, in addition there was an army officer and now an admiral —all on one little destroyer. At this stage we gave up thinking who they were and what they were doing. The Captain left the cabin with the official and we had a few minutes to collect our thoughts. Suddenly we realised how much we still had to do before we sailed. The absence of the Admiral in the town meant that there would be some delay. When the Captain returned we asked permission to go ashore and collect our belongings.

" Well, don't be long ; remember that we are due to sail at any minute. You go on your own responsibility."

The Commander with a wry expression put his head round the door and said to the Captain : " The Admiral has got a surprise for you. He sends his compliments and says will it be possible to take three English women on board ? Apparently it is important. They have been of the very greatest assistance to us and something must be done about them."

There were a lot of knowing looks all round and we imagined that they might be Secret Service agents. We were thrilled. Three lady " spies " ! We had visions of glamorous Mata Haris in black velvet and pearls. But the Captain was not so thrilled : " God, I'm terrified of women. What can I do with them ? Where shall I put them ? I suppose they will have to have my cabin."

The Naval Control official whom we met on the quayside warned us not to stay in the town for more than an hour. We went straight to the van A . . .'s but they had not yet returned from lunch. So we left a note for them telling them to come to the ship, took our ambulance and went off to deliver the nurses' letter at the Red Cross.

It was Sunday and there was nobody at the office, but the *concierge* gave us a number of addresses where we might find the Présidente. We tore through Bordeaux from place to place but with no success, eventually arriving at the Hôtel Splendide, where it was thought she might be lunching. But it was hopeless to look for one individual among the thousands who were trying to feed. Queues were forming in every corner, there was a fight for tables ; there were not enough waiters ; the *maîtres d'hotel* were distracted. Three or four enormous rooms were filled with people and even on the terrace outside there was no empty space.

We got back into our ambulance, left the letter at the offices of the Red Cross and drove back to the ship.

We started to unload our few belongings and carried them on board. We asked an officer if our small stock of provisions, our stretchers and our drum of petrol would be of any use. He told us that with the limited sleeping accommodation and the number of people on board they would be, but that we should ask the chief engineer about the petrol. He sent two A.B.'s to help us unload. Very soon the ambulance was almost bare ; even the few things we discarded the sailors begged from us. They were especially delighted with our dungarees. The only thing we left behind was the petrol. It seemed remarkable to us that the engineer should not want it, but we learnt the reason later. Our small cellar—two bottles of red wine, one bottle of brandy, and the remaining cherries in brandy—we sent as a present to the Captain. The remnants of our vodka we kept for ourselves.

We stood on deck dismally looking at our deserted ambulance which had been our home for the month of June.

Then the worst moment arrived. Our two comrades came running on to the *quai*.

" Well, what's happened ? "

" We're going," we said.

" And us ? "

" It's impossible, they can't take you."

There was a dreadful silence. Too many people were watching ; we could not continue this painful conversation from the deck. By now everybody knew our story. As we walked across the gangway we felt the whole ship was watching our meeting.

We explained as best we could what had happened, but they were silent. It made things seem much worse, but there was nothing they could say. It must have been the most awful blow to them. But they took it wonderfully ; there were no recriminations. Beyond their overwhelming disappointment they gave no hint of there being an alternative. They shook us by the hand and wished us luck.

We hastily discussed what they should do. In view of the Captain's message their best chance seemed to be in St. Jean-de-Luz. We asked them to report our departure, take charge of our ambulance and do what they thought fit with it. We handed over our requisition order for the wind-screen, the keys of the car and the drum of petrol. They drove off immediately.

As we walked back to the ship we saw a silent group of French officers staring dejectedly at the English destroyer.

Seeing two soldiers in French uniform about to embark they beckoned to us.

" Where are you going ? "

" To England."

" Can we go, too ? "

" Unfortunately, the ship is full." It seemed a very lame reply when they really needed help.

" How did you get on board ? "

" We're English." We felt as if we were denying the uniform we wore.

" You're lucky, you can go on fighting. We want to get to England, too. We won't give up like this. We'll go to any country where the fight is kept alive. If only there were a dozen ships in the harbour now we could fill them all with soldiers who feel like us."

Although the Armistice was only a few hours old, there were already signs that many people strongly disapproved and felt deeply humiliated by the surrender.

We promised to report their presence when we got on board. Perhaps at least they could be given advice.

It must have been 3 o'clock by now, the Admiral had not appeared and there was still no sign of the ship sailing. There was an air of excitement aboard and mysterious telegrams were continually arriving. We overheard one officer say : " If we don't get out of this river damn soon we'll never get out."

The Major in command of a detachment of soldiers who, to our surprise, were on board, also took a serious view of the delay. He said jokingly : " I could have taken the entire town with my men while we have been waiting."

Then an incident happened that made us realise that we were really back in England. The lady " spies " had caused a serious departmental crisis. A notice, which had to be solemnly initialled by every member of the Upper Deck, was passed round amid general laughter. The " heads " on the starboard side (" the left-hand side when facing the blunt end ") were to be reserved for the ladies, those on the port side for the officers. The effect of the lengthy technical description was so confusing that no one was completely certain what was meant. But the Major eventually worked out the conundrum : Ladies' lavatory on the right, Gentlemen's on the left.

At least another hour must have passed and, though

the Admiral had come aboard, there was still no sign
of our sailing. While we stood on deck talking to the
Major and the young Lieutenant, who by now we had
discovered was an Intelligence officer, one of the
sentries repeatedly reported other French officers
applying to be taken to England.

Suddenly van A . . . and van B . . . came running
along the quay. " It's no good," they shouted, " they
won't let us out of the town. The sentries turned us
back, we haven't got the right permits. We'll have to
find some other way. We've come to see you off."

" Tell them you're going to St. Yrieix," we replied.
" Use your permit, write some more if necessary. You
can always change your direction once you're outside
the town. But before you go try all those other ships
along the quay ; some of them may be going to try and
get out of the river."

It was the best advice we could give, but it seemed
hopelessly inadequate. They looked sadder and sadder,
conversation became more and more strained, we felt
increasingly depressed. If the ship had not cast off
almost at once we might easily have been so foolish as
to leave it again.

As they waved good-bye they looked infinitely
pathetic. Behind them we saw the little group of French
officers, motionless and mournful. It accentuated the
poignancy of our parting from our friends and from
France.

We all stood on deck looking our last at Bordeaux.
Now for the first time we saw all our fellow-travellers.
In addition to the officers, the Naval Control official
and the lady " spies "—who turned out to be three very
ordinary English women in mackintoshes and trousers
—there were a Scotsman who had escaped from Paris,
an Air Force Intelligence officer, and two wounded
airmen.

The order was immediately given for everyone to

put on lifebelts. We quickly gathered from conversation how dangerous might be our journey down-stream. The Scotsman had left Blaye in the early morning a few minutes before the arrival of the German mechanised advance guard. There was no doubt that the mouth of the river would be heavily mined, no one knew exactly the strength or the whereabouts of German batteries on the north bank and obviously trouble was expected as the decks were cleared for action. Despite the signing of the Armistice, hostilities were not due to cease until after agreement had been reached with the Italians.

Two French men-of-war lying at anchor saluted us as we passed and the crews waved enthusiastically. A large number of merchant ships were also anchored in the stream and at the docks ; on almost every ship the crews waved and raised a cheer of " *Vive l'Angleterre !* " or " *Bon voyage !* "

Quite soon we passed a large oil depot on the north bank. " There's the cause of most of our delay," someone said bitterly. The soldiers looked particularly glum.

This was such a curious remark that we timidly enquired its meaning. With certain reservations, since we never heard the official version, the story they told us was roughly as follows.

The destroyer, having been sent on destructive missions down the French coast, ahead of the German advance, had finally been sent to Bordeaux with a detachment of soldiers to blow up this important petrol and oil depot. The troops had been landed, the depot occupied, the explosive charges placed. The great moment had arrived. Meanwhile a wireless message from England had been received on board cancelling the orders, but the only officer not with the landing-party was the ship's doctor. The message had been handed to him and there was a rumour that, rather than cause intense disappointment to his fellow-officers, he had almost dropped it overboard by mistake. However, this was obviously a charming embellishment, because what he really did was to seize a bicycle and dash off to the scene of operations. He arrived as everything was set to go off. The anger of the frustrated saboteurs was intense ; however, rather than leave the supply intact, they had insisted on refuelling the ship and storing on board as much as they could carry. That accounted for the engineer's lack of interest in our drum of petrol.

The ship had then moved up-stream to the mooring where he had found it.

The fact that it had not sailed on the previous evening was easily explained. The story had a sequel which cannot now be told.

Anyhow, as a result we really were on the last ship to sail for England.

Everyone was in a bad temper and not encouraged by the thought of a long swim. The chief cause of the military's upset though was that for two days past and for two more days to come they had to face violent sea-sickness, without even the satisfaction of having done their job.

Despite all we began to wonder whether we might not have been safer had we stayed on solid ground with our two Dutch friends !

From now on for miles, on every landing-stage, on the parapet of the embankment, in every garden, in every window, people waved handkerchiefs and cheered as we sped down-stream. It might have been a triumphal progress. It was such a touching farewell to their Ally that everybody on board was visibly surprised and affected.

There was a call to dinner. We broke off our meditations on the landscape with its hundreds of historic vineyards and famous *châteaux* to go below. Regretfully

we remarked to each other : " How awful to think
that all this may be German by to-morrow . . . and
so much good wine ! "

As we went down the companion-way to the ward-
room, where we were housed, we noticed with a
shock an open trap-door and a chain of sailors handling
shells.

" Is this where we sleep ? " we asked.

" Yes, Sir, nice place, too, right over the magazine ! "

We wished for solid earth even more.

Inside the ward-room the midshipmen not on duty
were questioning one wounded airman. His experience of successive moves from hospital to hospital down
the length of France was not unlike our own, and
we listened intently.

Our fellow-travellers were a mysterious collection,
and they intrigued us more and more. We learnt that
the lady " spies " had escaped all the way across
France on bicycles. The Scotsman, too, obviously had
his secret. There were a number of unexplained naval
officers aboard. The Air Force Intelligence officer was
the most mysterious of all.

It appeared to us that we had fallen into the middle
of the Secret Service !

Only the Naval Control official seemed to have no
secret. But he was a hero of another sort, and on every
side we heard nothing but praise for his magnificent
impromptu rescue work. They all marvelled at his
courage and efficiency. He had left the town at the
beginning of the week on an English ship, had returned
of his own accord from Royan to help evacuate
refugees, had left again, met the destroyer on its way
up-stream, offered his services, changed ships and
returned a second time. It was he who, with the
Admiral, had reopened the Consulate and done
invaluable work there. But his greatest act had been

the saving of thousands of pounds' worth of valuable material.

Then the questioning turned on us. We were asked where we had been and what we were doing. Our attempts to tell our story in a few words must have created a rather confusing picture. After a little while we became conscious that the conversation had turned into an interrogation. A series of pointed questions were rapped out and the more truthfully we answered the less convincing our replies sounded even to ourselves, until finally we no longer knew who or what we were. Then we realised to our horror that our fellow-travellers regarded us with the gravest suspicions ! They clearly thought that *we* were spies ! After all, the unusual spectacle of two Englishmen in French uniform, the strange coincidence of our catching the last destroyer to leave Bordeaux, the incoherence of our replies due to vagueness and exhaustion, combined to produce this effect. In the end we were suspicious of ourselves.

We longed to ask each one of our fellow-travellers more about themselves, but under the circumstances dared not. However, we were able to discover details about the terms of the Armistice. They were as bad as our worst surmises and we gathered that they would not be published in France for a few days. It seemed so ironic that this little group of Englishmen sailing down the Gironde should be so well informed when most of the French nation was being kept in tragic ignorance.

We went back on deck to take one last look at France. Tired though we were it was impossible to tear ourselves away. It was 9.30 and we were practically out of the river. By a miracle we had escaped the notice of the German batteries and aeroplanes. It would not be very long now before we were in the open sea.

The wide mouth of the river was dotted with ships at anchor. There were large liners full of refugees, small merchant ships, some French, one Dutch, two

Belgian. The destroyer went round in circles, winding its way between their them and possible mines. A great deal must have depended on our de-gaussing jacket during those few moments. Every ship was crowded with hundreds of unhappy, stranded refugees attempting to escape from the Germans. On each, hands and handkerchiefs were waved and loud cheers raised. Poor creatures, they envied our good fortune.

The Pointe de Grave, on the south bank, is an enormous, open stretch of sand. Behind is a small hill dominating the river's mouth. On this is a vast erection like a lighthouse—it is the famous memorial to the first Americans to land in France in 1917. It stood there gaunt and defiant in the twilight, commemorating happier days. We thought of Reynaud's appeal. Now it reminded us of vanished hopes : a beacon whose light had gone out.

We circled almost from one bank to the other. On the north bank we could just distinguish a town, which must have been Royan. It was getting dark. We circled once more. Then we were in the open sea.

Doulce France, farewell ! For us this was a terrible moment. We watched your coastline disappear into the darkness with as much anguish as if we had been trying to hold on to our lives. We prayed that our return might be happier than our parting.

*   *   *

The next day was uneventful. With nothing but a calm and empty sea all round us and a brilliant sun overhead we had time to relax. We lay down unobtrusively in a corner of the deck and began to piece together the disjointed events of the past few weeks. We began to see things in their right perspective. Incidents and remarks which had seemed trivial or ridiculous at the time now took on their real meaning. We realised that, through no fault of his own, the

Colonel *had* been ignorant of what was happening. It had all happened so fast and so secretly. We remembered the *patronne* at St. Yrieix who had said so simply : " I will never be able to look an Englishman in the face again." A phrase of Reynaud's came back : " If I am told that only a miracle can save France now, then I will say that I believe in miracles." No one had guessed how serious nor how true it was at the time. Churchill's phrases took on a new significance : " . . . we shall prove ourselves once again able to defend our island home, to ride out the storm of war . . . if necessary for years, if necessary alone." Where was Reynaud now? and where Daladier? the men in whom the French had placed their trust. What would be the future of France ?—the future of the Entente? What would the English feel about the French?

Our fears had been aroused by the Scotsman. He had driven from Paris by car, a luxury refugee, and had already stated on board that there was strong resentment and anti-English feeling among the French *people*. Why had his experience been so completely different from our own ? We thought of the clamouring English crowds in Bordeaux and their behaviour to the porter and the *maître d'hôtel*. Their arrogant attitude would have provoked any nation.

We went back over our own experiences. We thought of the Aspirant in the hotel at Périgueux, and of the *patron*, too: of the *patronne* at St. Yrieix : of the nurses and members of our own Section : of all the soldiers with whom we had come into contact : of countless little friendly episodes which had seemed too trivial to record : of the three soldiers with whom we had lunched at Sézanne. We had never once met with unfriendliness, and in the last few days it had been positively embarrassing to hear the French apologise for the débâcle. A great nation does not lightly admit a failure on such a scale. Certainly, they had begun by trying to find excuses.

But the excuses had got fainter and fainter as they realised how much of the responsibility lay with themselves.

We could call to mind the excitement of numerous people when they thought that the English were present. Had the French expected too much from their ally? The fabulous exploits of the R.A.F. and of the Royal Navy were nowhere more appreciated than in France. The only criticism we could remember was the "Too late! Too late!" of the doctors in Limoges. Never once had we heard regrets expressed for the absence of the B.E.F. from France at this crisis in the Allied campaign. Yet they had needed and counted on the half-a-million men who had disappeared in the unforeseen disaster of Dunkirk.

We knew that no one could ever question the desire of the French soldier to go on fighting. We had had too many evidences of that. The determination to get to England of all the soldiers we had met since leaving St. Yrieix was yet another proof of this. We thought and thought: but nothing we could recall could shake the evidence we had seen and heard.

Nevertheless, the attitude of the Scotsman worried us. He was an intelligent man whose opinion carried weight in official circles. On what evidence was his opinion based? If his conclusions were really correct, how could we reconcile them with our own? Our conclusions were not the result of prejudice or perversion of facts; *we had, after all, seen and heard our evidence.* In this, we cannot have been unique.

Granted an anti-English clique, headed by Laval, which had wormed its way to power, also the indifferent and selfish class of *fonctionnaires*, what interest could anybody have in denying the sentiments of the vast body of the French *people*?

With a shock we realised that the Scotsman might represent a widespread English point of view. But why should the English want to disown the French? Such an argument could only be designed to serve as a pretext for the dissolution of partnership. Now we understood why the Ambassador had left France. Were the English already so proud that they preferred to fight alone? Was it another example of "the nation of shop-keepers" cutting its losses?

We thought and slept, slept and thought. The more we thought of the Scotsman's attitude the more it worried us. But of one thing we were convinced : that the English, with their cherished sense of fair play, would not and could not jettison the whole body of the French *people*.

* * *

It must have been 6.30 a.m. when we cast anchor in Plymouth harbour. A few minutes later a Customs launch drew alongside and an officer came aboard to inspect the papers of the few passengers. He gave them a cursory glance—they obviously meant nothing to him —and handed them back without a murmur. We were astonished that we were not questioned, nor did any-one ask for our English passports. It is true that both of them were in Paris, so perhaps it was just as well.

The Admiral took leave of us all and went ashore. The rest of us then thanked the Captain and his officers for their hospitality and climbed into a launch.

We were sorry the trip was over. For thirty-six hours we had been received by the officers of this destroyer in the most noble and generous manner. Both they and the crew had obviously suffered great inconvenience : they had given up their bunks, their living space, their food and drink, but never once had they allowed us to feel conscious of our intrusion.

As we reached the quayside we thought that we had reached the end of our adventures. " All we need is a travel warrant and we'll be in London to-night," we said cheerfully. But it was not to be.

We made for the large waiting-room of the maritime station which had been set aside for Transport Control. In the doorway was a canteen at which coffee, tea and Cornish pasties were being handed out. Down the centre of the hall were rows of benches crowded with excited, weary, unkempt refugees, male and female, military and civilian. Every conceivable language was being spoken. Across the end of the hall were tables at which sat officers; down each side were tables at which sat examiners. People seemed to be presenting themselves with their papers at these tables. The officials seemed to have been caught unawares; there was a general air of improvisation. We did not quite know what to do, nor did anybody know what to do with us. We put down our baggage and drank a cup of tea.

Finally we forced ourselves on an examiner's attention and were told that only the R.T.O. himself could deal with anything so unforeseen as the arrival of two Englishmen in French uniform.

There was a train for London in the station and all our friends from the destroyer were travelling on it. We wanted to do the same ; unfortunately, not having enough money, we had to ask for a travel warrant.

The R.T.O. paused among his telephones to receive us. He listened to our story, but had no time for individual or exceptional cases. We begged him to look at our few papers, which at least proved that we were English, but they did not seem to interest him. His mind was made up. "You can't go to London in a French uniform. Instructions have been received that all French soldiers—and about one hundred and thirty have just arrived—are to proceed to a place in the North of England. You will accompany them. There will be a train leaving later in the day ; the time is not yet fixed. In the meanwhile you will report for lunch at 12.30 at the Drill Hall with the rest of the French soldiers."

" But, Sir . . ."

" There are no ' buts,' you can't go to London in French uniform, even if you are English."

That settled it. However, official mistrust of us stopped abruptly there. The gates of the station were wide open and we walked calmly past the sentries and policemen out into the town.

Outside the gates were crowds of children flourishing scraps of paper or miniature note-books. " Autograph, mister ! Autograph, please ! " There was a chorus along the whole length of the main street. It seemed so odd that they should set any store by a collection of foreign names. But then another thought entered our heads : potentially, those little books could be an excellent source of information, especially for enemy agents. Most of the foreign soldiers arriving at Plymouth that day must have had the same thought ; every book had its Louis XIV, Greta Garbo or Sacha Guitry. It also seemed odd to us that we should be allowed to telephone or telegraph to London with the utmost liberty. If we had been spies or Fifth Column, what a gala we could have had !

We strolled about the town and met many French soldiers doing the same. Plymouth seemed so calm and unchanged, except for the barrage balloons hovering overhead, that we felt lost. It seemed as though the war had been left behind in Europe. We went to the hotel and had a bath and a drink.

There was a touching moment when the chambermaid, who had cleaned our boots and brushed our uniforms, refused our proffered tip. " I am happy to do anything I can for you," she said, " I have a brother still missing in France. It's nice to be able to help anybody who has come back. After all, we've all got to help each other in this war."

We found a copy of the *Western Evening Herald* in the bar. A headline caught our eye :—

" FRENCH HOSTILITY

Refused Refreshment Because He Was British."

Below was an interview with a " retired commercial journalist," who had left France " a week last Sunday," that is to say, Sunday, 16th June, the day before Pétain's first speech.

Amongst other things, he stated : " No accommodation could be obtained at hotels, but one or two cafés were open. Because he was British, however, they would not let him have any refreshment. The bulk of the French public were very hostile, even in the village where he had lived for many years, and the British were blamed for the present catastrophe."

We could hardly believe our eyes. Was this the way in which expatriate Englishmen expressed their gratitude to the country in which they had chosen to live " for many years " ? We thought once again of the English in Bordeaux and wondered what atrocity stories they were manufacturing ; they so obviously enjoyed being " heroes." We wondered, too, how many unsuspecting people in England would be taken in by these pathetic and treacherous histories. We wondered if they would take the trouble to enquire more closely into the facts. " What were you doing in France at all ? " should have been their first question. One thing seemed to us quite clear : the reason why so many English people had remained in France was that they had felt happy and secure behind the shield of the French Army.

Our fears of the previous day became more real. This was the second time that we had heard the French *people* attacked—not the politicians, nor the Army, but the French *people*. We were even more puzzled. Why had our experiences been so different from those of others ? Surely no one could have seen a wider or more representative section of the French people than we had ?

What would have happened if Hitler's troops had sailed from Dunkirk to England instead of going southwards into France ? Was England any more prepared than France ? Had England, too, been relying too much on her ally ? Was France to be condemned now because her cafés no longer had any food ?—how often had we seen Frenchmen turned away for lack of supplies !

The French could perhaps be accused of refusing " refreshment," but not of refusing protection. Would anybody dare to deny that for nine months the existence of the French Army had largely kept the German Army from the shores of England ? If England was better armed now than in September, 1939, it was mainly due to the protection offered by the French. No fair-minded Englishman would seek to deny this. Were his admiration, trust, regrets and extended hand of sympathy to be drowned in a flood of unthinking, jingoistic invective ? We could not believe that the Scotsman and the " retired commercial journalist " represented a majority. Hazlitt's words seemed to be still true : " The difference between the vanity of a Frenchman and an Englishman seems to be this : the one thinks everything right that is French, the other thinks everything wrong that is not English. The Frenchman is satisfied with his own country ; the Englishman is determined to pick a quarrel with every other."

Depressed and apprehensive, we went along to the Drill Hall for lunch. With the French officers, we sat at long trestle tables, drank tea out of billy-cans, and made a meal off paste sandwiches, an apple and a slice of cake. The unexpected guests were being given an unexpected reception.

After lunch we were told that the train would leave at about 6 o'clock from the town station. We fetched our belongings and waited there dismally. In the late afternoon a counter-order came. We were to go back to the Drill Hall. There we found four large buses. Were we all to travel by road ? Nobody was quite sure. Anyhow, the baggage was loaded on to the buses while large mugs of tea were dispensed all round.

Then a further order came. We were all to go down to the maritime station ; the train was to leave from there. Everyone was beginning to feel quite at home. The French habit of *ordre et contre-ordre* certainly had its English counterpart. We were formed into a column of threes and in the greatest disorder, carrying our baggage, we proceeded to march through the main street to the station.

The train had been composed for members of three Allied armies, each segregated. The Czechs were at the back, the Poles in the middle, the French in front. Our destination was more or less unknown. No representative of the English Army travelled with us, no foreign officer had been put in command. At 7 o'clock, like a herd of cattle, we steamed out of Plymouth towards an unknown destination.

Food in the form of tins of bully-beef and sea-biscuits had been issued to N.C.O.'s for distribution on the journey. They had given us solid food all right, but nothing whatever to drink ; there was not even any running water in the lavatories. The French, who were all overjoyed to be in England, made no protest, but we were furious. As the only two Englishmen on the train we took it upon ourselves to find the guard and ask him to have the train stopped at the first convenient station with a buffet. Tea, coffee or even water would do, we explained, but the soldiers could not be expected to travel all night without some form of liquid. He was sympathetic and quite understood, so the train pulled up at the next big station. The station-master, however, was not so sympathetic ; the buffet was closed, he was not prepared to organise a supply of water and tried to hustle " the foreigners " back into their carriages. We were obdurate and refused to continue our journey until water was running from every tap on the platform. *Gamelles*, water-bottles and mugs were hastily filled by the thirsty soldiers and we proceeded on our journey.

The first part of the night was spent in an exchange of escape stories. Each of the French officers and men had taken an independent decision and sacrificed a great deal by leaving their country. The more we listened to their tales, the more we remembered the officers in Bordeaux and the lack of shipping. " We were lucky to find a ship at all," one officer said. " We are so few, but for every one of us who has escaped there are a hundred with the same spirit left behind. While they remain alive the Germans will never conquer France."

Then suddenly the senior officer among us, a captain, said abruptly : " I might be a German."

We were all amazed and he laughed at our surprise.

" I have been visiting England for years," he said, " and every time I have arrived have wasted hours over formalities. This time, when I might be an undesirable person, no one has shown any interest in me whatever. No one knows that I'm not a German."

We talked for a little longer then, one by one, we fell asleep.

It was a cold, grey morning when we were turned out of the train, and there was a fine drizzle. No one was on the platform waiting for us, no one seemed to expect us.

" Are you sure we are supposed to get out here ? " we asked the guard.

" Quite sure," he replied, " my instructions were clear. The Poles were dropped at ——, the Czechs at ——, and the French here. Someone will come along for you soon."

After that poor consolation he got back into his van and the train shunted out of the station.

We waited in the cold and rain ; lost, hungry and miserable. After about twenty minutes a few who could bear it no longer set out to find a café. Almost immediately one of them brought back the news that a little shop had been discovered a few yards away. Leaving our baggage on the platform we besieged it in a body. Very soon the roadway was crowded with French soldiers with pots of marmalade, lumps of bread and Eccles cakes.

Suddenly, in the middle of this confusion, we noticed a distracted English lance-corporal, who was trying to make himself understood.

" What do you want ? " we asked him.

" Are you the French what was expected ? "

" We hope so," we replied.

" Then I'm supposed to take you all to the camp. I was sent to meet you on the wrong platform and found French sailors instead." He looked despairingly at the eating Frenchmen. "How can I get them to the camp ? " he said wistfully. " Will you help me ? They're not meant to eat here at all, they're meant to eat in the camp."

" We'll do our best," we replied, " but first of all we suggest that you let them finish eating. Then they must go and fetch their baggage, after that we'll follow you to the camp."

" Don't worry about their baggage," he said, " that will be collected."

" You'll never persuade them to believe that, it's all they have in the world."

At that moment a column of French sailors marched up towards the camp from the other platform. A number of soldiers from our group immediately joined their compatriots and disappeared down the road.

" I don't believe they're meant to do that," the lance-corporal said. He was getting really very unhappy by now, and we realised that if our help was to be effective we must do something immediately. We explained to the remainder of the group that we had to follow the lance-corporal to the camp, and that the baggage would follow. But as we had expected their first reaction was to return to the station and collect all that they could possibly carry.

" Will you get them into a column of threes ? " the lance-corporal asked us pathetically. We said we would do our best, but when at last we started to move towards the camp the column presented a most un-military spectacle.

For the next hour we marched round and round the camp, from office to office, each one giving us different instructions. Every time we moved on we lost a few more of our group. There was one awful moment for the lance-corporal ; he had disappeared into an office to make inquiries and on coming out found only two of his charges waiting. However, he was able to catch up the others who, having caught the marching habit, had gone plodding on.

We marched through rows of brown canvas tents, where little groups would stop and talk to French sailors already installed, until we arrived at a spot where sausages and tea were being distributed.

Two young English officers stood hopelessly looking at our group. " You must be having difficulties," one began, " I was in charge of the French yesterday. Some went for a walk and only a quarter of them came back. Then others, whom I was not expecting, arrived by another gate."

Eventually, we marched back to the main buildings. There were the usual delays on the way, but the lance-corporal had mastered the technique by now and, with patience and skill, managed to keep our group intact.

There was a pause. Obviously nobody had any use

for us at this camp. We could not have felt more useless, unwelcome or unwanted. London was the place for us. We saw an office labelled, " Camp Commandant." We knocked on the door and walked inside.

A little clerk, who some time before had spoken the only two French words we had heard uttered by an Englishman that morning, received us with a smile.

" Despite our French uniforms," we began, " we are English. However, we are in the French Army, attached to the *Section de Santé*. There is no unit of that Section here, nor can we find any representative of it. Quite clearly we must go to London to report. Will you please issue us with a travel warrant ? "

He consulted with an orderly in the office and they both seemed to agree that our request was reasonable. While the clerk started to write out our warrant the orderly, who had gone into an inner room, returned and asked for our papers. He disappeared again and the clerk went on filling up the form.

Suddenly the door of the inner room opened. In icy tones we were called in. The clerk took his cue and stopped writing. There was a hitch.

The Camp Commandant was sitting at his desk looking excessively remote and detached. Our papers were being examined by a genial Inspector of Police and a man in plain clothes. He was obviously a detective. Their expressions were grim and professional. Our consciences were clear, but our looks were sheepish and guilty. We were frankly terrified.

" Can you explain yourselves ? " Once again we embarked on our confused story. This time it sounded even more unconvincing.

We were cut short. " Can you produce anybody to identify you ? "

We were indignant at this. " Hundreds," we replied hotly.

" Can you get hold of them ? "

" Of course ; we can telephone to London immediately."

" Ah no, that won't do, they must come here and identify you in person."

" But that may take a day or two and what shall we do in the meantime ? "

" Haven't you any friends in the neighbourhood ? "

Our minds were a blank. " No," we stammered, searching for names. We were getting more nervous, the law was getting more formidable, the Camp Commandant even more remote ; London seemed a million miles away.

" Then I'm afraid you'll have to come with us to the police station and remain in custody until you can be identified."

Although it was not surprising that someone should at last be questioning our identity, which we were happy for our own sakes to prove, it did seem peculiar that the military should be handing us, two soldiers, over to the police.

They turned to go. The Commandant still said nothing. Not even by a gesture had he appeared conscious of our existence. Under escort—not arrest, that was carefully explained to us—we passed through the outer office. The little clerk, who had smiled at first, now cut us with a stare.

" Well, this is the first stage of our journey to London," we said to ourselves, " at least we have got out of this camp."

We got into a car and drove off. When the shock had passed we realised that this was the first display of official competence which we had met since our arrival in England, and told the Officers so. Their courtesy gave us confidence.

" Are you sure you don't know anybody in the town ? "

They were trying hard to help us. We thought and

thought, and by the time we reached the police station had remembered the name of V . . . P . . ., a friend of ours who was engaged on official business in the district.

The Inspector eagerly took up the telephone, but our friend was out. Messages were left at two or three addresses. It looked as if it meant the cells for a few hours, but at least V . . . P . . . was in the town. We were taken upstairs, not to the cells, however, and treated with the greatest consideration. Tea was provided ; the Station Superintendent came to enjoy the joke. By now everybody was in a very good humour. Our situation appeared more and more comic.

The police spared no pains to put us at our ease. In those calm and friendly surroundings we were able to collect ourselves and, for the first time, give full details of our story in a really convincing way.

Talk about France led the Inspector to mention that he was of Huguenot descent. The Inspector laughed when we told him that we were Cockneys. " I have an advantage over Cockneys," he said. " I was in the East during the last war and can speak Arabic. It's very difficult for a Cockney."

The time went pleasantly in conversation. It must have been two hours later when P . . . arrived. He had not been told for what purpose he was wanted, nor had our names been mentioned. Finding us, and in French uniform, he burst into fits of laughter, and almost insisted on hearing our story before we had been formally identified. It could not have been a nicer or more friendly welcome home.

The formalities took only a few minutes, but we insisted on one thing : a document establishing our identity and stating that our credentials had been properly examined by the police. The Inspector and the Detective-Inspector saw our point at once, but said a joint statement from them and the Camp Commandant was necessary. We said good-bye to the

Detective-Inspector and drove back to the camp with
P . . . and the Inspector. We commented on the fact
that no children were asking for autographs here, as
they had been in Plymouth.

" We stopped that at once," the Inspector told us,
" that sort of thing is much too dangerous."

That County Constabulary is very proud of itself,
but it has every reason to be. We waited in the rain
outside the Camp Commandant's office for some
twenty minutes, while the Inspector vouched for our
innocence, prepared the document and had our travel
warrant completed.

The little clerk, as he passed, smiled at us again.

The Inspector, too, was smiling when he came out.
He drove us to the station. It was 2.30, but P . . .
knew where to find oysters and champagne. It was
a perfect meal.

We left for London some hours later and arrived at
King's Cross at 10 o'clock on the night of Wednesday,
26th June.